The Left in China

"Ruckus has taken on the task of encapsulating for a Western audience the history of the left in China, where it stands today, and its prospects … The overview it provides is comprehensive, detailed, and strikingly insightful."

—Brian Chee-Shing Hioe, Founding Editor of *New Bloom*

"A must-read portrayal of the development of the left in China from the 1950s to the present, with important insights on how, despite its revolutionary rhetoric, the Chinese Communist Party has been an anti-left-wing force. Essential reading for global activists and scholars who believe a more egalitarian, democratic world is possible."

—Elaine Hui, School of Labor and Employment Relations,
The Pennsylvania State University

"In this riveting analysis, Ruckus rescues 'left politics' from the monopoly of the Chinese state and recenters the motor of history around social struggles from below—a much-needed perspective in understanding China from the international left."

—Yige Dong, Department of Global Gender and Sexuality Studies,
University of Buffalo

"With the left at odds over how to understand the Chinese party-state and its growing international influence, Ralf Ruckus's thorough but clearly-written new book does a great service by shifting our attention to the oppositional movements of Chinese workers, peasants, students, and women who have contested inequality and exploitation over the past century-plus, often in the face of severe repression."

—Manfred Elfstrom, Assistant Professor of Political Science at
the University of British Columbia, Okanagan, and author of
Workers and Change in China: Resistance, Repression, Responsiveness

The Left in China

A Political Cartography

Ralf Ruckus

PLUTO PRESS

First published 2023 by Pluto Press
New Wing, Somerset House, Strand, London WC2R 1LA
and Pluto Press Inc.
1930 Village Center Circle, 3-834, Las Vegas, NV 89134

www.plutobooks.com

British Library Cataloguing in Publication Data
A catalogue record for this book is available from the British Library

ISBN 978 0 7453 4295 5 Paperback
ISBN 978 0 7453 4451 5 PDF
ISBN 978 0 7453 4449 2 EPUB

Typeset by Stanford DTP Services, Northampton, England
Simultaneously printed in the United Kingdom and United States of America

This book is dedicated to Alina.

Contents

List of Figures and Tables ix
Abbreviations x
Preface xi
Acknowledgments xvi

1 **Introduction: Understanding the Left in the People's Republic** 1
Initial Questions and Perspectives 1
The Making of the (Global) Left 5
Visualizing the Composition of the Left 8
Early History of the Chinese Left 13
Structure of the Book 15

2 **Against Broken Promises: Workers Claim Equality and Participation in the Socialist 1950s and 1960s** 20
Workers' Struggles and Political Discontent 1956–57 21
Economism and the Rebel Movement 1966–68 31
Conclusion: Regime Betrayal and Class Resistance 46

3 **For a Better Future: Worker Movements Demand Democratic Reforms in the 1970s and 1980s** 48
The April 5 Movement 1976 49
The Democracy Wall Movement 1978–80 54
Workers in the Tian'anmen Square Movement 1989 64
Conclusion: Movements For and Against the Reforms 75

4 **Defense and Nostalgia: Social Struggles Drive Leftist Resistance in the 1990s and 2000s** 78
Peasant Struggles Against Reform Effects 79
State Workers Against Smashing the Iron Rice-bowl 85
Maoist Organizing and the New Left 91
Conclusion: Old Class Composition, New Leftist Mobilization 102

5 Social Unrest and Organizing: Challenges for the CCP in the Capitalist 2000s and 2010s 104
The New Working Class 105
The Recomposed Left 114
Women*'s Struggles Against Patriarchal Regimes 123
Feminists (Not) Challenging the Party State 129
Conclusion: Struggles Force the Regime to Adapt 137

6 Conclusions: Social Discontent and Left Opposition in Socialism and Capitalism 141
How Social Unrest and the Left Changed Since 1949 141
Dynamics of Struggles and Countermeasures 145
Visualizing the PRC's (Other) Left 149
The CCP's Anti-leftist Record 154
Lessons for Left-wing Strategies 158

Epilogue 162

Chinese Terms and Characters 164
Notes 168
Works Cited 203
Index 220

List of Figures and Tables

FIGURES

Figure 1: Simple left/right scale 10
Figure 2: Left-wing groups and other political forces in post-World War II (West) Germany 11
Figure 3: Left-wing groups and other political forces in the PRC during the socialist period and the early transitional period (1950s to 1980s) 151
Figure 4: Left-wing groups and other political forces in the PRC during the late transitional period and the capitalist period (since 1990s) 153

TABLES

Table 1: Periodization of social struggles, actors, and demands in the PRC since 1949 16
Table 2: Periodization of economy, politics, class relations, and leftist debates in the PRC since 1949 143

Abbreviations

ACFTU	All-China Federation of Trade Unions
ACWF	All-China Women's Federation
CCP	Chinese Communist Party
CCRG	Central Cultural Revolution Group
DWM	Democracy Wall Movement
GLF	Great Leap Forward
HFM	Hundred Flowers Movement
KMT	Kuomintang, Nationalist Party
LGBTIQ*	lesbian, gay, bisexual, transgender/transsexual, intersex and queer/questioning
NGO	non-governmental organization
PLA	People's Liberation Army
PRC	People's Republic of China
SEM	Socialist Education Movement
SEZ	special economic zone
SWC	Staff and Workers Congresses
TVE	town and village enterprises
WAF	Workers' Autonomous Federation

Preface

In the past two decades, the People's Republic of China (PRC) has become the second biggest economy in the world. It is now a core country for global capitalism—its main manufacturing hub that is closely connected to other world regions through supply chains and trade. Economic changes in the PRC, like rising wages or problems in the export sector, have effects on the living conditions of people around the world.

Therefore, everywhere, left-wing groups discuss their position towards the PRC's global role in the context of their concern for social conditions and struggles of workers, peasants, migrants, and women* in their own regions.[1] These groups are divided on how to assess the Chinese Communist Party (CCP) that has been in power in the PRC since 1949. Should they support the CCP's domestic rule and the PRC's position as an economic powerhouse in the global system of capitalist nation states?

Around the world, certain socialists see the CCP as left-wing or communist and a bulwark against U.S. imperialism. For others on the left, the CCP is the political organization of an authoritarian capitalism that exploits workers and represses labor unrest, feminist activism, environmental initiatives, and religious groups. Yet, many left-wingers have not made up their minds, often for the lack of information on China in general, and social struggles and left-wing organizing in particular. In addition, direct connections and exchanges with left-wing activists in the PRC have been difficult to sustain in recent years due to the harsh repression of left-wing activities by the CCP regime. It is all the more important, therefore, to provide an analysis of social struggles and left-wing organizing in the PRC over the past decades. That is the aim of this book.

The initial impulse for this project came from Martin Birkner, who invited me in 2018 to write a book on the left in China for his book series on the history of the left in different countries for the German-language publisher Mandelbaum in Vienna, Austria.[2] Later, when David Shulman from Pluto Press heard about the book project, he offered to publish the English version. Back in 2018, I was still working on my previous book *The Communist Road to Capitalism: How Social Unrest and Containment Have Pushed China's (R)evolution since 1949* (PM Press) that was eventually published in July 2021.[3] It covers the seventy years of CCP rule and analyzes the political, economic, and social contradictions in the socialist, the transitional, and the subsequent capitalist period. The historical overview provided in that book left no room for a more detailed analysis of left-wing movements, though, and Martin's proposal gave me the chance to plan a second book that takes up some of the general threads laid out in the first but focuses on the connection of struggles and left-wing organizing in the PRC.

Originally, I had planned to conduct a series of interviews with left-wing activists in the PRC and to dedicate a large part of this book to the left-wing activities and debates of the past decade. Then two things got in the way: repression and the pandemic. Until the mid-2010s, there had been at least some space for left-wing organizing and public debate, but, beginning in 2015, labor and feminist activists came under increasing pressure. This culminated in the summer of 2018, when Maoist activists supported factory workers at Jasic Technology in Shenzhen, Guangdong province. State security forces arrested and prosecuted members of left-wing groups, not just in Shenzhen but subsequently also in other parts of the PRC, and stepped up censorship of left-wing online content.[4] After this blow, most left-wing groups had to take cover and limit their (public) engagement. Any detailed presentation or description of what they discuss and do—or even just contacts and interviews with a foreigner—would have risked putting them in danger, especially if connected to political activity that tries to bridge left-wing activism in the PRC and elsewhere. In addition, the outbreak of the Covid-19 pandemic in Wuhan in early 2020 led to rigid travel restrictions. The CCP regime followed a "zero-Covid" strategy and basically sealed off the country, making it even harder to enter and conduct research.

So, the question was whether, in the face of these obstacles, I would still be able to prepare this book. I decided to go ahead because the harsh repression of left-wing groups and the disconnection of activists inside and outside the PRC due to the pandemic and countermeasures render it even more urgent to raise the issue of left-wing solidarity and support, and to intervene in debates on how to relate to the CCP, to left-wing or feminist activism, and to social struggles in the PRC.

Still, I had to reconsider how to prepare the book and how to frame and conceptualize my arguments. I conducted a dozen interviews with left-wing activists and observers, collecting their perspectives on the nature of the current economic and political system in the PRC. I used the notes from my engagement with left-wing individuals and groups in the PRC since the 2000s and the research notes for the book *The Communist Road to Capitalism* from English, Chinese, and German sources on social struggles as well as left-wing debates and activity these struggles produced in every decade since 1949. And, eventually, I had many discussions and exchanges on my book concept and different versions of the manuscript with helpful friends and comrades.

One topic that repeatedly came up during these discussions was the particular perspective I use in this book to describe and understand left-wing activities in the PRC. I explain this more in detail in the introductory chapter, so I keep it brief here: I neither focus on the CCP itself, its different factions, and its left-wing legacy nor do I provide a taxonomy of left-wing currents in the PRC such as Marxism-Leninism, Maoism, Trotskyism and anarchism. Instead, I am interested in social struggles with left-wing demands and practices against the policies of the CCP regime and how they inspired left-wing oppositional activity in the PRC.

This focus on the connection of social struggles and the left-wing opposition they inspire has been part of my own political history and practice in left-wing circles in Western Europe, Eastern Europe, North America, and East Asia. I learned that the power for change does not lie in the size or orientation of left-wing organizations but rather in the mobilization of social struggles and movements from below. Left-wing activists or organizations can have an influence on these movements and struggles but that can go either way: helping the movements to flourish or causing them to wither away.

Therefore, left-wing strategy and theory need to begin with the analysis of the ongoing social conditions, the composition and direction of social protests. We need to understand how left-wing groups learned from the social struggles, what role they played, and whether their political attempts facilitated or obstructed the development of collective social and political power. So the research of the development and connection of social struggles and left-wing initiatives structured the analysis of this book—not the ideological battles or historical succession of prominent left-wing individuals or organizations.

Using this method reveals that in the PRC, from the 1950s until today, frequent waves of social movements and struggles inspired deviant and oppositional left-wing currents, most of which were either not using any ideological self-description or adhered to some kind of Maoism. These social movements and the left-wing currents they produced attacked inequality, exploitation, discrimination, authoritarian rule, or cadre corruption. They occurred during the socialist period from the mid-1950s to the late 1970s, during the transitional period until the late 1990s, and during the capitalist period since. But they have often been ignored, mystified, forgotten, disclaimed, or defamed—above all by the CCP itself, which has a leftist origin and still claims to be leftist today. These movements and currents, the "other" left so to speak, are the subject of this book, as they need to be put back in the limelight in order to debate their importance and political meaning for the historical trajectory of the PRC.

I limit my analysis mostly to the developments after 1949 and on those in the PRC's "core." Left-wing history in China before 1949 has been largely left out here to limit the historical scope. The trajectories of the left in Hong Kong and Taiwan are considerably different from that of the left in the PRC and demand (and deserve) separate inquiries that could not be included here. "Peripheral" regions within the PRC, like Xinjiang or Tibet, are also omitted here as they, again, demand a special focus, especially, on the experience of socialist (settler) colonialism and socialist as well as capitalist enclosures organized under CCP rule and on related popular resistance and organizing.[5] Regarding social unrest per se, I look mostly at workers, peasants, migrants, and women* and their struggles, leaving out other movements that might have a left-wing agenda, for instance, environmental groups.

The oppositional or "other" left in the PRC has been neither a homogeneous group nor politically impeccable—just like in other parts of the world. Born in social struggles and mobilizations, it has repeatedly been split along political (or ideological) lines, and its desire and practice to improve social conditions or overcome exploitation and discrimination was, at times, mixed with exclusionary practices or thoughts. After all, shortcomings, mistakes, and wrong turns are as much part of the left-wing history as the strengths, successes, and steps forward—and both experiences can teach us how to avoid traps and defeats during future revolutionary attempts in the PRC and elsewhere.

Acknowledgments

I want to thank the numerous people who helped me to write and publish this book. David Shulman from Pluto Press encouraged me to hand in the book proposal. During the writing and publishing process, David has been very supportive all along. Anonymous reviewers of the book proposal gave me important hints on how to develop this project further. Friends and comrades from the Greater China area and elsewhere read and commented on different versions of the book draft. They should remain anonymous as the book content is considered sensitive by the Chinese authorities. All the more, I want to stress that their well-grounded critique helped me to develop my ideas. Without their inspiration and support I would not have been able to write and complete this book. Last but not least, I want to thank Melanie Patrick for the magnificent book cover she designed, Sophie Richmond for her thorough copy-editing work that made the book a lot more readable, Dave Stanford for his very good typesetting work and for not losing patience with me, and everybody else at Pluto Press who helped in publishing and promoting this book.

1

Introduction: Understanding the Left in the People's Republic

Left-wing mobilizations and politics carry the possibility of overcoming capitalist exploitation, patriarchal oppression, and other forms of discrimination and violence. The People's Republic of China (PRC) itself is the result of a left-wing revolutionary attempt led by the Chinese Communist Party (CCP) to accomplish that, but much has changed since its founding in 1949. The CCP regime has since gone through several transformations, abandoning its left-wing agenda and suppressing left-wing opposition on the way.

In this introduction, I lay out the terms and perspectives used in this book. In the *first* section, I discuss why a narrative and analysis of the history of the oppositional left in the PRC is relevant for left-wing politics today, and I outline the initial questions for my analysis. In the *second* section, I go back in history and describe how the global left emerged from the social struggles of the nineteenth and the twentieth century. In the *third* section, I lay out a method of how to visualize the left in graphs that show its composition in a particular period and region (Figure 1 and Figure 2). In the *fourth* section, I describe the origins of the left in China before and shortly after the CCP took power in 1949, and I use the *fifth* section to map out the main arguments of the ensuing chapters.

INITIAL QUESTIONS AND PERSPECTIVES

At first sight, the question of what and who is the left in the PRC might seem to be an easy one. Today's leaders of the CCP still refer to Marxism as their ideological base and claim that the PRC and its political and economic system are socialist. They draw on the strong position of the party and the state in the economy and on the promotion of welfare measures, two aspects which are often identified with socialism and left-wing politics. Liberal oppositional forces in the PRC itself, activists in the 2019 Hong Kong protest movement, and various observers outside the China circle also consider the PRC socialist today and describe the CCP as left-wing, referencing the authoritarian Leninist rule of the party, for instance.

Is the CCP a left-wing force? First of all, I use a broad and historical definition of what I understand as left-wing. I include most concepts or practices that have criticized capitalist exploitation and inequality as well as forms of discrimination and oppression from positions that are described or self-conceived as left-wing. I include actors who promote such left-wing concepts or practices regardless of whether they actually attack all forms of exploitation and discrimination or not.[1]

The CCP comes out of a left-wing tradition of social struggles in the 1920s and followed a Marxist-Leninist agenda with the aim of establishing a "worker and peasant state." After it came to power in 1949, the CCP regime under Mao Zedong set up a planned economy and "dictatorship of the proletariat" in the socialist period until the late 1970s. In that sense, the CCP can be considered left-wing in a Marxist-Leninist form during that period.

In the late 1970s, the CCP regime dominated by Deng Xiaoping started "market reforms." Subsequently, it gave up its Maoist class struggle strategy and rhetoric and orchestrated the country's full transition to capitalism up until the 1990s. Since then, the party has overseen the integration of the PRC's economy into the global economy, offering its vast (migrant) labor power for exploitation by domestic and foreign capital. As a matter of fact, in recent decades, the CCP leadership has become the core of a ruling class in a capitalist and authoritarian system and has used racist, sexist, and colonial forms of discrimination and oppression against its internal migrants, women*, and ethnic groups.[2] Thus, the party cannot be described as left-wing today.

What about other left-wing forces in the PRC's seventy-year history? My focus in this book is the complex dialectic of social struggles and left-wing organizing. On the one hand, left-wing issues, demands, and practices shaped social struggles. Workers, for instance, regularly fought for better conditions or attacked the cadres for their arbitrary or abusive management style and demanded (more) control over the means of production. These are progressive aims, but that does not mean that these workers and their struggles were not otherwise ambivalent and often contradictory with regard to left-wing goals.

On the other hand, when writing about *the* left in the PRC, I refer to the multitude of different individuals, groups, or currents that represent various left-wing positions and have been going through conflicts and splits. These actors, organizations, or currents are no less ambivalent, promoting left-wing politics as well as other positions that contradict left-wing goals, for instance, nationalism or authoritarianism.

In a country like Germany, for instance, the left includes a range of currents—social democrats, socialists, anarchists, and communists of various kinds. In the PRC, neither during the socialist period nor afterwards, did the CCP regime allow the open development of such organized political currents besides the CCP itself. However, during and after social mobilizations "from below," left-wing criticisms and demands were voiced—outside the party and its mass organizations, but also inside. Workers, peasants, women*, students, and others engaged in debates and protests promoting left-wing views and desires. They formed left-wing groups, movements, or currents, and demanded material improvements or even criticized the exploitative or oppressive nature of the CCP regime.

How do I analyze the PRC's "other" and oppositional left in this book? There are various ways to look at the trajectory of left-wing activity in the PRC. Some readers might expect a history of left-wing ideas and concepts or of the ideological battles between leftists inside and outside of the CCP, for instance, during and after the Cultural Revolution involving the "ultra-leftists" around the Gang of Four or during and after the transition to capitalism in the 1990s involving the New Left. Others might want to read how ideological roots in prominent leftist currents like anarchism or Trotskyism (re-)surfaced in social struggles or leftist debates, or how they challenged the CCP leadership's rather fluid interpretations of Maoism. Such a history of political thought and its reflection in political debates or organizations makes sense if the aim is to understand what certain politicians, intellectuals, or groups thought—it says less about what they did. Thus the ideological twists and turns are not my topic here. I do not want to discredit the analysis of ideological debates and their relation to historical events as such, but studying them is, at worst, no more than a mental exercise that earns an author academic credit.

I chose a different approach for this book. The focus of my narrative and analysis is on important social struggles and the left-wing debates, currents, demands, and practices they inspired.[3] In each chapter, I first describe the origins and composition of a particular (cycle of) social struggle, the forms of organizing and the protesters' demands. I then turn to the regime's reactions, its methods to diffuse or halt the struggle. This tells us about the dynamic of conflicting interests between social protesters with left-wing demands and the CCP regime that tried to strengthen its rule. And I also look at the involvement of left-wing actors, groups, or currents that the social struggle inspired or triggered, their positions, demands, and tools.

Why do I do organize the chapters in this way? One aim of this book is to provide a historiography of social struggles and left-wing currents in the PRC, their potentials and their limitations. I focus on those struggles and currents that stood in opposition to the CCP regime or, at least, the leadership of party and state. I use the terms "oppositional" and "left-wing" in many cases to interpret and describe struggles and currents, but they do not necessarily reflect self-descriptions of the protagonists. The role of (more or less) leftist factions or currents within the CCP—some with connections to extra-party movements or left-wing forces—are mentioned where necessary, but their positions and debates are not a central topic of this book.[4]

Another aim is to put the relation between struggles and the left in their correct configuration: it is the social struggles of proletarian subjects against those in charge of economic or political structures which form the ground on which left-wing ideas, debates, and practices develop. The latter might have an influence on further social struggles, but they are rarely the origin or the decisive impulse. The relation between social struggles or movements and the left has always been a central issue for those engaged in left-wing debates.[5] Leftists often imagine that the correct left-wing ideas and leaders constitute necessary conditions for struggles to spread and be successful, that they themselves could trigger and guide struggles, and surely many have tried to actually do that. Most often, though, that does not work.

The social struggles I analyze include different sorts of open protest, such as strikes or demonstrations, as well as more hidden forms of discontent and unrest. At times, they accumulated and formed protest waves or even more or less organized movements. Obviously, these social struggles were not necessarily left-wing as such but rife with discrepancies or contradictions, and they showed organizational or political limitations. In addition, participants (or activists and leaders) might or might not have had explicit left-wing agendas and might or might not have been part of the political left. Social mobilizations or workers' strikes could even include racist, sexist, and other discriminatory elements. However, most of the *larger* social mobilizations and protests in the PRC in the past seventy years, and certainly those I chose to look at in this book, included demands, tendencies, aims, or strategies that I understand as left-wing.[6] And some of them either explicitly expressed left-wing aims or clearly triggered left-wing currents.

Before approaching the history of the "other" or oppositional left in the PRC, I will first look at the history of the term "left-wing" and propose a way to understand and visualize left-wing forces using a left/right graph.

THE MAKING OF THE (GLOBAL) LEFT

The use of the terms "left" or "left-wing" as a metaphor for progressive or emancipatory politics has its roots in the late eighteenth century. The idea first appeared during the French Revolution and was used as a description of deputies in the National Assembly who were against the king (sitting on the left) versus deputies supporting the king (sitting on the right). The distinction between political left and right was adopted in other countries too, and continued to shape political competition and conflict throughout the nineteenth century. With the expansion of capitalist relations and the making of working classes, the conflicting left/right positions shifted from revolutionaries vs. royalists to socialists vs. reactionaries.

Regional factors shaped the specific dichotomies of left-wing attackers of the existing order vs. right-wing defenders of that order, and both camps developed different currents and positions. It should be noted that, besides the horizontal left/right metaphor, other metaphors and descriptions have been used to grasp the contradiction of social interests and classes or specific aspects of it: spatial metaphors like above/below, or front/behind; temporal descriptions like old/new or tradition/progress; functional descriptions like order/disorder, paternalism/emancipation, or hierarchy/equality; and epistemological descriptions like irrational/rational or natural/constructed. Limited space prevents me discussing all the similarities and differences here. After all, the left/right metaphor has been used more than others to specify, attack, or defend a particular political camp.

In the mid to late nineteenth century, when the political left consolidated and attacked capitalist relations and the state that defended them, it split into various currents. This took place not just in the core countries of capitalism at the time (among them Britain, Germany, France, and the U.S.), but also in peripheral or colonized parts of the world. Capitalist classes and working classes were both in the making, and the establishment of capitalist relations and their interconnection with patriarchal and feudal forms of oppression and exploitation created immense social misery. Also, they triggered social struggles in the form of strikes, riots, uprisings, and various forms of everyday resistance. These struggles involved fierce debates on ways of organizing in labor unions or parties, on strategies for reform or revolution, on collaboration with or rebellion against the state, and more. From the slave upheavals in Haiti in the late eighteenth century to the anti-colonial movements in African countries in the mid-twentieth century, struggles against slavery, feudal, colonial, or capitalist oppression produced groups or currents that critically debated and developed left-wing ideas and concepts.

Around the globe, the left repeatedly split into several parts, most of which go back to debates and conflicts in the mid to late nineteenth century. I do not address the multitude of different positions and nuances, so this will remain fairly rough: the first important division opened between a communist (and, at that time, social democratic or socialist) left on one side and various anarchist or libertarian left currents on the other. Most anarchists opposed, for instance, the communists' hierarchical forms of political organizing, their advocacy for the left's involvement in or usage of the state, their idea of gradual changes (in stages) on the road to revolution (rather than its immediate realization), and later their affinity with nationalism and national liberation.[7]

An important argument in the same period touched upon the role and rights of women*. The struggle was fought out in all parts of society and within all left-wing currents. While early feminists argued for enforcing immediate gender equality as part of revolutionary change, the positions of male*-dominated left-wing leaderships oscillated between opposing feminist demands, ignoring them, or treating gender discrimination as a secondary issue that would be solved in the (socialist) future.[8]

In the late nineteenth century and early twentieth century, when working-class movements in some countries consolidated and social tensions led to revolutionary outbreaks, another important split deepened between a revolutionary left and a reformist left over the direction and means of social and political transformation. The revolutionary left opted for rupture, an escalation of social and political struggles, and the replacement of class rule. Both anarchists and Marxist-Leninists considered themselves part of the revolutionary left, but anarchist currents have remained marginal or only popular for brief periods within oppositional movements over the past 150 years.[9]

It was the Marxist-Leninist camp which prevailed in important revolutionary movements as in Russia and China—and, when anti-colonial struggles from below pushed for changes after World War II, in many successful national liberation movements and postcolonial governments in the Global South. Marxist-Leninists typically argue for a transitional period between capitalism and communism in the form of socialism and a "dictatorship of the proletariat" that lays the groundwork in a given nation state for the establishment of communism in the (distant) future. When, in the twentieth century, Marxist-Leninist parties established "actually existing socialisms" under pressure from domestic and foreign hostile forces—like the CCP in the newly founded People's Republic in the early 1950s—the implementation of the "dictatorship of the proletariat" turned into the dictatorship of the party leadership. Oppressive policies or acts of domination that occurred during the socialist "dictatorship" in the name of the working class or "national liberation" could be justified by the future (communist) goal. Marxist-Leninist vanguard parties learned to defend the interests of a new socialist ruling class while keeping up their image as left-wing—even if they acted against domestic social or political movements with left-wing demands.

Meanwhile, the reformist left envisioned gradual change towards socialism through compromise with capitalist class rule in a parliamentary political system. Social democrats (or socialists) have dominated the reformist left and shaped government politics mostly in countries of the Global North with a "Western" democratic and capitalist system (built on colonialism). They wanted to improve the conditions of the exploited or repressed by adapting capitalist conditions (e.g. through welfare), and they looked for change within the existing system through elections and lobbying. In practice, social democratic parties' participation in governments has led to the development of a political caste that claims to be left-wing even though it benefits largely from its positions of power and influence in the capitalist state.

Despite their differing strategies for transformation, social democrats and Marxist-Leninists have had in common that they both have aimed to produce change through "modernization," industrialization, and "development," usually with nationalist programs and through state interventions. When they took over power and were confronted with social pressure from below and oppositional left-wing groups or currents, reformist social democratic parties as well as revolutionary Marxist-Leninist parties revealed their repressive character—and, as we shall see in this book, the CCP is a telling example.

VISUALIZING THE COMPOSITION OF THE LEFT

I now look at ways to differentiate and systematize various left-wing (and right-wing) political positions. My aim is to get a better picture of social unrest and the variety of left-wing opposition it inspired in the PRC. To use the term "left-wing" for a particular political position or the concept of "the left" for a specific political current or spectrum helps to identify political friends and foes. This identification is a basic condition for the debate and practice of left-wing political interventions.

The left is a mass that (potentially) works together in order to overcome patriarchal capitalism which has created global inequality, injustice, oppression, and misery. In the case of the PRC, the CCP claims to (have) overcome capitalism by establishing socialism. At the same time, the CCP regime has been the direct adversary of oppositional (or regime critical) left groups within and around social protests and movements.

So how can we clearly categorize the difference between a left-wing socialist regime in power and social struggles and left-wing groups that oppose it? As an analytical tool, I use a two-dimensional graph that illustrates the left-wing (or right-wing) political orientation of the various actors involved. Established forms of representing the composition and history of the left have mostly been applied to the left in capitalist countries, so the question I will pursue in this book is whether I have to adjust such representations of the left for the socialist or post-socialist PRC.

After World War II, it became common in politics, the media, and societies around the world to talk about the composition and relation of left-wing (as well as right-wing and centrist or moderate) political forces in countries with a capitalist system and, especially, those with a parliamentary form of democracy. Political parties, movements, or individuals were assigned to positions such as communist, socialist, liberal, conservative, or fascist.

These positions can be placed on a simple left/right scale (see Figure 1).[10] Such a categorization seems easy to apply. However, any group or individual on this scale features various attributes—positions on social (in)equality, organizational democracy, global politics, individual and collective rights, and more. In order to define the location of an individual or group on this simple left/right scale, these different attributes must be synthesized. As a result, Marxist-Leninists and anarchists, for instance, might find themselves at the same location on the scale, despite holding very

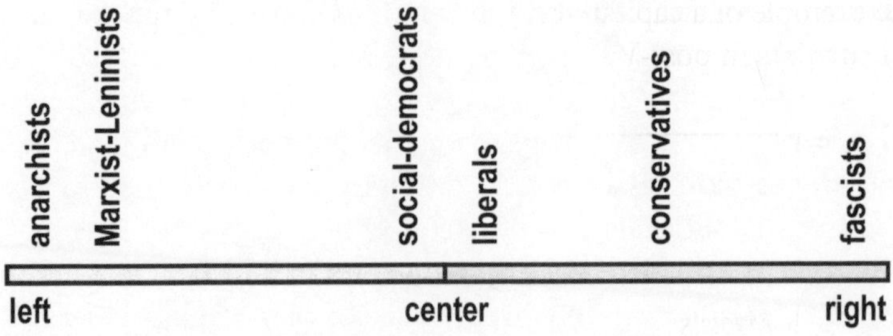

Figure 1 Simple left/right scale

different positions on organizational democracy, for instance.[11] Right-wing groups, meanwhile, advocate authoritarian, repressive, and discriminatory policies which place them on the far right of the scale but they might also demand more welfare or some kind of distribution of wealth similar to groups placed on the left side of the scale.

For that reason, I propose a two-dimensional graph (Figure 2) to visualize different political positions. I suggest the horizontal axis as the first dimension to determine a group's or an individual's position on exploitation and the distribution of wealth (with left-collectivist and right-exploitative as opposite attributes). The second, vertical axis and dimension shows the position on repression and the distribution of power (with egalitarian and authoritarian as opposite attributes).

The collectivist pole stands for non-exploitative, collective ownership of the means of production that promotes social equality and a society in which everyone is provided for according to their needs; the exploitative pole stands for supporting economic privileges by taking advantage of others, and for supporting the ruling classes' centralized control over the means of production and reproduction; the egalitarian pole stands for a non-hierarchical society in which people control and share power; and the authoritarian pole stands for people's lack of control over society and hierarchical rule.[12]

Such a two-dimensional graph can serve as a tool to illustrate and compare the positions of currents and movements placed according to their aims, demands, and practices. Figure 2 shows the example of a capitalist country in the Global North: the political currents in post-World War II (West) Germany.[13]

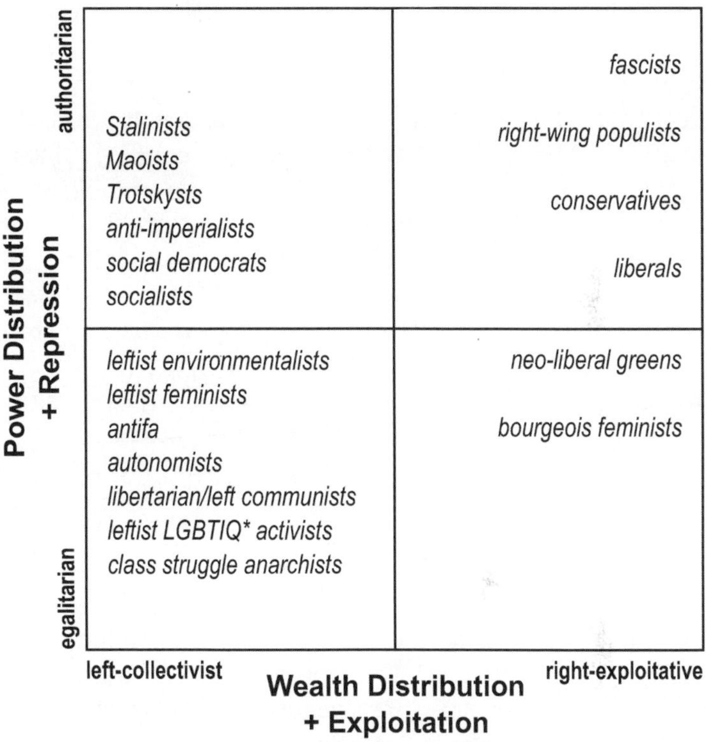

Figure 2 Left-wing groups and other political forces in post-World War II (West) Germany

The groups and currents shown in the boxes left-collectivist/egalitarian and left-collectivist/authoritarian were inspired by social movements and upheavals. Social democrat and socialist movements were born in social struggles and class confrontations in the late nineteenth century and early twentieth century, as were Marxist-Leninists, who later controlled the post-World War II regime in East Germany. Smaller groups or organizations of Maoists, Trotskyists, Stalinists, class struggle anarchists, as well as libertarian or left communists were largely inspired by the students' and workers' movements in the late 1960s and early 1970s (although some of them had earlier roots). Leftist feminists got a boost during the women*'s movement in the 1970s and 1980s, a time when the left-wing LGBTIQ* movement also became bigger. Autonomists, anti-imperialists, and later antifa were born out of the social movements (squatting, anti-war, anti-fascist, and more) in the 1980s.[14]

Such a diagram illustrates the relations of political forces in *capitalist* societies. These have existed in different forms of government, from what is usually called Western democracy to military regimes, both in the Global North and the Global South. The political spectrum in *socialist* societies in Eastern Europe or the Global South poses a challenge. What does it mean when the regime in power is (part of) the left or, at least, has a left-wing history? How do we grasp and visualize the relation between such a leftist regime and oppositional left-wing activities or movements? In the case of the PRC, an additional problem is that the regime changed its composition and strategy after the late 1970s, moving the political and economic system from socialism to capitalism by the late 1990s.

The underlying thesis of this book is that the two dimensions, wealth and exploitation on the one hand, power and repression on the other, can be used as markers to characterize political groups in both socialist *and* capitalist societies. *Before* the transition to capitalism in the PRC was completed in the late 1990s, left-wing political forces opposed the socialist CCP regime and attacked exploitation, oppression, and discrimination. This touched the economic realm and especially relations of exploitation, (re)production, and the distribution of wealth in a socialist society, as well as the relations of power, domination, and repression under the CCP regime. *After* the transition to capitalism was completed in the late 1990s, left-wing political forces opposed the capitalist CCP regime and attacked exploitation, oppression, and discrimination, again in the socio-economic realm of wealth distribution and the political realm of relations of power.

I return to this point and draw two-dimensional graphs of left-wing groups and other political forces in the PRC in the concluding chapter (Figures 3 and 4, chapter 6).

EARLY HISTORY OF THE CHINESE LEFT

Before discussing social struggles and left-wing currents in the PRC, I look at left-wing groups before and right after its establishment in 1949. In the late nineteenth and early twentieth century or late Qing period, the imperial regime attempted to develop and reform the country. Social tensions increased between the peasantry or the small industrial proletariat and the power holders. Anarchist, socialist, and feminist currents sprang up, often infused by experiences of urban Chinese students and intellectuals who had been abroad—many of them in Japan or France—and who translated or brought back literature from left-wing authors and currents in those countries. These early left-wing students and intellectuals opposed colonial occupation, feudal imperial rule, and, after the revolution of 1911, the regional warlord regimes.

The first organization promoting socialism was the Revolutionary Alliance (*tongmenghui*) formed in 1905, the forerunner of the Nationalist Party (*kuomintang* or KMT) founded under Sun Yat-sen in 1912.[15] A big boost for left-wing ideas came with the May 4 movement (*wusi yundong*) in 1919. Students mobilized against the government after it agreed to the Treaty of Versailles, which allowed Japanese forces to hold on to territories in China after World War I. The May 4 movement was part of a larger mobilization against "traditional" Confucian concepts and for a "modernization" of the country that influenced many of the activists involved in social struggles of workers or women* and in upcoming (left-wing) political endeavors.

Some of these activists previously influenced by anarchism or socialism and involved in social struggles founded the CCP in 1921. The Comintern (or Communist International) controlled by the Communist Party of the Soviet Union played a decisive role in setting up the CCP and influenced its development in the coming years.[16] The CCP quickly became the main organized left-wing force in China, actively involved in urban social conflicts and workers' struggles and integrating socialist and (at times) feminist positions. The Comintern pushed the CCP to form an alliance with the Nationalist Party or KMT from 1924 to 1927 to fight warlordism and unite the country.[17]

That alliance ended when the KMT adopted an anti-communist line and forced the CCP out the cities in 1927. The CCP regrouped, developed a peasant base, and built a peasant army for the fight against the KMT and other reactionary forces. In 1936, another alliance between CCP and KMT was formed, however, this time directed against the Japanese army that had occupied parts of China. After the Japanese army's defeat in 1945, CCP and KMT forces clashed again and fought another civil war that ended with the victory of the CCP in 1949.

After taking power in 1949, the CCP followed the Marxist-Leninist strategy and constructed a socialist economy and nation state as an intermediate stage on the road to communism. Trying to reach the economic level of "developed" capitalist countries, the CCP pushed for catch-up development through a massive industrialization program, capitalist technology, a hierarchical labor regime, and a gendered division of labor. The peasant army and the party, with its strong left-wing tradition, formed a new bureaucracy at the core of the authoritarian state. Opposition to the CCP and its policies was increasingly repressed.[18]

In the first half of the 1950s, land reform, nationalization of industries, and a new planned economy transformed social relations, effectively decomposing the landlord class and disempowering the urban capitalist class. However, the CCP subsequently installed a new rigid class structure with social hierarchies that involved economic and political discrimination, that is, higher income, better welfare, and better access to goods or services as well as more life opportunities and liberties for some than for others. The main fault lines existed between cadres vs. urban workers/peasants, urban workers vs. peasants, men* vs. women*, and Han Chinese vs. "minorities."[19]

The new divisions and inequalities triggered social conflicts and struggles as well as political critique, with the discriminated groups demanding better conditions and more control over their lives. While some opposition could be called right-wing, pro-capitalist, or pro-democratic in a "Western" sense, much of the dissent included critique and demands that can be called (oppositional) left-wing.

In this book, I focus on the latter, the story of social struggles and left-wing political dissent in the PRC, the motivation behind them, their position vis-à-vis the changing CCP regime, and their own contradictions and splits. I chose the social struggles and left-wing currents on the basis of their size, importance, and impact on the historical trajectory in the PRC. Obviously, this results from my own selection of cases of struggle and left-wing dissent, and does not make up a complete account.

STRUCTURE OF THE BOOK

Left-wing groups and currents generally develop out of social unrest and mobilizations (and influence them). The authoritarian rule and suppression of oppositional groups in the PRC meant that, during times of social unrest, left-wing groups and currents which addressed this unrest could not formalize and grow into publicly recognizable and lasting movements and organizations. They were often limited to informal and hidden methods of organizing and existed for just as long as the movement around them.

However, protests, mobilizations, and left-wing debates produced legacies that later currents could refer back to. Participants and activists from particular movements resurfaced and joined later movements, infusing them with their experiences and the forms of organizing and protest they had learned to use. And both the social movements themselves and some of the left-wing currents they produced, created substantial political pressure from below, provoked regime reactions in the form of countermeasures and reforms, and thereby shaped the trajectory of the PRC in each period—socialism, transition, and capitalism—from 1949 until today.[20]

The structure of the book follows the cycles of social struggle and left-wing mobilizations that can be observed in the history of the PRC. In each of the following chapters, I look at the main social movements in a particular period, the composition, discontents, demands, forms of struggle, results, and regime responses. This is followed by an account of the left-wing voices or groups that these movements produced at the time. The aim is to identify characteristics of struggles and left-wing currents in the respective periods, and to see how they changed when the PRC moved from socialism to transition and then to capitalism.

Table 1 shows each chapter, the corresponding period, and my characterization of the conflicts at that time (left column), the discontent, struggles, or conflicts I analyzed in that period (center column), and social or left-wing groups and currents that were involved in the conflicts or in debates about them (right column).[21]

Table 1 Periodization of social struggles, actors, and demands in the PRC since 1949

Confrontation and period	*Discontent and struggle*	*Actors and their social or political demands*
Chapter 2 Against Broken Promises: Workers Claim Equality and Participation in the Socialist 1950s and 1960s	Section 1: Labor discontent and strikes in 1956–57	Precarious workers demanding better conditions and attacking cadre privilege and corruption
	Section 2: "Economist" wave during the Cultural Revolution in 1966–68	Rebels or precarious workers demanding improvements; Maoist dissidents criticizing the socialist class society
Chapter 3 For a Better Future: Worker Movements Demand Democratic Reforms in the 1970s and 1980s	Section 1: Labor unrest and popular discontent in 1976	Workers in the April 5 Movement demanding democratic rights
	Section 2: Democracy Wall Movement from 1978 to 1980	Worker activists mobilizing for democratic reforms
	Section 3: Labor mobilization during Tian'anmen Square Movement in 1989	Worker activists independently organizing and demanding socialist democracy
Chapter 4 Defense and Nostalgia: Social Struggles Drive Leftist Resistance in the 1990s and 2000s	Section 1: Rural discontent and uprisings	Peasants fighting against cadre corruption and land theft
	Section 2: Protests in the urban state sectors	Urban state workers resisting effects of restructuring and destruction of their livelihoods
	Section 3: Leftist critique of the market reforms and their effects	Maoists and the New Left demanding improvements or return to socialism

Chapter 5 Social Unrest and Organizing: Challenges for the CCP in the Capitalist 2000s and 2010s	Section 1: Migrant worker discontent and struggles	Migrant workers fighting for better conditions and rights
	Section 2: Leftist support for migrant workers	Labor NGOs and grassroots activists organizing and campaigning for migrant workers
	Section 3: Women*'s everyday struggles	Women* fighting against sexist practices and for more control over their lives
	Section 4: Feminist mobilizations and campaigns	Feminists fighting against patriarchal discrimination and violence

In chapter 2, "Against Broken Promises: Workers Claim Equality and Participation in the Socialist 1950s and 1960s," I describe protests that were mainly staged by those who had a rather precarious status. They did not benefit much from the socialist welfare state as they were mostly not (permanently) part of a state economic institution or company. In the first section, I look at these workers' strikes for better conditions and against cadre privileges and corruption that broke out in 1956 and 1957, just after the establishment of the planned economy and the nationalization of industries. In the second section, I discuss precarious workers and youth who participated in the rebel faction during the Cultural Revolution in 1966 and 1968 and organized "economist" protests for an improvement of their lives. Some of these rebels and Maoist dissidents even formulated a harsh left-wing critique of the class relations in the PRC.

My reading is that, in this main part of the socialist period, protests were triggered by new social divisions and inequality. Social movements and oppositional leftists still took the left-wing legacy and revolutionary promise of the CCP seriously and demanded the improvement of working and living conditions as well as equal and just treatment of all workers and peasants.[22]

In chapter 3, "For a Better Future: Worker Movements Demand Democratic Reforms in the 1970s and 1980s," I first address the April 5 Movement of 1976, a short period of demonstrations expressing the critique and anger of workers and others over frequent CCP campaigns and purges as well as economic problems. In the second section, I analyze the Democracy Wall Movement of 1978–80, a mobilization of workers and others who, in part, demanded a democratic form of socialism. In the third section, I turn to the Tian'anmen Square Movement in 1989, and especially the workers' involvement and their demand for substantial political reforms and improvements.

I contend that, at the end of the socialist period and during the transition, workers and others had learned about the limitations of the authoritarian state system under the CCP and demanded an end to corruption and authoritarianism as well as more control, self-determination, freedom of expression and association, and better living conditions.

In chapter 4, "Defense and Nostalgia: Social Struggles Drive Leftist Resistance in the 1990s and 2000s," I analyze in the first section the struggles and "rightful" resistance of peasants against cadre corruption and land theft between the mid-1990s and mid-2000s. In the second section, I address the protests of urban state workers, the socialist working class, against the restructuring of the state sector and its effects in the late 1990s and early 2000s. In the third section, I discuss the revival of Mao, the new Maoist groupings, and the so-called New Left since the 1990s.

I suggest that, at the end of the transition period, the destabilizing effects of the market reforms as well as the cuts to welfare measures and work guarantees made it increasingly clear that the CCP regime was on course to establish a capitalist system. This, and the struggles of peasants and workers, led to the resurfacing of leftist ideas and practices of organizing.

In chapter 5, "Social Unrest and Organizing: Challenges for the CCP in the Capitalist 2000s and 2010s," I describe in the first section the struggles of migrant workers during that period for better conditions and an end to their discrimination. In the second section, I discuss the leftist supporters of migrant worker struggles in labor non-governmental organizations (NGOs) and other groups from the 2000s on. In the third section, I analyze the situation of women* in the PRC, the challenges they faced during the reforms, and their struggles for more control over their lives. In the fourth section, I turn to the different currents of feminism that were reacting to the changing patriarchal order and the struggles of women* since the 1980s: feminist NGOs, critical socialist feminists, and young feminist activists.

In my view migrant worker protests and the struggle of women* in the capitalist period were recurrent reactions to new pressures under the transformed (capitalist) CCP regime. They produced new generations of left-wing labor initiatives and feminist activism. Struggles and activism put substantial pressure on the regime which reacted with a mix of concessions, cooptation, and repression.

In chapter 6, "Conclusions: Social Discontent and Left Opposition in Socialism and Capitalism," I summarize the results of the analysis in each chapter. I then describe how left-wing mobilizations in the PRC, their composition and demands, have changed in the seven decades since 1949. I return to the visualization of the left/right spectrum and draw up graphs that include the (oppositional) left-wing currents in the PRC in the past seven decades. Next I focus on the CCP regimes' role and their explicit anti-leftist record. And in the final section, I discuss lessons from this analysis for left-wing strategies in the PRC and elsewhere.

In sum, the different social movements and left-wing currents that have emerged throughout the history of the PRC since 1949 reflect the changing nature of the CCP regime. Social unrest and oppositional left-wing critique, as spontaneous, erratic, or contradictory as they often were, still had a major impact on the trajectory of the PRC and could continue to pose a threat to the CCP regime. The global left is well advised to pay attention and learn about the (oppositional) left in the PRC, to establish connections with it, and to organize support.

2

Against Broken Promises: Workers Claim Equality and Participation in the Socialist 1950s and 1960s

In this chapter, I look at two workers' movements during the first decades of CCP rule. They show how, in the socialist period, groups of workers clashed with the leftist CCP regime. Workers asked the CCP to fulfill its socialist promises. Their demands were typical of a left-wing agenda: for material improvements, against discrimination, against cadre arbitrariness, for more (workers') control. The workers' struggles inspired various political debates, including a left-wing (and revolutionary) critique of the CCP regime. They also triggered a complex reaction of concession, cooptation, and repression that illustrates the antagonistic relations of regime and resistance.

In the *first* section, I focus on the unrest and opposition that occurred in the mid-1950s. The CCP leadership had just completed rural collectivization, the nationalization of urban industries, and the introduction of the socialist planned economy. Particular worker groups felt discriminated against and, in 1956 and 1957, organized strikes in several cities around the country—the first significant social unrest directed against the new socialist class system. The CCP leadership was alarmed, fearing worker revolts like those in socialist Poland and Hungary in 1956. It allowed open criticism during the Hundred Flowers Movement, voiced by intellectuals as well as workers. When the criticism went too far and included attacks on the CCP regime as such, the leadership started the Anti-Rightist Campaign to denounce and punish intellectual and proletarian critics.

In the *second* section, I analyze a particular part of the protest and opposition during the Cultural Revolution. In 1966, the CCP leadership faction under Mao Zedong attempted to regain full control over the party and called for mass mobilization during what it called the Cultural Revolution. Soon, disadvantaged and discriminated social groups such as apprentices, temporary workers, rusticated youth, army veterans, and victims of party campaigns used the opportunities to openly mobilize and protest. This morphed into an organized rebellion in Shanghai and other cities when workers and others demanded material improvements in a wave of unrest that the regime rebuked as the "economist wind." Some rebels even formulated a radical left-wing critique of the socialist class category system and the "red bourgeoisie." When the rebel actions threatened to get out of control, Mao's faction mobilized the army to crack down on the movement.

WORKERS' STRUGGLES AND POLITICAL DISCONTENT 1956–57

> [T]he Communist Party has come, but we still have to work like beasts of burden, from morning to night, from the beginning of the year to its end. [...] Does this mean "liberation"? Does this mean that [we are] the masters of the country? (Workers in Suzhou, 1954)[1]

The workers' struggles of 1956 and 1957 were the result of the social, economic, and political developments in the first transition period between the founding of the PRC in 1949 and the full implementation of the planned economy in 1956.

The leftist CCP regime managed to consolidate the PRC as a nation state, but it took some years to establish full control over all parts of the country. After taking power, leaders of the CCP and the revolutionary peasant army formed the new state bureaucracy. That bureaucracy presided over the "dictatorship of the proletariat," the temporary governance form for the transition from capitalism to communism. In reality, the new state was a kind of authoritarian "garrison state," with a security apparatus as well as campaigns and purges designed to control, punish, and eliminate any opposition, whether right-wing or left-wing.[2]

In 1949, large parts of the country's economic infrastructure were destroyed after years of occupation, war against the Japanese army, and civil war. The CCP leadership first tried to reconstruct the economy and secure the supply of basic goods. It carried out a land reform that dispossessed the rural landlord class but left the rural economy of private farms intact. It also collaborated with private capitalists as long as they did not oppose the new regime. In 1953, when the economy was sufficiently stabilized, the first Five-Year Plan prepared the ground for the full conversion to a planned economy. By 1956, agriculture, still the largest sector where the vast majority of the population worked, was collectivized. Urban handicrafts were cooperativized, urban industries nationalized. The CCP leadership followed the Stalinist plan for an industrial catch-up development which put more emphasis on investments in heavy industries and the production of machinery than on consumer goods production or the construction of housing. The surplus needed for the investments was drained from agriculture, or, more precisely, from the labor of agricultural workers, whose standard of living was kept far below that of urban workers.[3]

The CCP leadership orchestrated the disempowerment of the urban ruling classes close to the former KMT government and the rural landlord class. The social configuration changed substantially during this process. A socialist class system was installed that divided the population into class categories according to the social position of the male "head" of a household before 1949.[4] Over the next two decades, the CCP leadership added several political class positions to this classification, such as "revolutionary cadre" or "rightist." A categorization as "good" or "bad"—or "red" and "black"—determined the access of individuals and their family members to job positions, education, party membership, or housing.

The legal position of women* in families and society was initially strengthened in the early 1950s. While, before 1949, they had few legal rights and were largely excluded from work "out of the house," after 1949, their legal position was strengthened in the Marriage Law and they were integrated into the waged workforce. This, however, did not lead to the abolition of the established gender regime but, rather, to its socialist reconfiguration. Women* continued to do most of the (unwaged) reproductive work and were pushed out of or pulled into waged labor depending on the regional economic situation. They were paid less and mostly given unskilled and lower-status work positions, in urban industries as well as rural collectives. They also continued to be seen as inferior, had to deal with discrimination, and suffered sexualized violence—despite regular party propaganda celebrating women*'s liberation.[5]

Directly after liberation in 1949, workers expected rapid improvements in their material situation and their position in the work units (*danwei*). Many workers were involved in a wave of strikes—the first confrontation between workers with left-wing demands and the new regime.[6] Shanghai, for instance, saw more than 3,000 strikes or other forms of major labor disturbances from the arrival of the Red Army in June until December 1949.[7] Some unions supported what the CCP called "extreme leftist" tendencies among the workers and were reprimanded. The previously militant unions—all of which had to be part of the official All-China Federation of Trade Unions (ACFTU, *zhonghua quanguo zonggonghui*)—were subordinated to the party line, which cost them a lot of support from the workers' side.[8]

Meanwhile, several campaigns, like the Democratic Reform Movement (*minzhu gaige yundong*, 1950–53), the Campaign to Suppress Counter-revolutionaries (*zhenya fangeming*, 1950–52), the Three Antis Campaign (*san fan*, 1951–52), and the Five Antis Campaign (*wu fan*, 1952), aimed at weeding out those who opposed the CCP in factories and offices. Workers who supported the CCP were able to use these campaigns to push through material improvements as well as more control over management.

Under the impact of workers' discontent, the party leadership initially supported workers' participation in the work units. However, after it had consolidated its control over industrial enterprises with the help of mass mobilizations and campaigns, it established the Soviet One-Man Regiment model that gave the command in a work unit to one socialist manager.[9] Subsequently, workers' participation, for instance, through workers' congresses, was not high on the agenda any more.[10]

In sum, the basic structures of the socialist authoritarian state, the exploitative system, the social hierarchies, and the patriarchal order were developed and built from the late 1940s until the mid-1950s. In the next section, I turn to the major labor unrest that broke out when particular groups of workers began to feel the consequences of nationalization and the new forms of exploitation and social discrimination.

Rising Social Tensions

Several factors played a role in triggering labor unrest again, in the mid-1950s.[11] First, the economic problems inherited from the previous transitional period of the early 1950s made it difficult for the CCP regime to improve conditions for most workers according to their expectations. To control hyperinflation, it promoted austerity measures, which led to company bankruptcies and higher unemployment. When workers used campaigns to gain more control over company management—like the Three Antis and the Five Antis campaigns in private companies—this led to confrontations with capitalists who cut down their engagement and laid off workers. And the socialist transformation, starting with the first Five-Year Plan in 1953, produced wage cuts and stagnation in some parts of the economy, for instance, in trade. In sum, the "economic restructuring destabilized labor relations and led to the decrease in real income for workers."[12]

Second, the first Five-Year Plan included ambitious industrialization targets and, in order to accomplish them, the CCP regime adopted "certain new managerial practices that were potentially incompatible with the party's ideological goals."[13] Enterprises were under pressure to increase their efficiency and fulfill production targets. Subsequently, working conditions were often poor and, as little attention was given to work safety and labor protection, industrial accidents and occupational diseases were widespread. Workloads were often excessive, and workers had to do obligatory, often unpaid, overtime. Managers tried to maintain workplace discipline under these conditions, and that often meant they had to use coercion or force.

Third, the Soviet One-Man Regiment introduced in the PRC created hierarchically organized workplaces with limited workers' participation. Some managers who had already attained this position before 1949 kept their jobs well into the 1950s. Other managers were revolutionary veterans who came from the countryside and often viewed workers as "backward" because they "had not contributed to the revolution." Many workers viewed these managers as "despotic" and the management form as undemocratic.[14] The fact that the CCP propaganda continued to present the achieved socialist transformation in very positive terms, celebrating the workers as happy "masters of the factories," led to even more discontent.

Finally, the asymmetric configuration of the new planned economy, based on the extraction of surplus from the countryside and its channeling into urban producer goods industries, included a hierarchy among state-run work units and cooperatives according to type of enterprise, sector, and form of ownership. Full benefits and welfare were only given to workers in high-level state-run enterprises, and only to the formal and permanent workforce. These formal and permanent employed remained a minority of urban workers. Many others worked in collective enterprises and did not receive the full package. Still others were employed informally and temporarily, especially unskilled workers or peasants who were forced to return to the villages when unemployed. Workers were divided according to profession, employment status, and position in the workplace hierarchy and received different remuneration, benefits, and access to housing and services.[15]

The Wave of Strikes

The discontent led to a strike wave in 1956. The protests were widespread and took place in most larger cities, with Shanghai, the industrial center, being the most prominent location.[16] They continued in spring 1957 in many regions, from the northeast to the southwest.

The great majority of strikes occurred in newly formed joint-ownership enterprises, that is, private companies that were nationalized in March 1956. Their workers expected to enjoy the same wage level and benefits as workers in work units that had already been state-owned before.[17] They were shocked when wages, conditions, and labor participation even deteriorated.[18] In June, the CCP regime carried out a reform that raised the wages, but part of the pay rises were eaten up by inflation.[19] The increase of work targets in the fall of 1956 led to higher work pressure and another wage decrease—often the trigger for struggles.[20]

Usually, workers involved in the unrest were a minority in their respective workplaces. Many younger workers were involved. Like workers with rural backgrounds, they demanded the same welfare as older or formal workers in state-run work units. Apprentices wanted formal labor contracts and the same salary as permanent workers. In Shanghai, they even established inter-factory links to fight for their interests.[21] Temporary workers demanded long-term employment and the same conditions as formal workers. Women* workers wanted an end to discrimination as they often got jobs that were devalued, had lower wages, and did not allow them to be promoted. They also demanded better care facilities in the workplaces to lessen their burden of reproductive labor. Rusticated workers, that is, urban workers who had previously been sent to the countryside when the economy was slow, wanted to be allowed back to the cities and to get their original jobs back. Unemployed people also took to the streets to demand jobs and welfare.[22]

These discontented workers used different means of struggle. To voice their demands, protesters distributed fliers and used *dazibao*, big-character posters, or notes they put on blackboards explaining their grievances. In Shanghai, the disputes typically began with workers voicing suggestions and demands towards management. If these were ignored, they made formal complaints to higher authorities and set deadlines for when they expected a satisfactory offer. They also "often staged rowdy meetings to publicize their grievances. These initial steps were classified by union authorities under the rubric of *maoyan* or 'giving off smoke.'" If their demands were not met, the protest could "evolve into a strike (*bagong*), slowdown (*daigong*), a collective petition movement (*jiti qingyuan*) or forcible surrounding of cadres (*baowei ganbu*)—activities that were categorized as *naoshi* or outright 'disturbances.'"[23] Other forms of struggles were more restrained, like absenteeism, the refusal of orders to do certain work or tasks (*san bu gan*: dirty work, hard work, night shifts), methods of breaking the work rhythm (pace) and sabotaging quality, and "work according to the wage" (*an chou fu lao*).[24]

In a number of cases, protesters organized action committees and pickets or coordinated strikes in different factories and districts. And as the strike wave unfolded, workers even formed autonomous unions, "often termed *pingnan hui*, or redress grievances societies."[25] Given the low regard workers had for the official ACFTU and its union cadres, "it is not surprising that they were quick to abandon the official union organization whenever they felt the need to confront the enterprise leadership on an issue." While the ACFTU's enterprise unions "became an irrelevance in disputes," workers learned to take their problems and demands directly to their managers or to the CCP representatives, collectively and in an organized fashion.[26]

The Regime Hits Back

The regime's reactions to these workers' protests illustrate the dynamic of struggles from below and countermeasures from above, of demands for better material conditions and more control in work units and other areas of society versus the regime's attempt to defend its rule against these challenges and strengthen the new social and political hierarchy. The workers' demands and forms of struggle led to changes in the regime's reactions over time—and the regime's reactions led to new forms of critique and struggle from below.

In 1956 and the first half of 1957, state agencies like the labor bureau and work unit managements were quite conciliatory and often made concessions to protesting workers. Some official voices criticized workers for their "economism" (*jingjizhuyi*)—a derogatory term for (purely) materialist demands—and low level of "revolutionary consciousness." Cadres from mass organizations such as the ACFTU, the Chinese Communist Youth League (*zhongguo gongchanzhuyi qingnian tuan*), and the All-China Women's Federation (ACWF, *zhonghua quanguo funü lianhehui*) played a mediating role, even blaming enterprise cadres for "not trusting the working class."[27] They criticized the irrationality of managers and the indifference of many union officials towards the unrest.[28]

This wave of labor protests created enough pressure from below to push the CCP regime "to adjust the industrial system and managerial practices in a direction that was consistent with the state's 'image' (i.e. its ideological principles)."[29] The Soviet, strictly hierarchical "One-Man Regiment" was complemented by forms of worker participation and supervision through Staff and Workers Congresses (SWC, *zhigong daibiao dahui*) as well as collective leadership under party control. The CCP regime saw the danger of more open confrontation between alienated workers and the authorities in the work units and beyond. "[I]t was a recognition that policy had gone too far in the direction of only emphasizing production and neglecting democracy, welfare and workers' rights."[30]

The CCP leaders were concerned about the workers' uprisings against socialist regimes in Hungary and Poland in 1956, and feared similar protests in the PRC. In order to learn more about the domestic discontent and to provide a valve for letting off tensions, the regime launched the Hundred Flowers Movement (HFM, *baihua qifang*) or *daming dafang* ("big speaking out, big opening up") campaign in late April 1957 that allowed more open criticism.[31] The campaign followed a speech by Mao Zedong in February 1957 in which he emphasized that contradictions within the masses, rather than between the masses and their class enemies, were "non-antagonistic" in kind and could be resolved through debate, criticism, and self-criticism. The prime addressees of the HFM were intellectuals and white-collar employees or cadres who were encouraged to voice their criticisms. Still, the HFM also had an impact in workplaces like factories, even if production workers "remained on the sidelines" and the campaign was largely confined to technical and office staff.[32]

The criticism voiced by intellectuals and professionals exceeded what the party leaders had expected. Complaints about social or economic grievances were accompanied by attacks on party rule as such. The CCP was criticized for being authoritarian, exploitative, and living at the expense of ordinary people. Many of these criticisms were expressed from a liberal perspective, but similar accusations came from workers who felt betrayed by the establishment of an exploitative socialist system. Workers also used the opportunity given by the HFM to organize more protests and strikes at the height of the campaign in May 1957. They surrounded work unit offices, and attacked cadres verbally and sometimes physically. Some even called cadres "worse than the capitalists of the pre-revolutionary era" and cast the CCP as "rightist, corrupt, exploitative and privileged."[33]

Initially, the HFM was supposed to last for six months, but in early June the regime decided to stop it. It had underestimated the depth of the division between party leaders on one side vs. workers and intellectuals on the other, and realized that the criticisms and the campaign were getting out of hand. In retaliation, in July 1957, it struck back by launching the Anti-Rightist Campaign (*fanyoupai yundong*). Many of those who had raised criticisms of party rule or leaders during the HFM were severely punished. The CCP branded hundreds of thousands as "rightists," and stripped many of their positions or sent them to work in the countryside. This included intellectuals and professionals who could easily be attacked as "anti-socialist." Many union cadres were denounced, demoted, and purged after being "accused of making use of workers' narrow economic demands to 'incite workers to revolt' and of 'using the union to challenge the party.'"[34] The regime even reorganized and decentralized the union, and union cadres were subsequently subordinated to CCP workplace committees.

Many workers who had taken part in the strikes and criticisms were also punished with imprisonment or years of labor reform, but only a few were actually branded as "rightists."[35] "Most were distinguished from the intellectuals by being labeled 'bad elements' rather than rightists, a term which has criminal rather than political connotations."[36]

After all, it was an embarrassment to the CCP regime that after nationalization, which allegedly had cast workers as the "masters" of their work units, and after the installation of a socialist economy, labor conflicts did not disappear but escalated, as the CCP and the state had no organizational control over the working classes. Instead, the regime had to use various countermeasures like concessions and repression to halt a wave of strikes and criticisms before it could cause further damage to party rule.

Failed Expectations

In sum, the workers' struggles in the mid-1950s included positions, demands, and practices typically seen on left-wing agendas: discontent due to class divisions or social and political discrimination or economic exploitation; demands for equal treatment and improved conditions at the workplace; protests against authoritarian and arbitrary superiors (cadres); and forms of grassroots (and informal) organizing among interest-based proletarian groups.

The confrontation between temporary, migrant, or contract workers and the leftist CCP regime reflected the discrepancy between the regime's promises and the reality as experienced by workers. Many of them considered their situation miserable. They loathed the new social divisions and inequality, the discrimination against certain groups of workers, as well as bureaucratic apathy and indifference to the daily problems and living conditions of workers—conditions showing "the structural gap that [separated] the haves and have nots of the socialist economy."[37]

While in pre-1949 labor struggles employers or management were the main targets of protests and demands, after the transformation to a state-run economy from the mid-1950s on, the government was held responsible—a "new pattern of a worker reaction to adverse economic conditions."[38] Workers knew that the CCP and state cadres were responsible for the conditions in the work units. Most of their voiced demands were economic—for higher wages or better conditions—but "much of their wrath was directed against cadres in factory, government, Party and union positions."[39] This alarmed the government and was especially threatening, as it could not use an effective intermediate structure like the unions to diffuse tensions because the workers did not trust them (any more).[40]

The state came under attack because the policies of the CCP government "failed to meet the workers' expectations of what the new regime would mean for their economic interests," and because of "practices of state actors at the basic level that adversely affected the well-being of workers or nurtured daily discontent."[41] Part of this was a kind of "moral economy," as workers expected justice and equality from the state in exchange for them granting the regime legitimacy.

Even though the protests in 1956 and 1957 had no countrywide coordination or organizational core, on the local and enterprise level they showed the workers' ability to organize. These workers' protests threatened the legitimacy of the CCP's socialist regime "indicating the seriousness of the crisis in their relationship with the party only seven years after liberation."[42]

Subsequently, the CCP regime adapted the Soviet One-Man Regiment in the late 1950s and early 1960s to give the impression that there was more workers' participation, but the "discrepancy between the official rhetoric about the position of workers as the masters of enterprises and the actual experiences of workers in the workplace" continued to exist and created disillusionment and discontent.[43] The experience of the worker protests that threatened CCP legitimacy also contributed to the regime's decision to start a major reform in the late 1950s, the Great Leap Forward (GLF, *da yue jin*) that was meant to revitalize the socialist project.

In the next section, I will look at another workers' uprising that raised similar issues and left-wing demands for economic improvements and workers' control. This time, the struggles gave birth to left-wing mass organizing against and resistance to a CCP regime divided over the correct line of its leftist agenda and rule.

ECONOMISM AND THE REBEL MOVEMENT 1966–68

> The prolonged wage freeze, the delay in turning contract labor into regular workers, insufficiency of labor insurance, fringe benefits, and subsidies or employment for high school graduates, the assignment of dormitories, and overdue overtime compensation—in a word, all tumbled out as pressing problems. Like dried firewood piled up over the years, they burst into a raging flame from a single spark.[44]

In this section, I look at the workers' struggles during the early phase of the Cultural Revolution (*wenhua dageming*)—between

1966 and 1968. My account will not cover the whole history of the Cultural Revolution, and I will not look at the ideological and factional disputes involving Mao or the so-called "ultra-left" in the CCP leadership. My focus is on how new workers' discontent and struggles with left-wing demands and practices reflected the class divisions in PRC socialism at the time, and bred new currents of left-wing dissent and critique of the socialist class system.

Several developments in the late 1950s and early 1960s led up to the Cultural Revolution, the event that would eventually change the course of the socialist project in the PRC. In 1958, in an attempt to speed up the country's economic development, the CCP regime launched the GLF. The mobilization of peasants and workers for the construction of new infrastructure and industrial projects as well as the reorganization of rural collectives and urban work units largely failed. Problems of economic planning and reporting severely affected agricultural production, and the shortage of food led to a massive famine which killed millions, mainly in the countryside. CCP leader Mao Zedong had pushed the project and was seen as responsible for the failure. He had to take a step back while the now leading faction around Liu Shaoqi and Deng Xiaoping took back many of the GLF reforms. Millions of mobilized peasants were forced to return to the countryside and rural/urban migration was resolutely stopped through the *hukou* system.[45] At the end of 1961, the new leadership enacted the Seventy Articles, a document that entailed the return to pre-GLF economic policies and the One-Man Regiment in the work units.[46]

Meanwhile, the relations between the CCP regime and the political leadership of the Soviet Union deteriorated over the course of the 1950s. After Soviet leader Joseph Stalin's death in 1953, the new Soviet leadership started the de-Stalinization campaign and aimed for a "peaceful coexistence" with the main capitalist enemy state, the U.S. The CCP regime feared a similar "de-Maoization" and argued with the Soviet leadership on how to handle the uprisings in socialist Poland and Hungary in 1956. The GLF mentioned earlier can also be seen as an attempt by the CCP regime to follow its own version of "socialism in one country." In the early 1960s, it felt increasingly threatened by both global powers, the U.S. and the Soviet Union, and, in 1964, it started a massive project of moving industrial infrastructure inland, that is, away from vulnerable coastal and border regions. This so-called Third Front Construction (*sanxian jianshe*) would strain the economy and add to the social and political tensions of the mid- and late 1960s.

In 1962, the still powerful party faction around Mao Zedong, who had been occupied with the increasing "bureaucratization" of the party and the state elite since the mid-1950s, promoted another campaign, the Socialist Education Movement (*shehuizhuyi jiaoyu yundong*, SEM), also known as the Four Cleanups Movement (*siqing yundong*), which lasted until 1966. Work teams of party cadres carried out rectification measures against rural and urban cadres who were exposed as enemies from the old society or as "capitalist roaders" (*zouzipai*) responsible for the failure of the GLF. The SEM relied on the intervention of party cadres and was not as efficient as the Mao faction had hoped, especially not in mobilizing forces against the rival leading faction around Liu Shaoqi and Deng Xiaoping. The Cultural Revolution, the next campaign that aimed to challenge the rival faction and move Mao back into the driver's seat, therefore, would involve the mobilization of forces *outside* the party, especially students.

In the mid-1960s, the first post-liberation generation of middle-school and university students was faced with increasing problems of youth unemployment, blocked social mobility, hierarchical and authoritarian educational institutions, and a repressive system of class categories that produced a complex environment of privilege and discrimination. When, in 1966, the faction around Mao Zedong called for the mobilization against "capitalist roaders" in the party and reactionary forces in society to revive the socialist project under the leadership of Mao himself, many young members of this generation were ready to follow.[47]

In May that year, Mao's faction set up the Central Cultural Revolution Group (*zhongyang wenge xiaozu*, CCRG). Mostly made up of supporters of Mao, it was first responsible to the Standing Committee of the CCP Politburo, but in late 1966 and early 1967 the CCRG itself became the de facto leadership. After the mobilization started in the summer of 1966, Red Guards (*hongweibing*) were set up—sanctioned by the group around Mao Zedong—and began attacking teachers and cadres in schools and universities.

The CCP leadership around Liu Shaoqi sent work teams of party cadres to control these attacks and make sure they did not target the top leaders. At this point, the Red Guards were mostly offspring of party, state, and army cadres. They wanted to secure their own privileges as "heirs" of their revolutionary parents, and they referred to the so-called "blood-line theory" (*xuetong lun*) to legitimize the attacks. These were predominantly directed against the so-called "black categories," people with "bad" class background in schools and neighborhoods, on the basis that these were (allegedly) part of the old ruling classes or counter-revolutionaries. The group around Mao intervened in August 1966 with the "Sixteen Points" document, calling, instead, for attacks on "capitalist roaders in the party" and "bourgeois reactionary authorities." The Sixteen Points also emphasized the importance of production, as Mao's group wanted the Cultural Revolution to stay outside the work units so as to prevent any economic harm.[48]

Still, the Red Guard attacks on the "black categories" dominated the late summer's "red terror" (*hongse kongbu*) phase, with house raids, torture, and killings of many ordinary people, especially, in Beijing. Mao's circle intervened again in the fall of 1966 and emphasized that the struggle had to be directed against the "bourgeois line" in the party leadership. At this point, the dynamic of the Cultural Revolution changed. Many youths from the "black categories" used the redirection towards a "bourgeois line" to set up their own Red Guards. The Red Guard movement grew much bigger, with new organizations and meetings for which the young Guards traveled around the country. The new Red Guards began to attack not only cadres for being "capitalist roaders" and supporting the "bourgeois line" but also old Red Guards who defended those cadres. Young activists from the new Red Guards criticized the discrimination against the "black categories" and the exploitation of rusticated youth and others. Subsequently, the movement split into *conservative* groups (*baoshoupai*) defending the socialist order and party system and *rebel* groups (*zaofanpai*) attacking the socialist order and bureaucratic party leadership. With the new direction, the Cultural Revolution gained momentum and began to spread to the work units, something both factions in the CCP leadership had tried to prevent.

Discontented Workers

As in the mid-1950s, many of those who took the lead in the labor unrest of 1966 and 1967 were discriminated and precarious groups of workers. Their protests were the result of discontent accumulated in previous years.[49]

The group around Mao had promised to improve the status and situation of workers during the GLF in the late 1950s and early 1960s, but the GLF failed and no improvements were realized. On the contrary, to tackle the economic fallout of the GLF, in 1961 and 1962 the faction under Liu and Deng emphasized discipline, increased the pace of production and work quotas, and brought in austerity measures. By the time the Cultural Revolution began, many workers were disillusioned because wages had not been increased since the 1950s, many overtime hours had not been paid for years, and the housing situation was still miserable.

This did not affect all workers in the same way, though. Workers were still divided depending on type of industry, employment in state enterprises vs cooperatives, and status differences between senior and junior or permanent and temporary workers.[50] One of the main practices which fueled workers' unrest during the Cultural Revolution was the so-called "worker-peasant system" (*yi gong yi nong*) implemented since 1964. It was meant to set free more industrial surplus for accumulation by cutting costs. This was done by limiting the number of workers with permanent and higher-paid jobs and replacing them with rural temporary and contract workers with lower wages and fewer benefits, who were not allowed to bring their families to the cities and could easily be sent back. In the mid-1960s, it was not just workers employed on these terms who had cause for protest, but also many permanent workers who feared to lose their more secure status.[51]

When the Cultural Revolution started, the situation of many workers, permanent and temporary, deteriorated even further. Rusticated youth and former urban workers who had been sent to work in the countryside used the political situation to return to the city. In Shanghai, this massive population influx led to food shortages.[52] Many workers involved in Cultural Revolution activities were also laid off or suffered pay cuts after criticizing enterprise cadres.

Mass Organization and Struggle

Workers had many reasons to fight for improvements, but during the initial phase of the Cultural Revolution in summer 1966 they mostly stayed out of the conflicts and mobilizations. At first, the unfolding events looked like one of the previous rectification campaigns, and workers knew about the negative effects they could face if they attacked cadres or state authorities. In addition, the CCRG tried to keep the Cultural Revolution out of the work units and told workers to participate only in their free time. And when, in the late summer and early autumn of 1966, workers tried to get involved in Cultural Revolution activities—with the support of student Red Guards—enterprise cadres and party organs suppressed these attempts. The situation changed in November and December, when more and more workers got involved in mass struggles and set up their own organizations. On November 17, 1966, the CCRG legitimized these efforts, again unleashing the establishment of autonomous organizations, this time of workers, that were difficult to control thereafter.

The new movement reflected the divisions and antagonisms in the socialist society. Workers demanded higher wages, shorter working hours, better working conditions, secure employment, and better health care and benefits. In Shanghai, the CCP regime later criticized this as mere "economism." The composition of the movement was reminiscent of the labor protests in 1956 and 1957. Workers' rebel groups included apprentices who protested against prolonged training periods, wages which were often less than half the average, and their low social and political status.[53] Temporary and contract workers (among them many women*) were often performing the same work as permanent workers but received lower wages and fewer benefits, and were laid off when not needed any longer.[54] "They called for the abolition of the 'corrupt' system of contract labor, demanded that they be able to keep a higher percentage of their wages, and those who were laid off agitated for reinstatement and back wages."[55] Rusticated urban workers had been relocated to the countryside after the GLF and economic retrenchment in the early 1960s. Some of them were later re-hired by urban work units but only as temporary workers who had to keep their rural *hukou*. Many rusticated workers returned to the cities during the Cultural Revolution and demanded permanent jobs with higher wages and an urban *hukou*. Rusticated youth had been relocated to frontier or rural areas to do agricultural labor. The Cultural Revolution interrupted the rustication program and many rusticates returned to cities like Shanghai, formed organizations, and demanded jobs and an urban *hukou*. Demobilized soldiers also set up their own rebel groups. Compared to those demobilized in the 1950s, those demobilized after the GLF had lower wages and lacked job security. They demanded improvements and equal conditions now. Victims of various campaigns, for instance the Anti-Rightist Campaign 1957, also organized and demanded their rehabilitation and jobs that had been denied to them so far due to their "bad" class label.

All these groups started organizing and pushing for their demands in late 1966 and 1967. In their workplaces, rebel apprentices, temporary or contract workers were often the minority, also because many did not dare to stick their heads out by joining rebel groups. However, in Shanghai, for instance, many rebel organizations drew tens of thousands and more. They used various forms of struggle to put cadres in work units and government offices under pressure, among them demonstrations, sit-ins, blockades, and petitions to local authorities or even the center in Beijing.

The rebels were confronted by "conservative" worker groups dominated by permanent and skilled workers or cadres who drew on their members' experience of (party or union) organizing and their positions in the work unit hierarchy. They mostly defended the status quo and wanted to maintain production as their wages and bonuses depended on it. They also demanded "economist" improvements when temporary or contract workers got rises—as they wanted to keep their privileges.[56]

Concession and Repression

In late 1966, it became clear that workers' rebel organizations were rapidly expanding and had some support from the CCRG in Beijing for their struggle against the "bureaucratism" (*guanliaozhuyi*) of the faction around Liu and Deng. Many cadres gave in to the demands and made concessions to prevent being labeled counter-revolutionary. They paid out back wages, made temporary workers permanent, allowed rusticated youth or workers to return to the city, assigned jobs to unemployed youth, and raised the wage level even in rural areas.

In Shanghai, the participation of workers of different factions in "economist" activities as well as "political struggle" or factional organizing, debates, and conflicts led to widespread absenteeism (from workplaces) or de facto strikes. The disruption of production and transport, the overstretching of public and work unit funds by the payments of large sums to workers, and the vastly increased consumption triggered by these payments created an economic crisis. The old political party and state institutions had largely collapsed under the pressure from Red Guards and rebel groups. These developments led to the paralysis of the city in early 1967.

In this situation, the CCRG again changed the direction of the Cultural Revolution. First, it promoted the slogan "grasping revolution and promoting production" (*zhua geming, cu shengchan*) it had already used since November 1966. Maintaining production and restoring order became the prime target. The leadership subsequently attacked "counter-revolutionary economism," claiming that "capitalist roaders" had duped workers into leaving their workplaces and following their personal interests instead of collective interests.

Second, in January 1967, the CCRG made the vital decision to allow rebel groups to carry out "power seizures" (*duoquan*). At this point, the old party and state authorities had already collapsed. In Shanghai, the dominant rebel alliance in the city, the Workers' General Headquarters (*gongren zongbu*) tried to take over political power, and the CCRG feared that it would lose control over the course of the Cultural Revolution altogether.[57] The sanctioned power seizures had to be carried out by a "big alliance" (*dalianhe*) of rebel leaders, old cadres, and People's Liberation Army (PLA) officers, who formed so-called Revolutionary Committees (*geming weiyuanhui*). Such a Revolutionary Committee was first implemented in Shanghai where it replaced the more radical set-up of the so-called Shanghai People's Commune (*Shanghai renmin gongshe*) formed by rebel groups. Afterwards, such committees were established in other parts of the country. They were meant to crack down on economism and restore political and economic order.

Many rebel leaders were coopted into these new institutions. Mao Zedong himself, plus those in the CCRG who were later identified as "ultra-left" and some local rebel leaders participated in condemning workers' "economism." They insinuated that the material demands of workers were a plot of "capitalist roaders" in work units and local administrations "to sabotage the Cultural Revolution by diverting workers' activity into economic demands with 'bribes' of back wages and other payments."[58] Accordingly, the new Revolutionary Committees, often dominated by the PLA officers and old cadres, did not allow more concessions to workers' economic demands. The payment of back wages and bonuses was stopped, returned rusticates were told to go back to the countryside, and temporary workers' organizations were banned and their leaders arrested. The Revolutionary Committees also enforced the dissolution of other rebel organizations.

While many worker activists were arrested, on the work unit level, the conflicts about management practices connected to the Seventy Articles—labor hierarchies, strict rules, arbitrary management—remained unresolved and continued to simmer. "Economism" and protests by temporary and contract workers would reappear, even in industries that were under direct military control.[59] Many rebel workers were also unhappy about the return of large numbers of previously purged cadres, the dissolution of their organizations, and the dominant role of both cadres and PLA officers in the Revolutionary Committees.

During the summer of 1967, these conflicts were overlaid with battles between conservative and rebel groups, between different rebel groups, and between rebels and the army which, in most cases, supported the conservative faction. Depending on the location, these battles were more or less violent, and most centered around who would keep the political initiative, dominate the Revolutionary Committees, or resist repression.

The CCP leadership around Mao used the PLA, as well as political campaigns, to arrest, punish, and rusticate millions of rebels, for instance, the Cleansing the Class Ranks campaign (*qingli jieji duiwu*) against rebels among the workforce, or the One Strike, Three Antis campaign (*yi da, san fan*) against the "ultra-left."[60] As in other instances of popular dissent and resistance in the PRC, workers were punished more severely than students.

New Trends of Thought

The economist movement, as well as the organizing of rebel groups and power seizures in workplaces, temporarily shaped the course of the Cultural Revolution in early 1967 in Shanghai—and in different forms and varying chronologies in other cities as well. The leadership group around Mao used the Revolutionary Committees to reinstate cadres previously overthrown, coopt rebel leaders willing to cooperate, ban rebel organizations, and restore order in the work units. However, while the newly established power structures began to arrest, punish, and rusticate rebel leaders and activists, many rebels resisted and developed more radical ideas. The roots for these radical ideas lay in the complex and shifting political directions the CCP leadership faction around Mao Zedong had promoted since the early 1960s.

Before the Cultural Revolution, CCP leaders had attacked the Communist Party of the Soviet Union and its leader Nikita Khrushchev for having allowed the formation of a "privileged stratum" in society. "It was obviously a question in many people's minds when more and more Party officials were ferreted out as 'capitalist roaders' with the unfolding of the Cultural Revolution whether the concept of the 'privileged stratum' or 'privileged class' could be applied to China as well."[61] "Capitalist roaders" were first presented as betraying the revolution by supporting the return of the *old* ruling class. Accordingly, in the summer of 1966, the first wave of Red Guards turned mainly against the "black categories" and people with "bad class background."

In late 1966, the discourse shifted towards a critique of those whose privileges emerged from their status in the socialist society, the *new* ruling class. The CCRG promoted this change, at first, as it targeted the "capitalist roader" faction around Liu Shaoqi and Deng Xiaoping. For the CCRG, this was not a problem of the socialist system in the PRC, but only the problem of a few "bad apples" in the leadership who chose to "follow the capitalist road."

Radical parts of the rebel movement and the second wave of Red Guards took the attack on the material privileges of cadres and their children more seriously—as expressed by the writings of the young worker Yu Luoke and others—and they developed a critique of the new class hierarchy in socialist China.[62] In 1967, after the leadership turned against the rebel movement, many participants distanced themselves from the CCRG and decided to follow through with the new class analysis "and act accordingly."[63] Rebels began investigating the social situation in urban and rural communities and collected respective reports which revealed the exploitative nature of class relations in the PRC. "All these reports pointed to an important fact that exploitation did exist in Socialist China. What remained to be answered was who exploited whom. This question became clearer with the exposure of the luxurious and corrupt lives of some party officials."[64]

At the same time, rebels engaged in a debate on workers' control, attacked by the CCRG as a demand for "extreme democratization" or "ultra-democracy." This was infused with power seizures by rebel workers in work units in early 1967, who, in some locations, gained enough worker support to successfully withstand attacks from conservative workers, cadres, and military officers sent to control them. Popular among rebels was the Paris Commune as an example of workers' democracy that also played a role in the setting up of the Shanghai Commune in January 1967. For the CCRG, the problem with the commune was that it involved a form of direct democracy that left no room for the leading role of the Communist Party.[65]

The dissent between rebels and the regime found expression in the emergence of theory study groups from summer 1967 on, and later the development of left-wing theories by groups of young rebels like the April 3 Faction (*sisan pai*) in Beijing, the Anti-Restoration Society (*fan fubi xuehui*) in Shanghai, the Shandong Bohai Battle Regiment (*Shandong bohai zhantuan*) and the October Revolution Group (*shiyue geming xiaozu*) in Shandong and the Big Dipper Society (*beidouxing xueshe*) in Wuhan.[66] These groups were partially set up in reaction to Mao's call to study the theory of continuous revolution. "More importantly, however, after more than a year of dramatic changes brought about by the Cultural Revolution, people in general and the rebels in particular felt a strong need for an adequate and consistent theory to explain and to guide the current movement."[67] The groups developed what was called "the new trend of thought," that is, theories that differed from the dominant official ideology and that had a common ground in reinterpreting class struggle in socialism as the struggle against the new privileged class of CCP officials and not against the remnants of the old ruling class from before 1949.

The biggest and most prominent promoter of the new thought became Shengwulian, a coalition of rebel groups in Hunan province set up in late 1967.[68] As with earlier rebel coalitions, for instance, in Shanghai, Shengwulian was made up of various groups that had experienced exploitation (as temporary workers), discrimination (as ruralites), displacement (as rusticated), or exclusion (as people branded as "bad elements"). They now saw a chance to continue organizing and pushing for their demands: army veterans, teachers with "bad class background," workers from small factories, workers from light industry and the transport sector, peasants, college students and teachers, middle-school students, workers from collective enterprises, low-level party and state workers, and workers who had just graduated from vocational schools.

The coalition enjoyed large support in Hunan, but it became known in the whole of the PRC mostly because of various political texts produced by members of Shengwulian like Yang Xiguang. Shengwulian activists identified their political tendency as "ultra-left" (*jizuo*), discussed the existence of a privileged "bureaucratic class" or "red bourgeoisie," and saw the PRC as capitalist or state-capitalist. For them, the liberation in 1949 was a bourgeois revolution, leaving intact capitalist relations of production, followed by the establishment of socialism in the mid-1950s.[69] After the Great Leap Forward, they saw the formation of the socialist bureaucratic class that introduced capitalist methods and relations. These were characterized by powerful factory directors or heads of rural collectives who pursued personal gain, the exploitation of temporary and contract workers, work pressure in urban work units, and rusticated youth in collectives as new "serfs." Meanwhile the distribution of goods benefited the interest of the bureaucratic class. Exploitation was based not on property relations or ownership but positions and privileges.[70]

Against this, Shengwulian stood for continuing revolution. "Using phrases such as 'a greater storm of political revolution,' 'thoroughgoing revolution,' 'thoroughly smashing the old state machinery,' Shengwulian expressed its desire for a fundamental change of the existing system. It thus raised a series of radical political demands, aimed, ultimately, at overthrowing the bureaucrats as a class."[71] For Shengwulian activists, the promotion of Revolutionary Committees (of rebel leaders, old cadres, and PLA officers) by the CCRG as the new governance model of the Cultural Revolution equaled going down "the bourgeois reformist road."

Shengwulian's radical positions were echoed by groups in other parts of the PRC and were widely debated, especially, after the CCRG started attacking the coalition and distributed its material all over the PRC so it could be critically discussed. In January 1968, Shengwulian was openly denounced and attacked as "counter-revolutionary" and "reactionary," and its leaders were arrested. That was followed by harsh measures against the rebel groups already mentioned.

Averting the Left-wing Threat

In sum, two conflicts shaped the confrontation during the Cultural Revolution described here: Mao's faction aimed to regain control over the party and the state while infusing new energy into the socialist project; and the (rebel) movement of different actors from below used the space given to organizing and struggle and fought for the improvement of their lives. First students and then workers played the central role in the movement, which brought party and state to the brink of collapse. Both fundamental left-wing themes shaped the conflicts: rebel workers fought for economic improvements, associated with the "economist wind" of late 1966 and early 1967, and for self-empowerment and (democratic) control over workplaces, denigrated by the party center as "ultra-democracy." Mostly permanent, skilled workers, technicians, and cadres organized in conservative groups tried to defend their privileges, while mostly temporary and contract workers, apprentices and young workers formed rebel groups, and attacked managers and loyal workers in the work units.

Two understandings of class shaped the trajectory of events, the demands, directions, and forms of the movements involved. Conservative Red Guards identified "capitalist roaders" as members of the pre-liberation bourgeois class, the rebel Red Guards rather identified them as contemporary bureaucratic party leaders. The majority of the rebels considered these "capitalist roaders" in the party as morally and ideologically weak cadres. They thought the problem was not systemic but that of individual traitors. A minority of the rebels disagreed. Groups like Shengwulian attacked party and state cadres as part of the new bureaucratic ruling class or "red bourgeoisie." Their struggle was not against the "bourgeois line" or certain "capitalist roaders" alone any more, but about getting rid of the bureaucratic class of party leaders as a whole.

As the Liu–Deng faction in the leadership was weakened during the early phase of the Cultural Revolution, it was the CCRG under Mao that confronted and repressed the rebel movement when it got out of hand and threatened to undermine party rule as such. The CCRG promoted the new Revolutionary Committees set up in 1967 and 1968 that were dominated by cadres and army officers but integrated rebel leaders willing to cooperate. The cooptation of a part of the rebel groups or leaderships on a local, regional, and countrywide level divided the rebel movement into cooperative and defiant factions, and the former helped to rechannel the political discourse. The CCRG partially acknowledged the existence of an exploiting and privileged stratum but identified it with the Liu–Deng faction alone. It linked the economist struggle to the bourgeois-reactionary line whose protagonists had allegedly started that struggle. It denounced the workers' demands for more control in workplaces as "ultra-democratic" or "anarchist," and passed off the restoration of economic and political order through the "big alliance" of PLA officers, cadres, and rebel representatives as an accepted form of "rebellion."

The CCRG used the army as well as "conservative" groups to bring an end to the "economist" struggles, enforce the dissolution of rebel organizations, repress the rest of the rebel leadership, and re-establish order through arrests, punishments, and rustication of millions of rebels. The rebel struggles had neither created lasting forms of mass organization and mobilization nor had they fundamentally changed the hierarchies in the workplaces—even if the factional struggle continued and rebel workers made certain material gains.[72]

The rebel uprising and economist struggles failed or crumbled not just because of repression, cooptation, and concessions though, but also because of their inner contradictions: economist struggles often expressed specific situations and demands, and could not merge into a lasting powerful movement. Rebel students and workers shared the critique of conservative positions, but conflicts between these groups prevented further cooperation. Rebel students wanted to lead protests and workers did not trust the students, a theme that would come up again in later struggles. Rebel groups demanded the redistribution of wealth and power, but they had no common concept of what that would mean for the transformation of the socialist institutions.[73] Last but not least, the radical critique of bureaucratism (*guanliaozhuyi*) and "commandism" (*minglingzhuyi*) did not stop radical rebels from worshiping Mao Zedong or proposing "Mao Zedong-ism."

The mass phase of the Cultural Revolution ended in 1967 or 1968, depending on region. Two "ultra-leftisms" remained, one embodied by leftists in the CCP leadership who would play a role in the factional conflicts that shaped the first half of the 1970s, and the ultra-leftism of Shengwulian and the other groups who remained in opposition to party and state authorities, and who continued to suffer harsh repression, punishment, and rustication.

The experience of self-organizing and struggle, the left-wing critique of the socialist class society, and the repression by a leftist CCP leadership shaped a generation of young rebels, many of whom, even if punished or rusticated, continued to discuss their experiences in the years to come. The radical parts of the rebel faction condemned the Cultural Revolution for not going far enough or all the way. Their ideas diverged from the dominant Cultural Revolution discourse and questioned the political set-up of the PRC. Their new class theory, "with its emphasis on the inequalities and corruption of socialist China, served as the ideological basis of the democracy movements in the 1970s and early 1980s."[74]

CONCLUSION: REGIME BETRAYAL AND CLASS RESISTANCE

In this chapter, I looked at the specific ways in which social discontent and unrest from below produced oppositional left-wing demands and practices in the socialist mid-1950s and mid-1960s. In the two cases analyzed, the social divisions and the discrimination against particular groups—such as temporary and contract workers, apprentices, or rusticated youth who felt betrayed or treated unfairly by the socialist regime—led to discontent and demands for material improvements and more control in the work units. Both movements won (temporary) concessions but were eventually repressed.

The strike movement and political critique of the regime in the mid-1950s was a direct result of the establishment of the socialist planned economy and the full nationalization of industries. Certain groups of workers were disappointed that their wages were not rising as expected, that the piece rate system led to an intensification of work, and that the stratification of workers, with better conditions for some and worse conditions for many, was there to stay. The workers showed their ability to organize and strike, even when the union was opposed to their actions, but the strike movement did not manage to establish lasting organizational links.

The workers' rebel movement in the mid-1960s was part of a general mobilization triggered by the Mao faction against the Liu–Deng faction. However, it took on its own dynamic and at times evaded the control of the Mao faction. The rebel organizations were dissolved in 1967 and 1968, but rebel workers (and rusticated youth) would play a role in the factional struggles of the early 1970s and the democratic movements in the late 1970s and 1980s.

In both cycles of struggle, the left-wing issues of exploitation and wealth, as well as control and power, were important motivations for workers and rebels to take risks, organize, and struggle. Many workers were excluded from permanent jobs and encompassing benefits, and had to deal with unstable jobs and the possibility of being rusticated or called back to the cities (temporarily) at the whim of socialist cadres. They considered their working and living conditions unsatisfactory under a socialist regime. In addition, while, officially, workers should have been the "masters" of their work units, and the working class in charge of the society as a whole, in reality the socialist management was in charge of the work units and the CCP in charge of society.

The main addressee for workers' discontent and demands was the state and its representatives, in the form of managers and CCP party secretaries in work units and other institutions. The left-wing demands for material improvements and workers' control were made to a leftist regime that had established an exploitative and authoritarian socialist system. In a strictly controlled social and political environment, where organizing outside the control of the party or its mass organizations was banned, workers and other social players took risks to get together and openly criticize or even attack power holders. They took these risks despite the intimidation through regular rectification campaigns and severe punishments.

The CCP leadership made concessions with regard to some demands of discriminated workers, sometimes immediately, sometimes later.[75] However, eventually it repressed the larger mobilizations and organized critique that included left-wing demands, both in the late 1950s and in the late 1960s.

3

For a Better Future: Worker Movements Demand Democratic Reforms in the 1970s and 1980s

In this chapter, I look at three waves of protest in the PRC between the mid-1970s and the late 1980s. In all three, workers played a decisive role in confronting the CCP regime with demands for political reforms. Participants criticized authoritarian rule, corruption, austerity policies, and the deterioration of their living conditions—left-wing issues raised against the leftist CCP regime.

In the *first* section, I focus on the April 5 Movement (*siwu yundong*) of 1976. After the crackdown on the rebel movement of the Cultural Revolution in the late 1960s, factional conflicts and a series of political campaigns dominated the early 1970s. Growing discontent, labor unrest, and even political critique showed the exhaustion of Maoism as a mobilizing political concept by the mid-1970s. After premier Zhou Enlai died in early 1976, many people were dissatisfied with the way the CCP leadership handled his commemoration, and masses of protesters joined demonstrations that turned against the regime. Among them were many workers, including former activists with experience from the Cultural Revolution. The CCP regime repressed the movement before it could spread any further.

In the *second* section, I describe the Democracy Wall Movement (*minzhu qiang yundong*) of 1978 to 1980. Soon after Mao's death in September 1976 and the fall of the "ultra-left" Gang of Four (*sirenbang*), the CCP leadership was divided on the future political course. The new leader Hua Guofeng pushed for another massive industrialization campaign, while reformers around Deng Xiaoping planned larger economic changes. In 1978, a grassroots movement emerged in Beijing and other cities which demanded political reforms towards a democratic socialism. Again, workers and former rebel activists played a major role and helped to produce a series of unofficial journals and posters. At first, the movement was welcomed by the reformers in the leadership because it could use the pressure from below to push through their reform course. When the reformers had stabilized their grip on power, though, they harshly repressed the movement in 1980.

In the *third* section, I look at the Tian'anmen Square Movement (*tian'anmen guangchang yundong*) in 1989. By that time, the reforms had brought more economic opportunities to the countryside and cities, but they had also led to cadre corruption and the appropriation of public assets, economic problems like inflation, and a growing perception of job insecurity. In spring 1989, social discontent merged with demands for more democratic governance and social justice in the Tian'anmen Square Movement. In later stages, the mass mobilizations in several cities were dominated by workers. The CCP leadership saw their strong involvement as a threat to its rule and brought in the army to crush the movement.

THE APRIL 5 MOVEMENT 1976

> In the 1970s, it became apparent that forms of mass participation that could originally be manipulated were becoming increasingly difficult to keep under control after the experiences of the Cultural Revolution. More and more often, they resulted in spontaneous political expressions.[1]

The April 5 Movement expressed the social and political discontent workers and others had accumulated in the first half of the 1970s. It was too short-lived and too weak to change the political status quo right away, but the movement and the crackdown on it had an important impact on later protests and political changes in 1978 and after.

Several developments led to the mobilization in early 1976. First, factional conflicts divided the CCP regime and parts of the society in the first half of the 1970s. In the leadership, a "leftist" faction around Mao's wife Jiang Qing clashed with the "conservative" faction behind Zhou Enlai and later the rehabilitated Deng Xiaoping, as well as the "centrist" faction including Hua Guofeng. The leftist faction staged several campaigns against cadre privileges and corruption, but these campaigns were more top-down than the mobilizations during the Cultural Revolution.[2] The conservative faction tried to implement economic reforms, above all the Four Modernizations (*sige xiandaihua* or *sihua*) designed by Zhou Enlai, and pushed for the rapprochement with the U.S.[3]

Second, the pre-Cultural Revolution labor regime in the work units was largely restored in the late 1960s and early 1970s, with differences between industries and regions, and depending on the strength of rebels and conservatives among the workers and cadres of particular workplaces.[4] Concessions were made, like the permanent status given to temporary workers in 1971, but protests continued, often triggered by low wages, cadre arbitrariness, or housing problems. They included larger demonstrations and strikes in Guangzhou, Wuhan, and Hangzhou in 1974 and 1975. Factional conflicts and political campaigns had an impact on these protests, for instance, the Campaign to Criticize Lin Biao and Confucius (*pi lin pi kong yundong*) that was promoted by the leftists in the CCP leadership and that provided a pretext for workers' protests. Workers with a rebel background continued to play a major role in these protests and used their skills in organizing protests. The CCP regime suppressed the unrest, accusing participants of being counter-revolutionaries or class enemies.

Finally, several factors had led to the exhaustion of Maoism's mobilizing potential: these included the crackdown on the rebel movement in the late 1960s; the continued repression of rebels in the early 1970s; the harsh treatment of rusticated youth; the rehabilitation of cadres in work units and state administrations promoted by conservative forces; the leftist austerity policies; and the harsh living conditions for many workers and peasants. Some former rebel Red Guards dared to voice fundamental political critique publicly, for instance, a group called Li Yi Zhe.[5] In April 1974, it started to publish unauthorized posters in Guangdong which attacked leftist oppression, the cult around Mao, and cadre arbitrariness. They also wrote about a "newborn bourgeoisie" and its privileges, and criticized the wage freeze. Their posters circulated all over China and initiated a "poster war" in other cities that included attacks on cadre privileges and demands for the rehabilitation of people purged during the Cultural Revolution. Li Yi Zhe initially enjoyed some support from the conservative faction in the leadership, but its members were finally arrested and rusticated. The critique voiced by Li Yi Zhe and others who had a Red Guard background resembled that of Shengwulian in 1967–68 and was replicated to a certain extent in the Democracy Wall Movement in 1978 to 1980 (discussed in the next section).[6]

Factional conflicts, worker discontent, and regime critique all culminated in the events that shook the CCP leadership in spring 1976. These events formed a milestone in the demise of the leftist faction in the fall of the same year and the rise of the "reformers" soon after.

Spontaneous and Bottom-up Protests

Despite the growing social discontent, the April 5 Movement came as a largely unexpected spontaneous outbreak of anger. Different groups and interests confronted the CCP leadership with social, economic, and political demands. Even though much of the anger was targeted at the leftists in the leadership, the movement addressed problems with the CCP regime's authoritarian rule as a whole.[7]

Premier Zhou Enlai, for many a respected figure in the CCP leadership and an adversary to the leftist faction, died on January 8, 1976. The official handling of his death was seen as inappropriate if not disrespectful. In early April, for several days before and during the Qingming festival, when families traditionally mourn their ancestors, crowds gathered to commemorate Zhou in various cities, including Nanjing, Zhengzhou, Luoyang, Anyang, Kaifeng, Taiyuan, Changchun, Shanghai, Wuhan, Xi'an, Kunming, and Guangzhou.

The biggest gatherings—and the culmination of the movement—took place on Tian'anmen Square in central Beijing. On April 3 and 4, hundreds of thousands turned up with banners, wreaths, and posters. Many of them praised Zhou or criticized his leftist opponents in the CCP leadership. Some even targeted Mao Zedong, which had not happened in this open form even during the rebellious time of the Cultural Revolution. The authorities removed banners, wreaths, and posters during the night before April 5, which stirred up anger the next day and led to another assembly of tens of thousands on Tian'anmen Square, which turned into a riot.[8] During clashes with police and militia, cars were burned and government buildings around the square stormed and set on fire. In the evening, after most people had left, security forces were able to round up and arrest hundreds who had remained on the square.[9]

All in all, millions took part in the events, most of them in Beijing and Nanjing. Participants ranged from peasants to cadres, but the majority were young workers, with Nanjing as an exception where students dominated and workers supported them. Workers were also the biggest group among the smaller number of activists who initiated and pushed the protests.[10] They participated because they were disillusioned with factional conflicts, leftist campaigns, and obligatory study sessions. Economic demands were not prominently brought forward during the mobilization, but stagnating standards of living and especially the long wage freeze troubled many. The leftists in the leadership were held responsible for these problems as they objected to wage incentives and welfare measures. The hopes of many rested in the Four Modernizations that had been pursued by Zhou Enlai and Deng Xiaoping. The choice workers had at the time between the leftists and the conservatives resembled one between "no power and no money" and "no power and some money." In that way, it was "hardly surprising that after more than a decade of struggle and enforced austerity, most opted for the latter:" no power and some money.[11]

The movement was bottom-up and spontaneous, without central coordination or mobilization. The protesters used the death of a political leader and funerary rites to express their political grievances, "a well-established tradition" that would be repeated during the Tian'anmen Square Movement in 1989.[12] The forms of expression during the rallies and demonstrations included both mourning (flowers, wreaths, poems) and political statements and critique (red flags, slogans, singing the "International"). Young workers involved drew upon their Cultural Revolution experiences and referred to the right to "rebel" (*zaofan*) as well as the "four big freedoms" (*si da ziyou*): *daming dafang* (big speaking out, big opening up), *da bianlun* (holding big debates), *dazibao* (writing big-character posters), and *da chuanlian* (big linking up) that had inspired the Red Guard movement. They also drew upon more recent dissident discussions, like those about the posters of Li Yi Zhe that had emerged two years before.[13]

In all cities, the activities of the April 5 Movement were organized in and around work units. In some of them, up to 50 percent of workers in the same unit participated. Union cadres, managers, or even party cadres joined as well, or at least tolerated the activities. Although contacts were established between work units, and a few even coordinated their actions, this was not a widespread practice and the protests were rather cellular in nature. Many former rebel and conservative Red Guards took part. In some cases, they even cooperated (temporarily) although factional struggles had been heating up since 1974.[14]

The participation of conservative workers is not surprising as they opposed the leftist austerity policies and campaigns in the first half of the 1970s. However, the April 5 Movement was not just aimed at the leftists in the leadership but against authoritarian rule and lack of democratic control over the leadership as a whole. Rebel workers who had criticized Zhou Enlai during the Cultural Revolution now challenged the leftist leaders in the mid-1970s. They participated in the movement because the CCP leadership had changed and because the leftist leaders had become part of the bureaucratic class and promoted authoritarian policies that harmed workers' interests.

The Opening Salvo

In the days and weeks following the events around April 5, the CCP leadership organized mass assemblies and called for the denunciation of the movement's participants. In Beijing and other cities, tens of thousands were investigated, and several thousand arrested. In the capital alone, several hundred were even killed.[15] The CCP leadership branded many of those who were arrested during the movement as counter-revolutionaries and sent them to prison or work camps soon after. Most of those persecuted were workers.

The leftists in the leadership accused Deng Xiaoping of organizing the movement to challenge them, and he was subsequently purged again. Many of the movement's activists rejected the idea, however, "that they had been mere pawns or even marionettes of a powerful network." For them, "the meaning and significance of the movement lay in the very fact that it came from the grassroots, at a time when this seemed almost unthinkable."[16]

In sum, the April 5 Movement was an outbreak of tensions over the experience of the CCP's campaigns and purges as well as economic problems and stagnation. The movement was politically diverse but included left-wing demands for economic improvements and an end to authoritarian rule. It was quickly repressed and did not have time to develop lasting organizational structures.

Seen in historical perspective, the movement played an important role because the grassroots mass protests taught the leadership a lesson. Fundamental social and political changes were necessary to avoid an even larger movement that could destabilize CCP rule. The Deng faction, at least, seems to have understood this. Indeed, the movement is one of the events that led to (and justified) the coup against the "ultra-left" Gang of Four in October 1976. Equally important, it was the forerunner of the Democracy Wall Movement that began in late 1978.

After the crackdown in 1976, the poems, memories, and reports the movement's participants produced were collected and circulated secretly. They preempted the infamous "people's literature" (*minkan*) of the movement after 1978. And last but not least, it was the conflict about the rehabilitation of the participants in the April 5 Movement that eventually triggered the Democracy Wall Movement. The April 5 Movement was "the opening salvo" of the democracy movements described in the next two sections.[17]

THE DEMOCRACY WALL MOVEMENT 1978–80

> According to the concepts of Marxism-Leninism, the people should control the means of production. But ask yourselves, Chinese workers and peasants: Apart from the small wage which you receive each month, what do you control? What belongs to you? The answer is shameful: Others are your masters. In a social-

> ist society, the product of labor should belong to the worker. But what do you get? Just enough so that you can continue to work! Higher salaries have not sufficed to compensate for soaring prices, and our standard of living has not improved. (From a wallposter put up in Beijing in December 1978)[18]

At the end of 1978, the Democracy Wall Movement (DWM) began to express the social and political desires of a generation of worker activists and their demands for change. Deng Xiaoping's reform faction still had not secured the dominant position in the CCP leadership and coopted these demands for change, using their impetus to win the leadership battle and push through restricted and streamlined economic reforms. The authoritarian form of CCP rule was reconfigured but not abolished.

In the few years before, between the April 5 Movement 1976 and the beginning of the DWM in November 1978, the political situation in the PRC had changed rapidly. Mao Zedong died on September 9, 1976, and his Premier Hua Guofeng successfully rejected the leftists' claim to party leadership. On October 6, he and other leaders even staged a coup against the so-called Gang of Four: Jiang Qing, Zhang Chunqiao, Yao Wenyuan, and Wang Hongwen were arrested and later put on trial. In 1977 and 1978, the CCP leadership continued to force provincial or city party leaders who had been appointed by or connected to the Gang of Four to step down. Meanwhile, cadres who had been purged in various campaigns, from the Anti-Rightist Campaign in 1957 to campaigns in the early 1970s, were rehabilitated and often returned to their old positions. The leadership also sponsored a public debate on the crimes of the Gang of Four and the fateful policies during the Cultural Revolution.

After the coup against the leftists, the power struggle continued. The reformers around Deng Xiaoping pushed for changes in line with the Four Modernizations and the introduction of more markets, but they were confronted by the centrist Hua Guofeng and his supporters, and by an opportunistic "whateverist" faction. Following Mao's orders, Hua Guofeng became his successor. He promoted an industrialization program that did not diverge much from previous attempts to revive the economy by pushing major heavy industry and infrastructure projects. However, he stressed the "task of developing the economy" and "emphasized improving living standards and doing a better job of organizing the market."[19] For that matter, "Hua combined Soviet-style big push industrialization with an opening up to the capitalist world."[20]

Hua's big push plan quickly ran into crisis, but the Deng faction still had difficulties prevailing in the leadership contest. It was another popular movement that proved decisive. After Hua had taken over, the leftist austerity policies had been dropped and wages increased—measures that were popular among workers. However, workers' expectations were high, and certain groups began to voice their grievances. Among them were rusticated urban youth who wanted to return to the cities, peasants who had problems with local cadres, and other people who had been branded and purged in campaigns since the 1950s and demanded rehabilitation. It was at this moment that the DWM rose up and eventually helped the Deng faction to take control.

The Fight for a Political Opening

The DWM, from 1978 to 1980, asked for political reforms, and, especially, the introduction of democratic control and people's self-determination. The movement, dominated by workers, was not homogeneous but consisted of various tendencies ranging from those demanding a more democratic form of socialism to promoters of democracy modeled on that in Western countries.[21]

The spark that set off the DWM came from the struggle for the rehabilitation of those purged in connection with the April 5 Movement. Soon after the fall of the Gang of Four in October 1976, they demanded a revision of the regime's verdict on the April 5 Movement. In fact, many of them were released from detention in late 1976 and early 1977, but they kept their designation as counterrevolutionaries and were discriminated against accordingly. When the verdict was finally reversed, in November 1978, activists saw the chance to go public with their more general critique and demands.

Starting in mid-November 1978, big-character posters (*dazibao*) were hung up on a roadside wall just west of Tian'anmen Square in central Beijing. More posters and underground journals (*dixia kanwu*) soon circulated in Beijing as well as Guangzhou, Changsha, Wuhan, Taiyuan, Tianjin, Qingdao, Harbin, Shanghai, Nanjing, Guiyang and Kunming.[22] Leading groups with their own publications were April 5 Forum (*siwu luntan*), Beijing Spring (*Beijing zhi chun*), Masses' Reference News (*qunzhong cankao xiaoxi*), the Chinese Human Rights Alliance (*Zhongguo renquan tongmeng*), the Enlightenment Society (*qimengshe*), Exploration (*tansuo*), and Today (*jintian*).[23]

At the end of the year, activists had organized in groups to discuss and publish the posters and journals. These groups formed a "loose coalition" whose rallying point was democratization, the support of more reforms, and demands for "civil liberties, basic democratic rights, and a higher degree of freedom vis-à-vis state and party."[24] The activists were mostly in their twenties and early thirties. Those slightly older had already been involved in the Cultural Revolution as rebel and conservative Red Guards.[25] Those a bit younger had been part of the April 5 Movement in 1976. "Many of them had been arrested on that occasion. While in prison they developed a common attitude toward the necessity for reform and change."[26] While many others were still waiting to see what the regime under Hua and Deng would deliver, these April 5 veterans and the slightly older Cultural Revolution activists demanded immediate political changes.

Both groups were made up of state-employed workers, technicians, clerks, or teachers, some of them daughters and sons of high-ranking cadres. Notably, the intelligentsia (like authors, professors, or researchers) was not represented[27] and, instead, many factory workers played a big role. Not only did this work have a high social status at the time, skilled or unskilled factory jobs were also the best that activists from the Cultural Revolution could hope for, and many families tried to get their children jobs in urban factories as that was a way to avoid them being sent to the countryside.[28]

While workers' grievances were expressed in the DWM posters and journals, two other groups played a specific role at the time. The first of these was youth who had been rusticated, that is, young people sent to the countryside in the years before, who began to return to cities illegally in the late 1970s. Their conditions in the villages were harsh, and they believed the way they were chosen and "sent down" was arbitrary and discriminatory. After 1976, some of them were, in fact, allowed to return, but many more felt encouraged to move back to their home city in the wake of the DWM. After their return, they began to petition urban authorities for an official permit to stay in the cities.

They were joined by the second group, peasants, who came to the cities at the end of 1978. These peasants sought redress for injustices they had suffered in previous years or even decades. They saw cadres in their home villages as responsible for these injustices, and, as they could not get the desired recognition at home, they went to big cities to petition the authorities there. In Beijing, thousands of them gathered outside government buildings and asked for their cases to be heard.[29]

Together, rusticated youth and peasants formed the so-called *shangfang* or "petition" movement. They staged demonstrations, some of which even turned into riots. Because they were not part of the urban rationing system, they also had to use illegal means to survive in the city.

The Movements' Political Demands

The wall posters, written and hung up by individuals and groups, can be divided into three categories: those criticizing Mao Zedong or other leaders for their role in the persecution during the Cultural Revolution or the delayed rehabilitation of those purged; those complaining about personal arbitrary persecution and maltreatment during campaigns or personal hardships, for instance, of peasants; and those calling for democratic reforms of the socialist system or individual rights.

Demands and other content of posters and underground journals reflected most of the authors' background as workers and, in some way or other, Marxists. As workers, they brought up an "enormous backlog" of grievances that had been built up over the years.[30] Economic issues expressed included the urban housing shortage, inequality, unequal pay for equal work, unfair distribution of pay and bonuses, threats to workers' job security as well as welfare benefits, and worries over rising prices and inflation. Deng's Four Modernizations were often supported in the hope that they could improve the economic situation of workers, but authors added demands for the democratization of management, that is, workers' participation in running the work units. Among the concrete political issues criticized on posters and in journals were cadre privilege, corruption, and abuse of power.

As Marxists, activists demanded political reforms that aimed to overcome previous leftist politics (of the Gang of Four), the abolition of the bureaucratic ruling class, and the creation of a socialist democracy—but no abolition of socialism.[31] Democratization stood for the public supervision of the CCP government under Hua and Deng. To accomplish that, political reforms had to complement economic reforms.

Some Marxists had the idea that socialism could be merged with elements from bourgeois democracies as in the West, others rather referred to more consistent or direct forms of democracy, as during the Paris Commune. Radical voices demanded not only the right to elect low-level management cadres, as offered by the reformers, but that control over the work units should be passed from the party organization to the workers themselves.

In 1978, just two years after Mao's death and the coup against the Gang of Four, activists felt confident to criticize the shortcomings of PRC socialism because "nothing was sacred" any more. "Calls for a complete reassessment of the whole history of CCP rule were now commonplace"[32] as the reform discourse inside the party leadership opened up the opportunity to criticize the past and discuss the future. It is no coincidence that during the time of the DWM demands for workplace democracy were made and the bureaucratic class was critiqued as exploitative. Many participants had become rebels in the late 1960s. Some were familiar with the critique of exploitation and oppression by a new socialist ruling class, expressed by Shengwulian as well as by the texts of Li Yi Zhe and others who had voiced a systemic critique of actually existing socialism.

Another wing of the movement did not refer to Marxism and saw no possibility to realize democracy within the socialist framework. While it also attacked the privileges of the bureaucratic or technocratic ruling class, it demanded a multi-party system or even promoted the U.S. as a model of democracy. Many of these "abolitionists" were former conservative Red Guards.

Toleration and Repression

The *shangfang* mass movement of rusticated youth and peasants combined with worker activism and public political critique expressed in underground journals and posters posed a threat to the CCP regime and provoked a reaction. At first, the leadership faction around Deng Xiaoping largely tolerated the DWM publications. The movement offered a chance to demonstrate to the outside world (and the new trade partners) that the CCP could deal with mass mobilization and tolerate public dissent. More importantly, the movement mostly attacked the factional opponents in the leadership who resisted more fundamental reforms.

When the movement began in Beijing in November 1978, the party leadership was simultaneously holding a working conference (in preparation for the scheduled Third Plenary Session). The reformer faction around Deng wanted to reinstate the economic principles of the post-GLF readjustment policies (1962–65) but faced opposition from the centrists around Hua Guofeng and the faction that resisted radical change, the "whateverists." Deng's faction prevailed. The movement on the streets was obviously favoring Deng's side, and any decision against more reforms would have likely provoked more protests.

At this point, the socialist or Marxist wing of the democracy movement was dominant. However, in early 1979, the movement mushroomed and spread to other cities. The non-Marxist abolitionists began to dominate and voiced more fundamental criticisms of the PRC's political and economic system. Now even Deng's faction began to see the movement as a potential threat.[33] After all, he and other cadres had been purged victims of the mass rebellion during the Cultural Revolution and feared anti-systemic movements from below.

The gradual repression of the DWM began in early 1979 and continued in a more or less severe form thereafter. On March 16 and March 30, 1979, Deng gave speeches in which he defined the red lines for any public debate and critique in the form of "four basic principles" that had to be upheld: the leadership of the CCP, the socialist path, the dictatorship of the proletariat (renamed "the people's democratic dictatorship"), and Marxism-Leninism-Mao Zedong Thought.[34] Subsequently, the party press attacked the DWM and for its promotion of "extreme democratization" and "bourgeois democracy."[35]

The subsequent wave of repression largely hit the abolitionists, and several prominent actors of the DWM were arrested—including Wei Jingsheng, who had openly criticized Deng Xiaoping.[36] The Marxist socialist democrats were spared in this first crackdown, and their journals continued to be sold. However, even if the socialist democrats disagreed with the abolitionists' political positions, they opposed their repression by the CCP leadership. For them, the repression showed that regime and bureaucratic class were standing in the way of democratization as such. The activists were determined to continue their struggle. The movement blossomed again in late summer 1979. In February 1980, it even formed the National Federation of People's Publications. Later that year, the center of the movement shifted away from Beijing and to the south because there was less pressure on the movement in Guangzhou and other places.

The cross-provincial networking and cooperation alarmed the regime once more. In the same year, labor unrest increased, and protesting workers even called for independent unions during a spate of labor unrest and strikes in 1980 and 1981. This was spurred on by news about the Solidarność union movement in Poland, which showed workers in the PRC that they were not alone in confronting a socialist regime and that it was possible to gain mass support for an oppositional workers' movement. The reformer regime in Beijing had moved away from previous leftist austerity policies and ended the wage freeze but workers still objected to parts of the reforms. For instance, they opposed the widening gap the reforms had brought between different workers' incomes, and the fact that more power was given to managers but not to the workers. This gave DWM activists the chance to create more links with other discontented workers.

The regime, meanwhile, had already prepared the final crackdown. In February 1980, the "four big freedoms" (speaking out, holding debates, writing character posters, linking up) were abolished and removed from the constitution, and the sale of unofficial journals in public was finally banned. By now, the Deng faction had secured its position and begun ousting leadership members of the other party factions. That meant they could get rid of the remaining DWM journals of socialist democrats as they had no use for them any more.

In December 1980, still feeling the impact of Solidarność in Poland and its repercussions in the PRC, the CCP leadership officially branded DWM activists "counter-revolutionaries who were stirring up social unrest and trying to wreck the economic reforms." It launched a mass campaign against the "two illegals" (illegal publications and illegal organizations) and "this heralded the final round of arrests and closures of unofficial journals."[37]

As it had done after previous cycles of social struggle, the CCP regime also made limited concessions to the demands of the DWM and the workers' struggles in the winter of 1980–81. Workers had demanded better representation in Staff and Workers Congresses (SWCs) at their workplaces or—after reports about Solidarność in Poland—even the right to form independent unions. However, the new regulations for SWCs in mid-1981 only granted them consulting rights with no decision-making rights. The role of the ACFTU was also not changed much, except for "attempts to make the unions appear more independent of the Party."[38] And although the regime had allowed discussions about the election of lower managers by workers, it never implemented such regulations. In 1982, the regime even removed from the constitution the right to strike.

Deng's reformer faction drew a final line under the pre-1978 period with the show trial and conviction of the Gang of Four, and with the CCP's formal adoption in June 1981 of the "Decision on certain questions in Party history" that condemned the Cultural Revolution and the leftists.[39]

For a Different Socialism

The Democracy Wall Movement between 1978 and 1980 was the last major confrontation between workers with left-wing agendas and the leftist CCP leadership at the end of the socialist period as it marked the beginning of the transitional period (which lasted until the end of the 1990s). Many participants were workers who had already been part of the April 5 Movement in 1976 or rebel groups during the Cultural Revolution in the second half of the 1960s.

In 1978, they used the opportunity opened up by the leadership conflicts in the initial reform phase to stage protests and initiate lively political debates. These debates focused on the shortcomings of PRC socialism and an alternative (socialist) strategy that included people's participation and control. The movement expressed both aspects of left-wing concern—over the unequal distribution of wealth and other material problems, and over the unequal distribution of power in work units and the society as a whole.

As workers, they pushed for the improvement of living conditions. As left-wing activists, they attacked the bureaucratism of the socialist ruling class, a critique that was reminiscent of that of Shengwulian and others.[40] This time, there seemed to be a chance for change as a part of the CCP leadership wanted (economic) reforms, but what the movement expected did not match what the reform faction around Deng was prepared to offer.

The movement did not overcome its political divisions (for instance, between Marxists and non-Marxists) and suffered from constant pressure and repression on the part of the regime. While it managed to create links between political groups and discontented social groups such as rusticated youth, peasants, and workers, these links, and the impact of the struggles of these groups, were not strong enough to force the regime to make major and lasting concessions.[41] After all, large sections of the peasantry and the working classes still hoped for improvements through the reforms proposed by the regime—and they were tired of more social and political struggles that reminded them of the years before 1976.

Still, the regime understood the potential threat posed by a largely left-wing political movement organized by workers and the possible convergence with increasing labor unrest—after all, this happened just a decade after the major social unrest during the Cultural Revolution had brought the party to the brink of disaster.

The CCP leadership again used a mix of concessions, cooptation, and repression to divide, neutralize, and suppress the movement.

Social discontent continued throughout the 1980s, from workers' strikes to student demonstrations, often linked to the effects of particular reforms on people's livelihoods. The movement I will describe in the next section was the culmination of that discontent, and an escalation of social and political tensions between various parts of the PRC society and a CCP regime that was already on its way from authoritarian leftism (in the socialist period) to authoritarian rightism (in the capitalist period).

WORKERS IN THE TIAN'ANMEN SQUARE MOVEMENT 1989

> The working class is the most advanced class. We must be the main force in the democratic movement. [According to the Constitution] the Chinese People's Republic is led by the working class. We have the right to chase away all despots. Workers know better than anyone the role of knowledge and technology in production. So we will never permit anyone to harm the students, who are nurtured by the people. To destroy dictatorship and autocracy and to promote the country's democratization is a duty that we must not shirk. The source of our strength is unity; firm conviction is the source of our success. In the democracy movement, "we have nothing to lose but our chains, and a world to gain." (Workers' Declaration by the Preparatory Committee of the Beijing Workers' Autonomous Federation or Gongzilian, May 21, 1989)[42]

The Tian'anmen Square Movement 1989 continued the line of mobilizations for political reforms or a more democratic version of socialism. Started and dominated by university students in Beijing, the movement eventually opened up spaces for a second movement, the mobilization and self-organizing of other urban groups, above all, of discontented workers, some of whom organized in independent labor unions.

They confronted a regime that had already abandoned main parts of its leftist political agenda. Throughout the 1980s, it gave up its class struggle rhetoric and its (professed) focus on revolutionizing society and, instead, fully concentrated on the development of the productive forces. Economic growth, or even "some people getting rich first," became the main goal of economic reforms. In the eyes of the CCP leaders, these would take the country out of backwardness and poverty into an industrialized and prosperous modernity.

The gradual economic reforms of the 1980s, first in the countryside and then in the cities, produced some material improvements but also economic and social problems. The market reforms did not follow a ready-made blueprint; the CCP leadership started local and regional experiments with economic and institutional changes, and later introduced them elsewhere if they had been successful.

In the late 1970s and early 1980s, the process began with rural reforms. Communal land was contracted out to peasant households that still had to sell certain quotas of production to the state at fixed prices. These state purchasing prices for agricultural goods were increased, though, and peasants were allowed to sell excess production on markets for higher market prices. This dual-track pricing system (*jiage shuangguizhi*) pushed the gradual commercialization of agriculture, led to an increase of output and peasant incomes, and "made possible large increases in food consumption in both urban and rural areas."[43]

Urban reforms started more slowly and took effect in the mid-1980s. State control over enterprises was decentralized, and another dual-track pricing system allowed for the sale of excess production on markets. In 1986, the Factory Director Responsibility System (*changzhang fuze zhi*) gave more decision-making power to managers, who could also lease an enterprise for a fixed period. In addition, the CCP regime introduced a system of contract labor for newly hired staff.[44]

The urban reforms created new problems, for instance, more cadre corruption. State cadres and work unit managers used their new powers to take control of state assets and fill their own pockets. While urban income increased in the first half of the 1980s, real wages of many urban households decreased due to price hikes and inflation in the second half. This even led to panic buying.[45] Work unit closures and bankruptcies made many urban workers unemployed, and the introduction of labor contracts produced a sense of insecurity among others as they feared losing their lifelong jobs. In the second half of the 1980s, the situation of urban workers fell short of what they had expected, especially when they compared it with the improvements for peasants. Many grew increasingly discontented. By 1987, strikes and slowdowns were on the increase again.[46]

Students staged demonstrations in late 1986 and early 1987, first in Hefei, then in other cities. The issues ranged from campus conditions to the slowness of the reforms. Students demanded more democracy and attacked the authoritarianism of the CCP regime. After one month, the regime suppressed the movement.[47] Throughout the 1980s, students grew increasingly discontented because of the relatively low status of intellectuals in society, the low wages for intellectuals' jobs, and the blocking of chances of advancement. All these issues contributed to the outbreak of student protests in April 1989.

The Urban Uprising

Students in Beijing and other cities started the Tian'anmen Square Movement and played a major role in demonstrations, debates, and even negotiations with the government. The series of events involving students will be presented briefly here, but a special focus will be the participation and agency of workers, which is often neglected or obscured.[48] They joined the movement to support the students but later self-organized and developed political demands that went far beyond the rather moderate course and aims of most of the students.[49]

As in 1976, it was again the death of a CCP leader that triggered the mobilization. Politburo member Hu Yaobang passed away on April 15, 1989. Many students saw Hu as a party leader who was willing to reform the economy and the state and who had been wrongfully demoted two years earlier. In January 1987, Deng Xiaoping and conservative forces in the CCP leadership had forced the reformer Hu to resign as general secretary because of his failure to handle the student demonstrations back then.

After Hu's death, students organized mourning events where they also attacked CCP leaders for corruption and nepotism, and demanded political reforms and democratic rights. The protest spread quickly. Increasing numbers of students staged demonstrations in Beijing and other cities. In Xi'an and Changsha these even led to clashes with the police. Students also organized class boycotts and set up independent student unions.

Deng Xiaoping attacked the students' mobilization as a "counterrevolutionary riot." Already in late April, units of the People's Liberation Army (PLA) were mobilized to Beijing, a sign of a possible imminent crackdown. By now, though, it was obvious that the students enjoyed widespread support among the urban population, and the demonstrations continued despite the threats. At this point, the rift in the leadership widened between hardliners, who wanted to repress the movement, and reformers, some of whom even sympathized with students' demands for political changes. Hu Yaobang's successor as CCP general secretary Zhao Ziyang chose a moderate course toward the students and even agreed to begin a public dialog and negotiations with student leaders.

In early May, the student movement lost impetus and declined because the students "did not know what to do next and were hesitant to escalate further."[50] Some radical students began a hunger strike on May 13 and successfully mobilized thousands of students again who occupied Tian'anmen Square in Beijing. To the embarrassment of the regime, this meant that when the general secretary of the Communist Party of the Soviet Union Mikhail Gorbachev arrived on May 15 for the first Sino-Soviet summit since 1959, the official meetings had to take place at the airport. The hunger strike continued for several more days, and hundreds of participants had to be treated in hospitals. But the student movement stagnated again.

It was the widespread support for the hunger strikers by other people, many of them workers who organized their own rallies (see the next subsection "Workers' Involvement"), that increased the pressure on the CCP leadership. On May 19, General Secretary Zhao Ziyang and Premier Li Peng visited Tian'anmen Square. Zhao promised more negotiations and a search for compromises.

However, the hardliners in the CCP leadership took the initiative. On May 20, Li Peng declared martial law in parts of the capital and tens of thousands of PLA troops entered the city to rein in the movement. To the surprise of the regime, tens of thousands of Beijing people, again many of them workers, started building barricades and roadblocks, effectively preventing the troops from advancing to the city center. Subsequently, large demonstrations in favor of the movement were also held in other cities, among them Shanghai and Guangzhou.

The blockade of PLA troops by the people of Beijing continued on May 21. At this point, some cadres from within the CCP leadership, and even some PLA officers, opposed a military attack on the movement. The troops retreated temporarily to positions outside the capital. Massive demonstrations in support of the students and their demands continued until the end of May, while much of the city was brought to a standstill as transportation workers and others refused to work and joined the movement.

On June 3, PLA troops made another attempt to reach Tian'anmen Square. Again, masses of people blocked their way and, when troops pushed on, many resisted with rocks and bottles. In some locations, military carriers were even set on fire, and some soldiers died during the confrontations. Clashes continued throughout the night, when tens of thousands of PLA troops used their weapons to retake Beijing's city center, killing hundreds and possibly thousands of people, most of them on roads leading to Tian'anmen Square. After the square was reconquered on June 4, security forces began with the arrest of student leaders and other participants of the movement.

The PLA attack was a shock to many Chinese, who had not expected that the CCP regime would use the army against the population (again). Massive demonstrations against the crackdown took place in Shanghai, Wuhan, Changsha, Xi'an, Hangzhou, Chengdu, and Shenyang in the following days. However, the regime continued to repress the movement which eventually ran out of steam. When order was restored, the CCP leadership punished its reformer leader. On June 24, Zhao Ziyang was officially removed from his position as general secretary of the CCP and replaced by the Shanghai party leader Jiang Zemin.

Workers' Involvement

Workers were involved in the 1989 movement in different ways, organizing support or protesting in the streets or in their work units, agitating other workers and forming independent unions, or self-organizing in their neighborhoods or elsewhere like for the defense of the city of Beijing against army attacks during the time of martial law.

In Beijing, workers began supporting the students' protests in the second half of April. A small group of young worker activists met for informal evening discussions on their situation in the work units, problems with cadres, inflation, and wages. They distributed a first flier protesting police violence against students on April 20. Around that time, they also began using Gongzilian (Beijing Workers' Autonomous Federation, BWAF) or similar names.[51] Other independent workers' organizations referring to themselves as Workers' Autonomous Federations (WAF) were set up in Changsha, Fuzhou, Guangzhou, Guiyang, Hangzhou, Hohhot, Jinan, Kunming, Lanzhou, Nanjing, Shanghai, Suzhou, Wuhan, Xi'an, and Xining. These groups differed in composition and size.[52]

In Beijing, the membership of Gongzilian grew rapidly, and reached 20,000 at the time of the suppression in early June.[53] The members were mostly workers between 20 and 40 years old and from Beijing.[54] Older workers, as well as low-level work unit cadres and union staff from state factories, and even the ACFTU itself, came out to support Gongzilian, but most of them were too afraid to get involved in a more active manner. In Beijing and other cities, some of the workers involved in organizing and protesting came from bigger state-run work units, a sign that the results of the reforms throughout the 1980s had affected them as well. Others had less secure statuses or jobs. For instance, in Chongqing, recently laid-off workers from state-owned factories, laid-off construction workers with a peasant background, and unemployed teenagers took part in the movement.[55]

The core group of Gongzilian in Beijing grew until early June to about 150 workers from different work units. Most of them had not been involved in political activism before and were "ordinary young workers with little education [...] from steel mills, railway yards, machine building plants, and construction companies."[56] While most students and intellectuals "kept their distance from the workers" during the 1989 movement, a few intellectuals supported (or advised) these core activists.[57]

At the beginning of their engagement, many workers shared in the mourning for Hu Yaobang and supported the students when they were attacked by the regime. Soon they formulated their own agenda, though, and criticized cadre privilege, corruption, and the negative effects of the reforms on workers' lives. Even though many of the issues raised by the WAFs touched on workers' material interests, the direction of their main demands was political and focused on the lack of workplace and political rights, as well as the need for independent union representation so they could fight for their interests. While this had also been a feature of previous confrontations with the regime, "in 1989 it was given even greater emphasis."[58]

Soon after the continuous occupation of Tian'anmen Square had started on May 13, Gongzilian activists openly declared the existence of their organization and established a permanent presence on the square, with makeshift tents, large banners, and a loudspeaker system. Until that time, students had dominated the movement, both in numbers on the street and in a political sense. This changed in the second half of May and especially after the declaration of martial law in Beijing on May 20.[59] The participation of students dropped, while workers and other urbanites came out in scores for demonstrations, and Gongzilian was very visible during these. It turned up with several vehicles that had been lent to the activists after they had made requests on wall posters. Their banner was prominent along those of delegations from various state-run work units.[60]

As Gongzilian played an increasingly prominent role in the movement, it expressed distinctively confrontational positions towards the CCP leadership and the reformer faction, as well as towards the student movement leadership. Many students and intellectuals supported the reformists in the CCP leadership behind General Secretary Zhao Ziyang, who had backed the marketization of the economy in recent years. Workers, meanwhile, shouted "Down with Zhao Ziyang!" or even carried portraits of

Mao Zedong "as a symbol of Spartan virtue and egalitarian ideals against a corrupt and cynical Dengist regime."[61] In fliers, Gongzilian attacked the regime for exploiting and suppressing the people, not just in the reform years, but in the past forty years since the founding of the PRC. In one document, Gongzilian also pointed to the previous cooptation of a popular movement by the CCP regime and Deng Xiaoping, the April 5 Movement in 1976, and warned the regime not to try to coopt and use the 1989 movement as well.[62]

During Martial Law

The declaration of martial law on May 20 changed the dynamics inside the movement and produced new confrontations in which workers took the lead. In the early morning of that day, workers and other ordinary people staged a successful blockade of army units. "[M]ass resistance to the government was suddenly a reality."[63] Outraged over martial law and the PLA activity, more workers now came out to participate in the movement. They were the main force confronting the PLA units when they advanced into the city center in Beijing. "Workers erected barricades and assembled human walls. They brought water and food to soldiers to fraternize with them and convince them to abandon their arms and stop their march."[64]

Gongzilian organized demonstrations almost every day, starting on May 20, and its loudspeaker system on Tian'anmen Square:

> turned out to be the most popular of the organization's activities, and the one with the highest profile. Ordinary workers, disgruntled journalists and government office workers, even disaffected cadres and soldiers, submitted statements to the broadcasters—often exposés of official duplicity or wrongdoing—and these were read out to large and appreciative audiences every evening.[65]

Other worker groups were set up, in workplaces and beyond. "Workers started organizing self-armed quasi-militias, such as 'picket corps' and 'dare-to-die brigades', to monitor and broadcast the whereabouts of the military."[66] In many factories, workers organized strikes and slowdowns.

All this activity had its limits, though. Two attempts to organize a general strike (on May 20 and on May 28) did not materialize, and the period between the increased worker involvement and activity in mid-May, and the crackdown in early June was, apparently, too short to establish reliable links and structures to take the workers' struggle further and shut down the (urban) economy for a longer period.

Workers' activity was also hampered by the students' attitude towards worker involvement in the movement. The student leaders simply did not want strong workers' participation because they thought that would lead to immediate repression, whereas the regime would respect the students' and intellectuals' right to protest. Another reason for the unwillingness of many students to allow the participation of other social groups in the movement was their arrogance and their contempt for the intellectual or political capabilities of workers.[67] The workers, meanwhile, not only distrusted the CCP leadership, but increasingly recognized the arrogant behavior and disrespect of the student "elite" towards them, and the similarity between the "elite" behavior of CCP leaders and student leaders: power struggles, factionalism, hierarchy, secrecy, privilege, conflicts over money, and corruption. Thus, students and workers never formed a common front against the regime. Only at the last minute, when the military attack was already under way on June 3, students ran "over to the workers' headquarters and asked them to call a general strike. By then, it was too late."[68]

On June 3 and 4, workers bore the brunt of the brutal repression in Beijing when many of them confronted the PLA units on their way to the city center. In the aftermath of the crackdown, the CCP regime ordered the arrest of large numbers of those who had participated in the movement and the resistance on the street, and many workers were arrested, tortured, or even killed during detention.[69]

Meanwhile, Gongzilian and other WAFs were banned, as were the student associations. However, in the immediate aftermath of the crackdown, and despite the obvious danger, many workers continued to come out to join protests against the military attack in Beijing. More WAFs were founded or announced, and mass absenteeism and strikes occurred in a number of places, as "roads, bridges, and railway lines [were] blocked in cities all over China."[70] In some regions, the regime allowed these activities for a few days, in other regions, they were quickly repressed. At the same time, the CCP leadership launched a media campaign to present the non-student participants as criminals, unemployed, or a "floating population" (of peasant migrant workers), making use of racist prejudices among urbanites against people with a poor or peasant background.

The Attempt Failed

Had workers not intervened during the Tian'anmen Square Movement in 1989 and had they not developed their own political agenda that threatened to undermine CCP legitimacy and power, the crackdown might not have happened (in this way). Some reformers in the CCP leadership around party leader Zhao Ziyang sympathized with students' demands, as they hoped a certain degree of democratization would stabilize the country and party rule. They engaged in negotiations with the students, offering concessions and attempting cooptation. A compromise and cooptation of the movement by the reformist faction around Zhao Ziyang seemed possible until mid-May. The situation changed when the student mobilization ran out of steam and more and more workers joined the movement. The workers' involvement and threat weakened the part of the leadership that sympathized with the student movement and tipped the advantage towards the hardliners in the factional leadership conflict.

Deng Xiaoping and these hardliners around Li Peng, already feeling humiliated by the student movement, pushed through the military crackdown. The top leaders were "terrified"[71] because they had their own experiences with previous workers' movements, as during the Cultural Revolution. They also witnessed the weakening of socialist regimes in Eastern Europe, above all in Poland, through the movement around Solidarność. The subsequent military crackdown was meant to prevent an escalation of workers' struggles and to avoid the Polish scenario.

Most of the reports on workers' struggles during the Tian'anmen Movement in 1989 cover Beijing and other big cities, but workers in small cities took part, too.[72] The state and the ruling class were the clear adversary, and the mobilization of workers and the setting up of WAFs was an indication that the specific connection between the urban permanent workforce and the CCP leadership had broken as a result of the effects of the reforms. Many workers had already lost or feared losing their status after reforms that strengthened the position of managers in the work units, who then began undermining the welfare and job guarantees of the "socialist" working class. The clash between the urban workers and the regime in 1989 was a harbinger of the confrontations from the mid-1990s on, when the regime began the restructuring of the state-run enterprises and laid off millions of workers.

What started in the late 1980s and appeared also in 1989, when workers took pictures of Mao to the demonstrations, was also the beginning of a redefinition of the image of Mao Zedong (and of Maoism to a certain extent). Workers seemed to cherish "the memory of the late chairman not because they liked his doctrine of ubiquitous and perpetual 'class struggle' or his policies during the periods of the Great Leap Forward and the Cultural Revolution. What they really missed [was] an egalitarian ideal."[73] The moral economy involved was meant to remind the leaders that it was indeed egalitarianism the CCP had promised (even if it had never been realized).

Workers also took as an inspiration Solidarność's success in forcing the socialist regime in Poland to compromise. The setting up of the WAFs was the first promising attempt to establish an independent union movement since 1949. Had the efforts to establish an independent union movement, and the self-organization and struggles of workers on the street and in their workplaces during the period of martial law between May 20 and June 4 lasted longer, and had the participants been able to generate their own political agenda, this might have been the beginning of a revolutionary process. As it was, the new union movement did not seem to offer a left-wing revolutionary alternative, but rather stood for left-wing reformism.[74]

The WAFs' language attacked the ruling class in clear terms ("bourgeoisie"), and in this way they were in line with striking workers in 1957, Shengwulian in 1967–68, Li Yi Zhe in 1974, workers from the April 5 Movement in 1976, and activists during the Democracy Wall Movement 1978–80.[75] Just like radical (rebel) currents during the Cultural Revolution:

> Gongzilian was profoundly anti-elitist and anti-bureaucratic. Yet the workers' populist rhetoric in 1989 was blended with new political conceptions: institutional restraints on managerial power in workplaces, within a framework of union representation and collective bargaining, and, more vaguely, a role for an independent union in national policy-making and an institutionalized right to "supervise" the Communist Party's exercise of power.[76]

These were concepts for a reformed socialism, with more control for workers over management and state administrations but no expressions of a revolutionary desire to establish a different kind of social structure and society. As socialism had already been reformed for a decade, and as the reconfigured class rule in the transition to capitalism took shape, workers were on the defensive and only demanded better conditions and more influence.[77]

CONCLUSION: MOVEMENTS FOR AND AGAINST THE REFORMS

This chapter looked at the specific conditions under which social discontent and unrest triggered opposition. This opposition included left-wing demands and practices against a regime that slowly changed its nature after the mid-1970s. Three larger popular mobilizations confronted the rule of the CCP leadership and demanded some form of democratic control of work unit managers, party cadres, and state officials.

The April 5 Movement in 1976 reflected the anger and exhaustion felt by many workers due to frequent campaigns and purges associated with the leftists in the leadership and due to pressing economic problems they attributed to the CCP regime's austerity policies. The trigger was the handling of the death and mourning of premier Zhou Enlai, a leader who stood for opposition to the leftists in the CCP leadership. The mass movement was soon repressed but it showed the CCP leadership that some change was necessary.

The repression and later rehabilitation of April 5 Movement activists triggered the Democracy Wall Movement from 1978 to 1980. Workers played a leading role in this movement. They collaborated with discontented youth and peasants, pushed debates on the unequal distribution of wealth and power, and attacked the regime's bureaucratism. The movement was not strong enough to challenge the CCP regime or win major concessions, though. From the start, it had to grapple with pressure from the authorities. The reformers around Deng Xiaoping tried to use it in order to win the power struggle in the leadership, but as soon as they had a strong grip on power, they harshly repressed the movement.

The Tian'anmen Square Movement in 1989 was surely the strongest challenge to the regime since the rebel movement during the Cultural Revolution about twenty years earlier. During its first weeks in April and early May 1989, the movement was dominated by student mobilizations asking for political reforms. The students, many of them children of party, state, and army cadres, demanded democratic rights like freedom of speech and freedom of association, mostly in the hope that a democratization of the regime would help to overcome corruption, nepotism, and the appropriation of public assets by cadres. The students were backed by sections of the political classes who aimed for more reforms and more control for intellectuals (and the growing urban middle class) over the political realm. However, when workers joined the movement in great numbers, it became a threat to the CCP regime. Workers were at the core of the mass movement after the declaration of martial law; they took over Beijing's streets, set up independent union structures, and resisted the army's advances. However, they did not manage to prevent the crackdown. After the neutralization of CCP leader Zhao Ziyang, who had negotiated with the students and promised concessions, the hardliners around premier Li Peng prevailed and ordered the army to use violence to finally crush the movement.

In all three movements, former Red Guards and left-wing rebels, and their experiences and forms of struggle, played a role, even though their political perspectives and aims had changed with the transition of the PRC's economic and political system. In each movement, protagonists attacked the authoritarian nature of CCP rule and demanded more political freedom as well as better working and living conditions. Workers took a big stake in these movements. Their idea of a kind of socialist democracy had a different meaning from what that term usually describes in countries with a representative form of democracy in capitalism.[78] It related directly to who has control in the work units and in the state.

The CCP leadership's reaction to all three movements, again, illustrates the relation between movements from below that included left-wing practices and demands, and the regime that tried to stay in power. This regime was in its own transition from a leftist authoritarian regime in socialism to a still authoritarian but now rightist regime in the capitalist period that began in the late 1990s. Repression was used against all three movements, in the first and the last case more swiftly and brutally as the movement from below and their political demands challenged the respective regimes more directly. While the Democracy Wall Movement could be coopted to a certain extent by the reformer faction around Deng Xiaoping, and also helped push for economic reforms (which can be understood as a concession), the immediate cooptation of the Tian'anmen Square Movement by reformers around Zhao Ziyang was blocked through their neutralization by hardliners around Li Peng.[79]

The April 5 Movement and the Democracy Wall Movement can be seen as catalysts that strengthened the reformer faction so it could introduce economic reforms. The Tian'anmen Square Movement was a reaction to some of the market reform effects. It was the last uprising of the working class in the transition period. The crackdown on workers, students, and their supporters, and the subsequent wave of repression, was a decisive win for the newly composed ruling class and opened the way for the harsh attack on the conditions of urban state workers in the mid-1990s.

4

Defense and Nostalgia: Social Struggles Drive Leftist Resistance in the 1990s and 2000s

In this chapter, I follow the struggles of peasants and urban state workers during the final transition to capitalism in the 1990s and early 2000s. Both groups staged largely defensive protests—from demonstrations to riots—against negative effects of the market reforms. These struggles and the obvious establishment of capitalist relations inspired (new) left-wing currents among workers and intellectuals, a revival of left-wing organizing that mostly used the legacy of Maoism and adapted it to the new capitalist realities.

In the *first* section, I discuss the situation of peasants. Their living conditions improved with the rural reforms in the early 1980s. That changed in the following decade, when they faced mounting economic difficulties, high taxes, cadre corruption or arbitrariness, and land dispossession or theft. Several waves of peasant unrest followed from the first part of the 1990s until the mid-2000s.

In the *second* section, I focus on the fate of urban workers in state enterprises. The reforms of the 1980s had already undermined their position in the work units. The systematic restructuring of the state sector in the mid-1990s scrapped their special status and "iron rice-bowl" (*tie fanwan*) of social guarantees and welfare. Millions of workers were even laid off. This attack led to a wave of state worker mobilizations in the late 1990s and early 2000s.

In the *third* section, I describe political currents that formed in reaction to the dismantling of the socialist economic structures and the shaping of capitalism in the 1990s. Worker groups who participated in the fight against the capitalist restructuring of state enterprises attacked the CCP regime with arguments reminiscent of the rebel movement of the 1960s. Meanwhile, leftist intellectuals, disillusioned by the CCP leadership's crackdown on the popular uprising in 1989 or disappointed by the regime's road to capitalism, began to criticize the reforms, neoliberalism, and the restructuring of the state sector.

PEASANT STRUGGLES AGAINST REFORM EFFECTS

> Down with the new landlords of the 1990s! (Protesting peasants in Anhui, 1993)[1]

In this section, I focus on peasant unrest in the 1990s and 2000s. At first, the post-1978 economic reforms brought changes to rural households that many peasants welcomed. The situation changed in the late 1980s and early 1990s. Facing mounting problems, peasant discontent grew as they raised issues like tax burdens or cadre abuse of power and started engaging in protests.

Peasants had been at the heart of the revolutionary process before 1949. They had suffered immensely from exploitation by the landlord class in Imperial and in Republican China. So it is no surprise that, when the CCP was pushed out of the cities by the KMT in the late 1920s and regrouped in the countryside in the 1930s and 1940s, it enjoyed the support of many peasants who hoped for a better future. When liberation was accomplished in 1949, their engagement seemed to pay off at first. In the 1950s, the CCP's land reform and collectivization eliminated the rural landlord class and improved the living conditions of the rural population.

However, most peasants were to remain relatively poor. In the 1950s, the socialist industrialization project was carried out on their backs. Through a set of price regulations and taxation—including the regulation of agricultural markets through "unified purchasing and marketing" (*tonggou tongxiao*)—rural surplus was channeled into urban sectors, and the living conditions of most peasants were far worse than those of most urban workers. The limitation of rural/urban migration through the infamous *hukou* (or household registration) system made it very difficult for ruralites to leave the village and find a better living situation in the city.[2]

The Great Leap Forward (GLF) in 1958 to 1961 failed and led to mass famine. While millions of people died in the villages, the supply of food to the urban population was mostly kept up. Due to their desperate situation, peasants began to hide or steal agricultural produce and clashed with local cadres. The experience of the GLF (partially) destroyed the trust of the peasants in the CCP leadership.

In the early 1980s, as a consequence of the reforms, the income of many peasant households increased. The rural collectives were largely dissolved, and peasant households leased the (still collectively owned) land and were responsible for production, profits, and losses through the rural Household Contract Responsibility System (*jiating lianchan chengbao zeren zhi*) officially implemented in 1982.[3] In the mid- and late 1980s, peasants (especially in areas close to urban centers in the east and the southeast) benefited from access to urban markets, and new domestic and foreign-invested urban industries and the (attached) growing rural industrial sector of town and village enterprises (TVEs) offered jobs for rural (excess) labor.[4]

In the late 1980s, peasants were less affected by the economic problems in the run-up to the Tian'anmen Square Movement. Most of them stayed out of the confrontation, and the movement was most active in cities. However, in this period, new problems began to loom.

Rightful Resistance

Most of the burdens peasants faced in the late 1980s and in the 1990s were directly linked to state policies.[5] Peasants had to pay high state taxes as well as other fees to the village and townships after earlier tax reforms had channeled financial resources away from the villages and counties to the center. The peasants saw the taxes and fees imposed by local and regional cadres as "arbitrary, unpredictable, and open ended."[6] Their income side did not look much better as the state paid low procurement prices for grain and inflation devalued peasants' earnings. After the mid-1980s, it became "increasingly unprofitable to farm," and the state often paid in IOUs rather than cash.[7] Reacting to peasant discontent, the state raised the procurement prices several times, but, in the mid-1990s, it again, "forced peasants to grow cheap grains through the 'governors' grain bag responsibility system.'"[8] The restructuring of the state industries had just begun and led to massive lay-offs of workers (see the next section, "State Workers against Smashing the Iron Rice Bowl"), and the regime feared that high grain prices would increase the chances of outbreaks of urban unrest. "The rural remained, therefore, a sphere into which the state could shift urban problems and costs."[9]

To support the rural industrialization drive that began in the 1980s and continued in the 1990s, local governments also requisitioned land from peasants. This happened especially in eastern and southeastern provinces and in suburban areas. The problem was not only that peasants lost their land, but that they often did not get (properly) compensated. Other pressures included the enforcement of birth control measures and the One-Child Policy (*dusheng zinü zhengce*) by local cadres which also led to conflicts, especially when cadres unfairly allocated birth quotas.[10]

In the mid-1990s, as the rural economy stagnated and other problems mounted, rural protests escalated. The unrest was triggered by conflicts over peasants' living conditions, the official appropriation of their produce, the collection of taxes, and the peasants' sense of being exploited. The protests took on different individual and collective forms, among them "[d]emonstrations; violent altercations between individual peasants and cadres; riots; wrecking of Party-government compounds; setting up of road blocks; sit-ins; holding officials captive; blocking of railroads; burning automobiles; and killing of cadres or police."[11] Clashes with security forces resulted in injuries and deaths.

Most protests were "localized and small scale,"[12] often occurring as immediate reactions, for instance, to government officials entering a village to collect taxes. Others were based on organized initiatives, like collective petitions (*jiti shangfang*) or planned demonstrations. Informal leaders could play a key role, and the demonstrations could escalate into violent clashes if officials made no concessions to peasants' demands. Some protests even involved the setting up of peasant committees or councils that reflected the peasants' demand to have their own independent organizations.[13] Waves of protests occurred between 1993 and 1997, including large-scale riots in Renshou County, Sichuan, in January, May, and June 1993, and a major wave of unrest in Hunan, Hubei, Anhui, and Jiangxi in May and June 1997.[14]

The struggle of peasants against unreasonable burdens like high taxes has a long tradition in rural China, and resistance against unjustified demands of officials has long been seen as "rightful."[15] This was the case in the 1990s as well. Resistance was most often directed against *local* officials, those seen as directly responsible for the peasants' misery, while *regional* or *central* authorities were often called on to support peasants' demands.

In other cases local cadres actually supported the peasants, as in 1993 during protests in Anhui that included references to the socialist ideology and legacy as expressed in slogans like "All power to the peasants" or "Down with the new landlords of the 1990s."[16] The same goes for protests in Shanxi, Henan, and Hunan in 1995, when party cadres promoted slogans like "End the exploitation and oppression of the peasant class," and in Jiangxi in 1997 with slogans like "Down with the urban exploiting class" and "Divide the wealth of the new rural despots."[17]

The peasant struggles in the 1990s thus reused class struggle rhetoric from the socialist period and references to the Cultural Revolution. This manifests the revival or "popular counter-remembrance of the Maoist period" as a time when peasants and workers enjoyed more social guarantees and more political influence.[18] Therefore, mostly ordinary and older villagers felt nostalgia for mass campaigns against cadre corruption as an effective way that they "could at least periodically call [cadres] to account for their misdeeds."[19]

Peasants demanded new regular campaigns to rectify rural cadres and to revive the four "big freedoms" (speaking out, holding debates, writing character posters, linking up).[20] "Rural nostalgics [...] claim that Mao was hard on cadres and the current leadership is not, and that Mao had faith in the masses and the current leadership does not."[21] In this way, protesting peasants used a reference to power from below and a leftist agenda they attributed to the pre-reform CCP regime.

From the late 1990s on, struggles over land and land seizures became the central grievance of rural protests. Local authorities, looking for new sources of income, began to sell land or land use rights for commercial or infrastructure projects. Peasants were forced to give up their land and often were not even compensated according to the regulations. Because land seizures "destroy peasants' livelihoods and basis for survival, they have had a more profound impact than tax and fee abuses, and thus have lain at the root of an escalating spiral of violence and resistance." Many peasant struggles to defend their land use rights ended in failure, though, resulting in an increasing number of "landless" peasants.[22]

Repression and Improvements

The state's immediate reaction to demonstrations and other forms of collective rural resistance was usually harsh repression, but it also made attempts to lessen the burden of the peasants through concessions and reforms.[23] In 1992 and 1993, it introduced legal measures limiting local government-imposed fees and taxes, and giving peasants the right to refuse the payment of excessive fees and taxes. It also repeatedly changed the urban grain pricing system to increase peasant incomes and tried to eliminate IOUs as payments.[24]

In the early 2000s, the central leadership, faced with continuing militant rural protests, acknowledged that it was losing ever more credibility and publicly declared that the social unrest in the countryside was a threat to its rule. Subsequently, it adopted more measures to lower the peasants' burden in order to defuse the situation. From 2003 to 2007, the early years of the Hu Jintao leadership, the CCP regime "slowed modernizing reforms in order to deal with rising tensions around peasant income and welfare, and growing rural-urban income inequality."[25] Most importantly, after a tax reform had abolished most local fees in 2002, the regime eliminated the agricultural tax in 2006, relieving the burden of the peasants. As part of the 11th Five-Year Plan (2006–10), it started a policy called "Building the New Socialist Countryside" (*jianshe shehuizhuyi xin nongcun*), which included monetary transfers from the central to rural governments (to compensate for the loss in taxes), the construction of rural infrastructure, and resources for the improvement of education, medical services, and the resettling of peasants into better housing.[26]

Against Land Theft

However, in 2008, the regime changed its focus again. "The global food crisis of 2007–2008 and then the global financial crisis or Great Recession of 2008 gave more urgency to agricultural modernization reforms and urbanization."[27] The regime saw further modernization of agriculture as a precondition for the further economic development of the country, and modernization meant increasing the efficiency, scale, specialization, and vertical integration of the sector.

Reforms of the *hukou* system and other policies aimed to facilitate more rural/urban migration and push up the urbanization rate further.[28] The regime set tighter "red line" rules for domestic grain self-sufficiency and a minimum amount of arable land. It relaxed land transfer rules which resulted in the concentration of land and the rise of larger, commercial farms. It also supported intensified vertical integration through specialized cooperatives and so-called dragon-head firms that "are supposed to lead Chinese peasants to agricultural modernization and industrialization by vertically integrating households—mostly through contract farming—with processing and product markets, inputs and agricultural technology."[29]

All this led to further pressure on the peasants, and the number of protests against land seizures continued to rise, peaking between 2013 and 2015.[30] After 2015, that number declined. Harsher repression seems to be the main reason. The police use of force against rural protests had already increased since 2000, but after Xi Jinping became CCP leader in 2012, "local governments faced with collective land seizure protests have been adopting harsher countermeasures than previous administrations. The Chinese government has resorted to repression more frequently than before."[31] Other reasons include the slowdown of economic growth during the 2010s, which also slowed down "land acquisition for public infrastructure and urban development,"[32] and concessions made by local governments in an attempt "to accommodate the economic demands of peasants who were victims of land seizure" and "to preserve stability before aggrieved peasants swarm the streets."[33]

In sum, after having benefited to a certain extent from the early market reforms in the 1980s, the living conditions of peasants deteriorated in the late 1980s and 1990s, leading to waves of rural unrest that continued in the new millennium. Peasants used petitions, demonstrations, blockades, or even riots against what they saw as effects of market reforms: high taxes, cadre corruption, or land theft. Some peasants referred directly to the pre-1978 socialist past and used Maoist slogans when staging their demands.

These demands included material improvements as well as issues of power and control over social, economic, and political affairs, the two dimensions of left-wing politics. This mostly small and localized unrest did not lead to lasting organizational structures. It was met with the selective repression of the immediate unrest, but, in the long run, the regime also made concessions like reducing the peasants' material burden by cutting rural taxes and by introducing the program "Building the New Socialist Countryside" in the mid-2000s. Still, pressure on peasants has remained high in the years since, especially because of the gradual capitalization of agriculture and rural land expropriation that robbed many peasants of their land.

We will see in the next two sections, how workers, too, made nostalgic references to the Mao era, as well as to the (imagined) greater extent of social equality and popular control during the socialist period, and how that was taken up by new Maoist groupings and New Left academics.

STATE WORKERS AGAINST SMASHING THE IRON RICE-BOWL

> No to capitalism, yes to socialism! (Urban state workers during a protest in the 1990s)[34]

In this section, I look at the labor unrest among urban workers in the PRC's rustbelt of heavy industries in the central and north-eastern provinces in the late 1990s and 2000s. It was triggered by the restructuring of the state sector and its effects on workers' livelihoods.

Besides peasants, urban state workers had been the second important social group for the socialist development project after 1949. From the establishment of the socialist planned economy in the mid-1950s until the first reform years in the mid-1980s, they were considered the "masters of the factories" and enjoyed relatively good conditions in comparison with temporary workers, migrant workers, or peasants. Then things began to change.

As described in chapter 2, economic problems triggered by the market reforms, such as inflation, began to reduce workers' real wages in the second half of the 1980s. In the same period, their job security diminished through the introduction of labor contracts and the new possibility for companies to go bankrupt. Their position in the work units weakened vis-à-vis managers while they also faced growing corruption and appropriation of state assets by cadres.

As a result of the mounting problems, state workers became increasingly dissatisfied. In 1988, workers organized a series of strike actions, and, as we saw, urban workers also played a major role in the last phase of the Tian'anmen Square Movement in 1989 when they demanded better conditions, the freedom to organize independently, and more democratic rights in society and the economy. During the crackdown, the regime attacked participating workers especially hard. Not only was their vision of a development towards a democratic socialism destroyed, the crackdown and the subsequent repression of worker opposition also cleared the way for further reform attacks on the urban workers.

Defensive Struggle

The CCP regime's attack on the state sector, the core of the planned economy that was restructured, put the lid on the transitional period. It was the reform that eventually transformed state-run enterprises into capitalist entities (whether state-owned or private) and that established capitalist labor relations for the majority of workers. The struggles of the urban state workers against this attack heralded the beginning of the capitalist period.[35]

In 1992, CCP leader Jiang Zemin declared that the regime's reforms aimed to establish a "socialist market economy." In 1995, the CCP regime began privatizing, closing, and declaring bankrupt small state-run work units and collective enterprises. In 1997, it officially promoted the privatization of small state-run work units in the whole country, and after 1999, this was extended to medium-sized and even some large work units.[36] This set the stage for a dramatic restructuring and downsizing of the state sector, and the massive (defensive) struggle of urban workers to defend their working conditions and welfare.

In the course of the restructuring of the state sector, tens of millions of state workers were laid off from the mid-1990s up to the early 2000s.[37] Many of them were so-called *xiagang*, workers who were out of work but remained linked to their work unit.[38] While younger and skilled state workers could often find new employment in the growing private sector, many older and unskilled state workers remained unemployed for years or had to accept informal and low-paid employment in the cities. Women* constituted a high proportion of unskilled workers and were especially hard hit by the lay-offs.

The restructuring and privatization of the state-run work units meant that laid-off and remaining workers lost their previous status and a large part of the welfare provisions, the "iron rice-bowl" they had been provided with through the work units: health care, child care, pension, and more. The new urban social safety net that was meant to replace the work unit services "turned out to have more substance on paper than in reality." Allocations for *xiagang* and pensions were low and paid on an irregular basis or not at all, which was also the result of widespread corruption. "As a result, many workers experienced a sharp reduction of income."[39] *Xiagang* and pensioners faced poverty, while those still working "were constantly confronted with the threat of lay-offs, an increasingly hazardous working environment, and low wages."[40]

The effects of the restructuring produced different reactions. Many workers accepted the changes.[41] Others reacted with everyday forms of resistance,[42] and some engaged in open resistance or struggles. Between 1998 and 2002, the number of demonstrations staged by laid-off state workers was around 100,000 per year.[43] Most of these proved short, involved a limited number of people, and were not connected to each other. In many cases, retirees who had not received their pensions or *xiagang* who had not received their benefit payments demonstrated, while those who still had jobs protested less.

The demonstrations and protests were organized, often involving "leaders" who had a background as work unit or union cadres, and relied on social networks of employees in a particular work unit. To justify their demands and protests, workers often referred to their (supposed) position and status as "masters" of the work units within the socialist state. They tended "to lean on the laws and repeat publicly their own attachment to the regime, thus avoiding framing their action in an idiom of confrontation."[44] During demonstrations workers would employ the "ideological arsenal of socialism" and put emphasis behind their demands by using terms like "working class," "proletariat," and "socialism." Slogans included "Long life to the working class!" or "No to capitalism, yes to socialism!"[45] Retired state workers saw the denial or delay of their pension, or cuts to it, as a violation of their rightful political status and as a failure of the state to deliver on its obligation.[46]

The cycle of urban state workers' struggles peaked in 2002, when large-scale, organized demonstrations hit several cities in the PRC's northeast. This "series of worker protests [...] illustrated the potential for localized and dispersed activism to develop into more coordinated unrest."[47] To give just a few examples: In Liaoyang, Liaoning province, after years of conflict over corruption and cuts, metal workers of a large state-run enterprise demonstrated on and off for ten weeks. They protested against wage arrears, benefit arrears of *xiagang* workers, and other forms of economic deterioration, as well as the arrests of some of their leaders by the police. In Daqing, Heilongjiang province, laid-off oil workers staged demonstrations for three months against changes in severance agreements. The police and army troops were called in to stop the actions. The protests spread to oil fields in Xinjiang, Liaoning, and Hebei provinces. And in Fushun, laid-off miners and workers from cement, steel, and petrochemical plants repeatedly blocked rail lines and roads in protest against problems with their severance payments.[48]

Taking the massive impact on the livelihood of millions of workers into account, this resistance still seemed muted as many workers did not protest. The main reason is that the government was, in fact, prepared for the struggles of state workers as it had introduced measures to soften the impact of the changes and to diffuse discontent. It showed relative tolerance when confronting workers' struggles and used the new processes for grievance expression and conflict resolution it had implemented, including the legal framework of the Trade Union Law (1992), the Labor Law, and the Arbitration Law (both in 1995). The provision of compensation and reemployment programs for *xiagang* cushioned the effects of the restructuring. Reemployment projects and welfare provisions designed to provide *xiagang* with new jobs were insufficient, poorly implemented, and suffered from lack of funds and corruption of local cadres and work unit managers.[49] However, they still managed to divide the workers, diffuse the criticisms to different agencies, and offered promises for a better future. Besides, repressive means were also used against workers' mobilizations, especially when other measures did not work: police interventions, arrests, and punishments. Such measures were mostly deployed against activists or protest "leaders" but also worked as a threat to those groups of workers who were likely to resist.[50]

The CCP regime feared the loss of legitimacy, especially since the socialist working class, the former social vanguard, was affected. As we shall see in the next section, nostalgic reminiscences of the Maoist past began to spread throughout the 1990s, and state workers used them to make claims. In response, and with the help of liberals and reformers, the CCP leadership used mass media to promote images of state workers with a "socialist" mindset as "backward," "inefficient," and "idle"—adjectives which were also used against the state sector as a whole to justify the restructuring.[51]

The Restructuring Continues

To sum up, in the mid-1990s, the CCP regime under Jiang Zemin intensified the restructuring of the state-run work units with closures, mergers, and privatizations: the decisive attack on the socialist working class. Millions of urban state workers lost the set of wages, welfare, and benefits termed the "iron rice-bowl," either because they were reemployed under different terms or because they lost their job altogether.

The bigger struggles of state workers took place mostly in regions with a concentration of large state-run enterprises like the northeast. The confrontation between the regime and workers was different from the earlier cycles of struggle in 1967 or 1989 as they neither started when the regime was already in crisis nor produced a new crisis. Despite the fact that the regime kept using socialist rhetoric, it was also obvious that the character of the economic system had changed. While in the 1950s, 1960s, and 1970s (discriminated) workers fought for the realization of what the regime had promised, in the 1990s (formerly privileged) workers fought against the abolition of conditions they had enjoyed under socialism. In their struggles against these effects, some of the workers also used Maoist rhetoric to defend the material benefits and social position they had had previously due to their relative privileges as the "masters" of the work units during actually existing socialism.

Younger and skilled workers had a better chance of keeping their job, but they were also more likely to find a new job if laid off. So it was older and unskilled workers, especially women* among them, who suffered most. Those who were able to organize struggles referred to a kind of "moral economy," asking for the wages, benefits, or pensions they had been guaranteed, and using the new official channels of complaints and mediation, as well as the labor laws, to press for their demands.

Even though the overall number of struggles was high and some protests were massive, they could not generate enough pressure to stop the reforms. While the regime, at first, reacted with indifference and inactivity in many cases, leaving it to the enterprises to work out solutions, or used violence and judicial measures against protest leaders to weaken the workers' struggles, it also made concessions in the form of welfare programs and a slower progress of the restructuring.

In any case, the protests were an important statement in the struggle over wealth and power, and they had an impact on state policies as they (and the migrant worker struggles discussed in the next chapter) pushed the regime to start the campaign for the Harmonious Society (*hexie shehui*) formulated in the mid-2000s.[52] That campaign showed the regime's increased recognition of workers' and migrants' economic problems and its attempts to defuse social discontent through a range of welfare measures, minimum wage increases, improved labor rights, and more in the mid- and late 2000s.

The struggles of urban state workers (and peasants) also contributed to the revival of Maoism and new organizing attempts. I turn to those in the next section.

MAOIST ORGANIZING AND THE NEW LEFT

> [M]any officials have become very rich while most of the people still have to live plainly and frugally. The gap between the rich and the poor is so wide that it is hard to describe it. Many people in Beijing are talking about the necessity "to liquidate corrupt officials." In Mao's days, there [were] no such things. (Beijing bus driver, May 1989)[53]

In the 1990s, several factors contributed to the revival of leftist debates in general and Maoism in particular: the new capitalist relations, the struggles of peasants and workers against reform effects, and the transformation of the corrupt ruling class of party and state cadres. Workers and peasants drew upon leftist discourses and references to Maoism and the past socialist period during their struggles and organizing attempts, and intellectuals, like those of the so-called New Left, were inspired by the capitalist transformation and new social struggles and engaged in new discussions about leftist political positions.

The revival of left-wing references and discourses in the PRC in the 1990s and after is linked to domestic changes brought about by the market reforms implemented since 1978, as well as by the global transformations in the late 1980s and early 1990s. After the crackdown on the Tian'anmen Square Movement in 1989, the CCP regime cleared out from the state and party leadership elements who had supported Zhao Ziyang's reformer faction, or even the movement itself. The CCP leadership under Jiang Zemin (with Deng Xiaoping still holding the strings in the background) tried to consolidate party rule and organized campaigns and purges aimed at "bourgeois tendencies." This was not a return to the socialist or Maoist politics of the 1970s and earlier, even though some leftists hoped for exactly that.

After all, the CCP regime had already changed its class politics in the late 1970s and 1980s. It had abolished the system of class categories, stopped using the class struggle rhetoric characteristic of the socialist period, and reduced its understanding of socialism to the development of the PRC's productive forces under the rule of the CCP. While the party continued to use a changed version of "Marxism" to explain and justify its policies, this proved increasingly hollow in view of the social and economic changes that these policies brought about. The CCP's farewell to class struggle changed the perspective left-wing activists in struggles from below as well as leftist intellectuals had on the CCP and the economic and political system of the PRC.

The CCP leadership, as well as old and new leftists, also carefully observed the economic and political crisis of the countries of the "socialist eastern bloc" that deepened in the course of the 1980s and led to popular movements demanding fundamental improvements and change. Most Communist Party regimes faltered under pressure in 1989 and 1990, and new governments took over which, in most cases, established some kind of "Western democratic," nationalist regime and launched (more or less intense) economic shock therapies. These shock therapies led to the integration of these countries into global capitalism as semi-peripheral economies and brought the degradation and impoverishment of large parts of the population.

In the PRC, the impact of the market reforms on people's livelihoods—especially less job security and social welfare, further growing social inequality, and rampant cadre corruption and appropriation or privatization of public assets by the ruling class—produced dissatisfaction and anger among the working classes and peasants through the 1980s and even more so the 1990s (as described in the previous two sections). Dissatisfaction and anger were also reflected in demands during social struggles and taken up in debates among old and new leftists.

The Maoist Revival

The revival of Maoist ideas and concepts started in the late 1980s and continued in the 1990s. Workers, peasants, academics, and others—some with experiences in the rebel movement in the late 1960s, in democracy movements in the 1970s, and in the mobilization in 1989—rediscovered and re-imagined Maoist discourses. They used them for new organizing attempts, both during social confrontations and struggles and left-wing political activism since the 1990s.[54]

In the late 1980s, nostalgia for the socialist period or for parts of Maoist thought began as "a new 'Mao Zedong fever' among Chinese working people."[55] Since then, the usage or referencing of Maoism or Mao has taken on different forms. A cultural "Mao craze," "[d]ivested nearly entirely of its original class, ethical, and political dimensions,"[56] led to the commercial usage of Mao or Cultural Revolution memorabilia (for instance, Mao books and badges or other souvenirs).[57] Among students, reading Mao's works and wearing Mao badges became fashionable in the early 1990s, and particularly around Mao's hundredth birthday at the end of 1993.[58] A series of museum exhibitions in the early 1990s on the history of the sent-down movement,[59] the generation of Red Guards or urban "educated youth" (*zhiqing*) who had been rusticated in the 1960s and 1970s, marked the beginning of a collective nostalgia regarding the remembered experiences during the pre-1978 socialist period. The re-release of songs from the 1960s and 1970s, the publication of books on the fate of the generation during this period, and even "homecoming" trips to the villages they had been sent to followed.[60] Exhibitions, book projects, and social gatherings brought members of this generation together, and they shared their stories and emotions regarding their rustication experience.

Many people imagined Maoism, Mao himself, and the socialist period as part of a mystified alternative to the reformed system, with its rising inequality, class distinction, cadre corruption, and other problems. Nostalgia in the form of exhibitions, documentary films, and social gatherings became a form of "cultural resistance," in which the experiences of the present (the 1990s) were "typically characterized by materialism, excessive rationalization, and a lack of meaning and purpose in life"[61]—in contrast to a past that had given a generation a sense of purpose through enduring hardships for a greater cause. The forms of nostalgia differed, from the yearning for better material conditions as during the socialist period to the support of the political program behind CCP socialism.

Debates and Networks

The Mao revival among workers and peasants in the 1990s was accompanied by new leftist political debates and organizing. In the second half of the 1980s, liberal ideas had dominated discussions among intellectuals and had substantial influence on the CCP leadership. After the crackdown in 1989, things changed. While socialist terms and concepts reappeared in official CCP statements, Deng Xiaoping accused "rampant bourgeois liberalism" of being responsible for the Tian'anmen Square Movement, and leftists saw their chance. Within one year of the crackdown, "three leftist periodicals came out in Beijing with a declared goal of anti-bourgeois liberalism and defending socialism."[62]

The CCP leadership was alert though, and tried to stop the spread of leftist critique of the economic reforms. During his infamous southern tour in 1992, Deng Xiaoping "called for getting rid of the ideological entanglement with 'isms' and accelerating the reform."[63] "Preventing leftism" (*fang zuo*) or "anti-leftism" (*fan zuo*) was part of this.

At this point, leftists close to or within the CCP mostly agreed with the leadership on the policies of a strong state, CCP rule, and ideological control of the masses, but they disagreed on the (relaunch of the) market reforms.[64] These reforms were deepened further in the mid-1990s, with the restructuring of the state sector and lay-offs, wage and welfare cuts for urban state workers (see the previous section, "State Workers against Smashing the Iron Rice Bowl").

While workers (and peasants) protested and made claims based on the socialist past, leftist circles in and outside the CCP began criticizing the market reforms while reassessing the Maoist heritage. An example that involved more established proponents are the four so-called *wanyanshu* (literally "10,000-words articles") that circulated in Beijing between late 1995 and 1997. "Attacking market reform and questioning the CCP's current policy direction, they represented the boldest de-Dengization statements since the reform."[65] The articles were written by people who had close connections to the party leadership, including Deng Liqun, who had been a close ally of Deng Xiaoping but grew increasingly critical of the reform course.[66] The articles called for the continuation of the state-controlled economy, and "warned that the decline of state industries would help capitalism prevail over socialism and would impoverish the workers. In opposition to Deng's non-ideological approach, they continued to stress the ongoing struggle between capitalism and socialism."[67] The leftists involved referred to anti-capitalist discourses the CCP itself had used before the reform. As the CCP leadership still insisted it was following the socialist path and was carrying out the reforms in the name of socialism, the leftist critique of pro-capitalist reforms even seemed "justified." Ironically, "Deng Xiaoping became the most cited person in leftist writings, where the 'orthodox' part of his words was frequently used against many current practices."[68]

Another example is the debates triggered by the theater play *Che Guevara*. Staged in 2000 and 2001 in various theaters, it attracted thousands of spectators—students, workers, CCP members, and intellectuals.[69] The play "interprets today's China and the world from a macrohistorical perspective, centered on a rich/poor antagonism." It criticizes U.S. imperialism, rejects globalization "as a serious intrusion of foreign capital and as camouflage for Western economic and cultural hegemony," and denounces "Western liberal or neoliberal discourse as nothing but justification for exploitation and oppression."[70] The heated discussions around the play mostly avoided a direct critique of the CCP or the state in the PRC, but they raised the issues of markets, globalization, the U.S.-dominated world-capitalism, and the actuality of revolution.[71]

The debates around *Che Guevara* were not only influenced by the arguments of the New Left of intellectuals (see the next subsection, "The New Left") but also new debates among grassroots Maoists. The latter staged larger conferences in the early 2000s and discussed whether to participate in CCP politics to change the system from within (i.e. to turn it back to a leftist line) or to form new organizations or parties. Rather than unifying the Maoist left, the debates led to a range of splits and different practices.

Meanwhile, leftist worker activists pushed on with struggles of state workers, which continued through the 2000s. An example is the case of the "Zhengzhou Four." During a struggle at a paper mill in Zhengzhou, Henan province, that began in 2000, "workers used 'Cultural Revolution' methods, according to one activist, in forcing out the managers, seizing the factory, preventing the removal of equipment, and instituting worker control." During another struggle in the city, in an electrical equipment factory, workers put up a banner with the slogan: "Continually uphold Mao Zedong Thought."[72] In September 2004, four Maoists—Zhang Zhengyao, Zhang Ruquan, Ge Liying, and Wang Zhanqing—wrote, printed, and distributed a leaflet that criticized the CCP leadership for corruption, for abandoning the interests of the working class, and for the restoration of capitalism in the PRC. The leaflet demanded a return to Mao's "socialist road." The two Zhangs were sentenced to three years in prison. The trial drew the attention of leftists from around the country, who came to Zhengzhou to protest.[73]

Another example was the worker unrest in Xi'an, Shaanxi province, like Zhengzhou a city affected by the restructuring of state-owned enterprises and mass lay-offs. From the early 2000s on, it saw workers' protest through the use of demonstrations and traffic blockades. In 2008, state workers—most of them in their forties or older—from several Xi'an companies, formed the "Shaanxi Study Group of Mao Zedong Thought" and, in the same year, the "Shaanxi Trade Union Rights Defense Representative Congress."[74] They used conventional organizing methods as well as online resources like leftist blogs, discussion boards, and Maoist websites to promote their agenda.

Throughout the 2000s, leftist debates found new platforms and multipliers on the internet that enabled many more people to interact directly and push these debates. Among the more prominent websites were Utopia (*wu you zhi xiang*, set up in 2003)[75] and Red China (*hongse zhongguo*, set up in 2005). The online exchanges were instrumental in creating a new composition of leftisms in the PRC. Part of the Maoist "old" left inside and close to the CCP continued to oppose the reform course and was especially agitated about the acceptance of capitalists in the party in 2001, at the end of Jiang Zemin's time in power. Many of these Maoists had been urban students and workers politicized during and after the Cultural Revolution. They criticized the reforms initiated by what they saw as rightists or "capitalist roaders" like Deng Xiaoping; they attacked the CCP for dumping the class struggle discourse in the 1980s; and they supported working-class actions like the state-sector workers' movement in the 1990s and after. They were—at least, rhetorically—also supportive of strikes of migrant workers against both the state and private capital (see chapter 5).

Apart from this part of the old left, grounded in the CCP's socialist history and ideology and active inside and outside the party, another leftist current developed out of political debates in the aftermath of 1989 and was influenced by the CCP ideology as well as other leftist tendencies: the so-called New Left.

The New Left

The term "New Left" (*xin zuopai* or *xin zuoyi*) was applied in the mid-1990s by liberal opponents to a loose and "heterogeneous group of scholars and intellectuals (some of whom resisted the label)."[76] During much of the 1980s, liberal (and right-wing, neo-authoritarian) discourses had dominated political, public, and intellectual debates. In the early 1990s, a number of intellectuals were still involved in different liberal discourses on economic and political reforms—supporting marketization, capitalist relations, or Western democracy.[77] New Left intellectuals formulated a critique of these liberal positions. The intense arguments between the two sides led to the formation of opposing currents, even though they were never clear-cut and some participants in the debates resisted their categorization as one or the other.

By the end of the 1990s, Wang Hui, Cui Zhiyuan, Wang Shaoguang, and Gan Yang were seen as the "big four" of the New Leftists, but many more have been involved or included.[78] The "New" in New Left set them apart from the old left. "Old" referred to older Maoists, who were still promoting rebel positions from the time of the Cultural Revolution, but also to the CCP leadership itself that was (and is, till today) seen by many observers in the PRC and elsewhere as part of the (old) left.

Several New Leftists had, actually, been reformist or liberal intellectuals in the 1980s, and some had sympathized with or participated in the Tian'anmen Square Movement in 1989.[79] They changed their positions after 1989 and developed "anti-liberal" as well as leftist positions that ranged from "Social Democrat to Economic Nationalist to Maoist."[80] Some had studied in the U.S. or other Western countries and used their versions of Critical Theory and certain academic strands in vogue at the time (like postmodernism, postcolonialism, or post-structuralism) for their analysis of the situation in the PRC.

Throughout the 1990s and into the 2000s, New Left ideological positions or general arguments were further developed in debates and in arguments with liberal intellectuals.[81] They included the upholding of the CCP's socialist legacy, that is, of Maoism and socialism as a political project; the critique of neoliberalism (i.e. the promotion of free markets and privatizations), Western "modernity," capitalist globalization, and the post-1989 global "end of history" discourse; the critique of the marketization of the rural economy; the promotion of a strong state able to control the effects of marketization and maintain stability; the critique of Western liberal democracy and parliamentarism as a form of capitalist rule; the denunciation of developments in the PRC that contradict the socialist cause and are seen as characteristic of capitalist societies, such as greed and corruption or social inequality; and the promotion of economic democracy, social equality, as well as demands for better working conditions, education, and welfare provided by a (strong) state.

Some protagonists of the New Left did engage in social struggles, like those of peasants and urban state workers in the 1990s and 2000s already described. Others did not and, instead, limited themselves mostly to intellectual attacks on their counterparts, the liberals, and, to a lesser extent, on other leftists inside and outside the CCP. In the late 2000s and 2010s, many from the New Left moved closer to leftist, nationalist circles inside the CCP (the "old" left). Parts of the New Left (and some of the Maoist activists) even supported CCP leaders, first Bo Xilai and his version of neoliberal policies, prettied up by Maoist folklore, and later Xi Jinping and his vulgarized and depoliticized form of Marxism (see chapter 5).

The New Left has not been, "strictly speaking, an oppositional force."[82] It has been "nationalist in orientation, identifying with the state's goals of national rejuvenation and self-determination in a geopolitical environment still characterized by U.S. hegemonic threats to Chinese sovereignty."[83] New Left positions on the PRC's standing in the world have come to resemble those of the "old" left which has been extremely nationalist all the way.[84]

Confronting the Leftist Challenge

Throughout the socialist period and even after, CCP leaderships kept up a leftist rhetoric. At the same time, they were critical of leftist deviance and opposition inside and outside the party, and leftists were frequently purged and punished. The reason is simple: leftists, especially those rooted in social movements, are able to politically express and use the discontent of workers or peasants, and have done so, for instance during the Cultural Revolution and the Tian'anmen Square Movement, when CCP rule seemed seriously threatened.

The Mao revival and folklore in the 1990s and after did not pose such threat to the CCP regime as long as references to the socialist past and Mao remained quite nostalgic and did not question the central role of the party. The regime was sensitive to workers' or peasants' references to the socialist past during their struggles. It often made limited concessions to their economic demands but used repressive means against activists or leaders.

The regime still closely observed leftist activity and was alarmed when leftists (inside and outside the party) employed a type of class struggle Maoism to attack the reform course, the establishment of capitalist social relations, or the party itself for its anti-worker tendency. It used its security forces to criminalize and repress; for instance, the few initiatives to establish alternative communist parties ended with leading figures receiving long prison sentences.[85] In a similar fashion, the regime punished worker activists who tried to mobilize and organize workers in independent union groups.

Surveillance and censorship became an even bigger issue in the 2000s, when the left began to use the internet to discuss and mobilize. Websites like Utopia were repeatedly closed down. Many leftists, including those of the New Left, knew what the limits were and neither attacked the CCP leadership openly nor (publicly) founded new political or labor organizations. They often criticized the economic reforms, marketization, or exploitation in terms that did not include a direct critique of the regime. And some positions shared by many around the New Left did not contradict the official CCP line: the support of a strong state, arguments for the defense of national interests, demands for a welfare state, and the promotion of social stability.

Referring to the Socialist Legacy

In sum, leftist topics and debates resurfaced in the late 1980s and early 1990s. The marketization of the economy had devastating effects on the urban state workers and created harsh conditions for migrant workers in the expanding private sector.[86] The emerging Mao nostalgia was partially triggered by a popular yearning for better, socialist times in the face of new social challenges like insecurity, inequality, corruption, and more. Workers (and peasants) resorted to Maoist slogans and reminiscences of the socialist period in social conflicts. They assumed that this would support their claims for the defense of standards or their demands for improvements. Their struggles, again, touched both dimensions of left-wing politics: the distribution of wealth (here the defense of the "iron rice-bowl," the demand for compensation for those losing jobs because of restructuring, or the protest against taxes) and the distribution of power (here the defense of their status and position in the workplace and their attacks on cadre authority, arbitrariness, and corruption).

Leftist activists, among them intellectuals and workers with experience of previous movements in the 1960s, 1970s, and 1980s, reorganized in the late 1990s and early 2000s. They used the impetus of the Mao revival and the state workers' and peasants' struggles to push for debates on market reforms, capitalist relations, and a possible return to the planned economy. Meetings, printed literature, and, later, the internet were platforms for discussing the present reality of capitalist exploitation as well as the political movements and experiences of the socialist past. Some Maoists came out of the struggles of (urban state) workers or were involved in them, and a few of them engaged in alternative party building. New discussion platforms and networks were established in the 2000s, when internet access became available to large parts of the population. Moving debates online helped to promote leftist issues and include more people. This was before the regime had established fast and effective censorship mechanisms.

A specific group was the New Left, a loose circle of leftist intellectuals who never formed a homogeneous group but became a reference point for leftist debate and critique in the PRC. They criticized the global neoliberal turn and its growing impact on the PRC, the effects of the market reforms, and the restructuring of the state economy, and spoke out for the defense or revival of Chinese socialism or Maoism. The New Left appealed mostly to academic circles and largely stayed out of actual social struggles, but it had an impact on leftists within the CCP and engaged in debates with leftists abroad. While pushing a left-wing agenda regarding the dimension of wealth distribution, they promoted (right-)authoritarian positions like a strong state, Chinese nationalism, party rule, ideological control, and the regulation of society from above.

The positions and debates of the Maoist current of workers and the New Left overlapped and later resulted in the shaping of several leftist (and mostly Maoist) currents that differed, for instance, in their loyal or critical position towards the CCP and their nationalist or anti-nationalist attitude regarding the PRC.

Even though a large part of these leftisms did not undermine the regime (and sometimes even strengthened its legitimacy), the latter was still nervous as it had faced serious challenges from the oppositional left in previous decades. For that reason, the regime kept a close eye on leftists and possible leftist mobilizations, especially when they were connected to social protests (of workers or peasants). It reacted with harsh repression when they tried to establish organizations or larger networks. But it was also willing to make concessions when material demands were made. How the regime also coopted leftist actors and demands will be described in the next chapter.

CONCLUSION: OLD CLASS COMPOSITION, NEW LEFTIST MOBILIZATION

In this chapter, I looked at how, in the changed economic and political landscape of the 1990s and early 2000s, new social struggles with left-wing demands broke out and inspired New Leftist currents. The CCP regime accelerated the market reforms after a short period of consolidation from 1989 to 1992, and intensified its efforts to restructure the economy throughout the 1990s. The reforms and their effects changed the class composition and conditions both in the countryside and in the cities.

Peasants faced mounting economic problems, including tax and fee burdens, and the relations between local cadres and peasants deteriorated as the latter were fed up with cadre corruption and abuse of power. In the mid-1990s, rural conflicts and peasant resistance escalated, with demonstrations and even riots leading to clashes with the police. Peasants used references to the socialist period and Maoist rhetoric to justify their resistance. While the CCP regime repressed the unrest, it also introduced reforms to lessen the burden on peasants and to improve the economic situation in the countryside. However, conflicts over land theft continued, and even amplified, in the late 2000s and early 2010s, as the regime kept pushing forward the reform and marketization of agriculture.

Urban state workers suffered a frontal attack on their working and living conditions in the mid-1990s, when the CCP regime began restructuring and partially privatizing state-run enterprises. Permanent workers not only lost their lifelong employment by either being sacked or given a work contract, they also lost most of the welfare package that had been granted to them in the socialist period. Like the peasants, they utilized Maoist rhetoric and emphasized the rightfulness of their resistance to the restructuring through demonstrations, street blockades, and other forms of protest. The regime made concessions, such as compensation and reemployment programs, but it continued the restructuring.

The movements of peasants and urban state workers were defensive struggles against the increasing commodification of their labor power.[87] They marked the final transition to capitalism in the PRC. Meanwhile, Mao and Maoism experienced a revival in popular culture and contributed to the emergence of different new leftist currents. Many people began to refer to the socialist past and Mao Zedong as the (imagined) symbol of equality and the defense of working-class interests. The emergence of various leftist activities among different social groups—workers, intellectuals, party members—and the nostalgic revival of Mao as an icon of equality under socialism stand for the specific form of left-wing dissent and debate in the late transitional and early capitalist period. Maoist grassroots groups got involved in workers' struggles and attempted to organize and coordinate activities. New Left intellectuals attacked liberal opponents, the marketization of the economy, and global neoliberalism while positively reassessing the PRC's socialist past.

The CCP regime itself continued to use leftist rhetoric and references to the socialist past to strengthen its legitimacy but continued the reform course, the attacks on the old socialist working class, and the massive industrialization program that brought in foreign capital and created a new working class of rural migrant workers. In the next chapter we shall see, how the struggles of this new working class created another generation of leftist activists while, on a second front, women*'s struggles connected to new feminist currents put even more pressure on the regime.

5
Social Unrest and Organizing: Challenges for the CCP in the Capitalist 2000s and 2010s

In this chapter, I look at the new forms of social unrest and resistance in the PRC in the 2000s and 2010s. After the establishment of capitalist relations, migrant workers and women* developed forms of defiance and resistance against the exploitative and discriminatory conditions. Their pressure from below inspired left-wing and feminist activism. The regime made material concessions, but also cracked down on organized forms of workers' and women*'s support.

In the *first* section, I describe the increasing discontent of (rural) migrant workers. Labor migration of (mostly young) ruralites began in the 1980s and accelerated in the 1990s, when the PRC became the "factory of the world" and migrant workers were needed in manufacturing, in the construction sector, and for service jobs including care work in private households. The number of labor conflicts involving migrant workers increased continuously after the early 1990s and reached its peak in the mid-2010s.

In the *second* section, I discuss leftist activism in support of migrant workers and their struggles from the mid-1990s on. It was often organized by labor NGOs and later grassroots groups of left-wing students and activists. They all faced surveillance and repression from local state authorities with close connections to capital interests.

In the *third* section, I focus on the situation of women* and their everyday struggles in the PRC. In the socialist period, the CCP regime integrated women* into the workforce but they continued to be discriminated against and treated as lower-status citizens.

In the transitional period, the regime tightened the control over women* with the One-Child Policy, women*'s employment rate dropped, and the gendered division of labor was reinforced. In the capitalist period, the regime eventually relaxed the One-Child Policy as demographic problems loomed that began to undermine the success of the PRC's economic model. In all periods, women* resisted discrimination against them and tried to gain more control over their lives.

In the *fourth* section, I take a look at feminist mobilizations in the past thirty years and their position vis-à-vis state feminism in the PRC. Women*'s NGOs spread in the 1990s and 2000s, when they campaigned for an end to violence and discrimination against women*. A small current of mostly academic critical socialist feminists emerged in the late 2000s, who criticized the strong influence of "Western" feminism on feminists in the PRC and argued for the recognition of the success of state feminism in the socialist period. In the 2010s, a new current of young feminists organized small street actions and online campaigns against domestic violence, sexual harassment, and other forms of violence against women*. The feminist movement won some concessions, but also faced harsh repression, especially in recent years.

THE NEW WORKING CLASS

> At the lower middle school, we read some Marxist theory. When the teachers explained to us the contradiction between productive forces and the relations of production in a capitalist society, they also referred to the inhuman exploitation of workers. At that time, we did not understand that. Then I came to Shenzhen to work here, and then I gradually understood how the capitalists oppress and exploit women workers. (Young female migrant worker)[1]

In this section, I describe the formation of the migrant working class and its struggles against exploitation or discrimination and for improvements of working and living conditions in the capitalist period. Most of the immediate demands and goals of workers in their struggles were economic in nature and presented no open political challenge for the CCP leadership. However, the demands for material improvements implied left-wing positions vis-à-vis a regime that had abandoned its leftist agenda, and they produced substantial pressure from below. The CCP regime wanted to defuse social tensions and reacted not just with repression, but also with political and legal reforms.

In the 1990s, the PRC had become the "factory of the world" for consumer goods. The boom in manufacturing, construction, and other sectors was built on the vast supply of migrant labor power from the countryside. The CCP leadership created the conditions necessary for capital to tap the PRC's rural labor power. The regime could rely on its experience with employing (temporary) rural labor in the decades before. During the socialist period, it had restricted (permanent) migration through the *hukou* system, used rural labor power on a mass scale in urban sectors when it was needed—and had sent it back to the countryside when it was not needed any more. These rural migrants usually received lower wages and fewer benefits than urban workers. This injustice and the discrimination against temporary workers triggered social conflicts and struggles, most notably during the "economist" unrest in the Cultural Revolution.[2]

In the early 1980s, the CCP regime slowly reformed the *hukou* system as part of its market reforms. Rural migrants were allowed to move to urban areas and newly founded special economic zones (SEZ), where foreign capital started setting up factories. These migrants kept their rural *hukou*, though, and did not gain urban *hukou* and the attached rights and benefits. In that way they continued to have a temporary status in the cities, their urban residence permits ran out when they lost their jobs, and they remained "outside the system" (*tizhiwai*), mostly working for private companies or with precarious employment relations.

In the early 1990s, the conditions were set for a rapid increase in migration. The regime further loosened the *hukou* laws, and millions of rural migrants moved to the cities and new industrial centers in the east and southeast. They filled the jobs of new or expanding urban sectors, mostly doing the dirty, dangerous, and arduous work in factories, on construction sites, and in urban services.[3] The status of rural migrant workers in the cities remained precarious. Under the Custody and Repatriation system (C&R, *shourong qiansong zhidu*) rural migrants without a valid temporary residence permit were detained and returned to their villages. The system was abolished in 2003, after a migrant worker named Sun Zhigang died due to physical abuse in C&R-detention in Guangzhou.[4]

Until the 2000s, migrant workers' proletarianization remained mostly unfinished or incomplete. With their rural *hukou* they kept the entitlement to a piece of land in their home villages (which was often farmed by their parents or other family members).[5] However, many migrants increasingly felt the effects of land enclosure. Farming did not generate enough income to support a family (i.e. migrants' remittances were needed), and more and more peasants lost their land due to land confiscation and the increasing capitalization of agriculture in the 2000s and 2010s.[6]

In the urban areas, migrant workers experienced extreme forms of exploitation, such as long working hours, low wages, high work intensity, dangerous and toxic work environments, brutal management practices, and racist as well as sexist discrimination (by managers and state officials or police). Employers, eager to keep a flexible workforce and using hire and fire practices, regularly ignored labor laws and left workers without labor contracts. Many migrants lived in dormitories close to their factories or construction sites, a form of substandard housing (without families). In that way, not only were workers easier to control and housing costs kept low, but also this "dormitory labor regime" enabled employers to pay even lower wages as the larger share of social reproduction (childcare, education, care for the elderly) remained in the countryside (at lower costs).[7]

Migrant Worker Protests

Labor unrest in response to the harsh conditions started in the 1980s and 1990s, with sporadic strikes in factories and on construction sites as well as short strike waves in provinces on the east coast and, especially, Guangdong.[8] This unrest included hidden forms of everyday workplace resistance (sabotage, slowdowns, and what James Scott calls "weapons of the weak").[9]

The number of visible workers' protests increased after 2003.[10] By that time, migrants had gotten used to labor regime and industrial work, and some of them acquired the ability to organize strikes and other forms of collective resistance. Even the dormitory labor regime worked in favor of organizing resistance in some instances, as workers took advantage of the fact that masses of workers met and interacted all day.

In the first half of the 2000s, most of the demands of the migrant workers' actions were rather defensive, asking for compliance with labor laws (e.g. regarding working hours, overtime, or minimum wages) or the payment of wage arrears. More migrant workers used the legal channels installed earlier, like arbitration boards and labor courts, to push through their demands. Still, the pressure from below on enterprise managements and local authorities was palpable.

In the second half of the 2000s, migrant workers' confidence and experience had grown, and they began fighting for real improvements (and not just for compliance with labor standards).[11] The offensive or more ambitious demands included wage increases, more respect from managers, better working hours, and sometimes even collective bargaining or proper worker representation.[12] Larger migrant worker protests took place, mostly in light manufacturing, construction, and transportation—sectors that bring workers together on a mass scale or give them particular disruptive capacities. Workers exploited the fact that labor shortages in labor-intensive sectors on the east coast, coupled with high labor turnover, had improved their bargaining power since the mid-2000s.[13] Their wildcat strikes were also more disciplined and better organized, with coordination through informal networks of workers and worker activists using telephones and internet platforms. The most spectacular strike wave took place in the auto industry in 2010, starting with a strike of Honda workers in Guangdong and spreading to other companies and provinces. By this time, given the number and spread of strikes, the PRC had become the "epicenter of world labor unrest."[14]

The number of labor protests continued to increase until 2015, when it began to drop slowly.[15] The nature of protests altered, too, with ongoing sectoral, spatial, economic, and generational changes.

Following the tertiarization of the economy, more service workers (e.g. in transportation, education, banking, and IT) were involved in labor conflicts than before. And in the wake of the relocation of industries due to higher wages on the east coast, more protests occurred in central and western China.[16] With the slowdown of economic growth, restructuring and relocation, workers staged more struggles against redundancies, and for compensation and, due to the aging of migrant workers, many of whom were then in their 40s and 50s, more protests demanded social insurance contributions (e.g. for pensions). In many cases, workers were again better organized and even more proficient in using smartphones, social media, and other media, and in some cases they managed to coordinate across companies, cities, and provinces: during the Coca-Cola workers' strike (2015), the crane drivers' strike, and the truck drivers' strike (both in 2018).[17]

Forms of Resistance

The workers' struggles touched upon the two main left-wing themes—the improvement of working conditions, and more control in the workplaces and beyond. Their forms depended on various factors and the region: the particular situation of the workers, the form of labor, the composition of capital, or the role of the local authorities.

First, forms of "contained resistance" have been used by hi-tech or high-skill workers with urban *hukou* or a secure status in the city (as well as some migrant workers), and they dominated in regions or provinces without prevalent militant or large-scale industrial disputes.[18] Workers made quite small and legally based claims, used formal state channels (like mediation or arbitration bodies, or labor courts), and refrained from organizing beyond the workplace. Contained resistance has steadily increased since the 1990s as more institutionalized forms of conflict resolution were provided by the CCP regime.[19]

Second, workers in low-tech, low-skill, and labor-intensive industries employing migrant workers with rural *hukou* have often used "boundary-spanning resistance" and demanded improvements irrespective of legal standards. This form of resistance involved strikes, street protests, and even riots, and was more prevalent in particular provinces, like Guangdong. The participants were sometimes organized loosely and, in some cases, had legal support from labor NGOs. Often these struggles started with contained resistance and escalated when demands were not met, and workers who developed organizing skills in previous confrontations took the lead. Since this form of resistance goes beyond the dispute resolution processes provided by the regime, it attracted more state intervention, like officials pushing for mediation, for trade union intervention, for management concessions—or even resolving the conflict with state resources. Boundary-spanning resistance began to increase in the early 2000s and continued into the 2010s.

In some cases, migrant workers have also resorted to "transgressive resistance." They demanded substantial improvements of their conditions or even institutional changes; made connections between different companies, sectors, or even provinces; and sought direct support from labor NGOs or leftist networks. Transgressive resistance began to be used more in the late 2000s and early 2010s, before the increased repression and other factors led to a drop.

In all three types of resistance, often team or line leaders, or older and experienced workers took the initiative in pushing for workers' demands, challenging higher management, or even escalating the form of struggle. Women* workers were involved in the resistance, usually to the extent they were represented in the workforce, and they took leading roles, too. During the 2000s, it was often young migrant workers of the "second generation" who organized protests and participated.[20] They wanted to stay in the cities, had learned from the experience of the "first generation," and benefited from the wider tacit acceptance of labor unrest by state unions and labor authorities.[21]

All migrants' workplace struggles were wildcat actions, that is, self-organized and autonomous actions. Strikes are not legally sanctioned or protected in the PRC, and the CCP regime does not allow the setting up of independent labor unions. The official union ACFTU, the mass organization of the CCP in workplaces, has union structures in many companies and regions, but it stays loyal to the regime and opposes strike actions. The CCP regime's ban on independent worker organizations, whether unions or political groups, prevented the formation of formal or official working-class groups, meaning that the PRC has seen "class struggles without class organization."[22]

In the 1990s and 2000s, the basis of self-organization was often the common place of origin of migrant workers, who came from the same village or region. In the course of the 2000s, when migrants slowly settled down in the urban areas (even without getting urban *hukou*), more protests were organized on the basis of common interests as workers in a particular job, department, plant, or company.[23] However, when their struggles were spreading in the 2000s, migrant workers had no clear language to talk about them in left-wing or class terms. In public debates, the language of class (*jieji*) and class struggle (*jieji douzheng*) had disappeared in the 1980s, abandoned by the CCP and most scholars and analysts, and had been replaced by a Weberian, bourgeois discourse on social strata (*jieceng*).[24] Migrant workers did not even use the term for workers—*gongren*—as it was still reserved for workers in urban state-owned enterprises. They used other terms like "working girl/working boy" (*dagongmei/dagongzai*) or "peasant worker" (*nongmingong*)—expressing their insecure and temporary status in the cities and demonstrating the lack of class language or a "discursive dyslexia."[25]

Adapted Countermeasures

In the long run, the mobilizations and struggles of migrant workers have been successful to a certain extent because, on the one hand, workers gained experiences in organizing strategies and protest tactics and, on the other hand, the pressure from below led to the improvement of their status and conditions. This was no smooth process, though, and the CCP regimes also reacted with repression to this pressure.

In the 1990s and early 2000s, when the economy was restructured, the regime under Jiang Zemin was often not able to respond to social unrest in a consistent and planned way and sent in the police, which provoked more conflicts and even riots. From the mid-2000s to the early 2010s, the "golden age" of economic boom and rising wages, the regime under Hu Jintao developed more means of concession and cooptation.[26] For most of the 2000s, for state and private capital, strikes were often not a big issue as wages were low and the economy was booming, so there was room for (small but continuous) concessions. Local or regional authorities tolerated labor protests as long as they were restricted to one company. However, strike organizers among the workers were usually dismissed, and attempts to set up independent labor organizations were rigidly repressed. Local authorities also intervened (repressively or otherwise) when labor struggles spread beyond company limits, involved clear political aims, or could not be resolved quickly. They also channeled grievances and conflicts into institutionalized mediation processes to atomize the workers and undermine class formation processes.[27]

In the late 2000s and in the 2010s, the state machine was much better prepared to use policing or political measures. It had gradually developed its "repressive capacity" as well as its "responsive capacity":[28] more and better trained police, new forms of surveillance and (online) censorship, new regulations on NGOs and other support groups, new (and better enforced) labor laws, labor arbitration and courts, more active ACFTU intervention and organizing, more "pro-worker" government propaganda (including the Harmonious Society mentioned in the previous chapter). During the "golden age," workers and supporters (like labor NGOs) were given space for experiments in collective bargaining but these were limited or brought to an end by the regime in the mid-2010s.

The regime under Xi Jinping (after 2012) continued to use institutionalized methods of labor conflict resolution and control, but, at the same time, it began to use more repressive forms against social unrest—as the economic growth slowed down and wage increases were limited. Factory closures, their relocation to the Chinese hinterland or Southeast Asia, and problems connected to the aging of migrant workers triggered an increasing number of conflicts. The main issues involved were redundancies, compensation, and social insurance payments, which involved large sums of money. Yet, the employers' space for concessions had become smaller. Migrant workers were left with fewer options in the 2010s, as the state cracked down on support networks and censored reports on social unrest. The repression of larger, transgressive, and spreading unrest included the sacking, blacklisting, or even arrest of worker activists, "leaders," and supporters. Which form of containment was used depended on "regional models of control," the level of unrest, the "bureaucratic incentives" for cadres, and the regime's counterinsurgency programs.[29]

Workers against Capital

In sum, from the 1990s, migrant workers had new opportunities to move to the cities and industrial zones and earn more than meager peasant incomes, but they also faced harsh working and living conditions in their urban jobs. At first, the number of protests increased slowly as the workers were still adapting to the new situation; when they had accumulated more experience, the number of protests increased substantially. However, even in protests, migrant workers were often not unified but separated along the lines of origin, skill, gender, sector, and region.

The struggles of migrant workers were aimed at private and state employers, and often also local state authorities. These were, on the one hand, closely connected to local factions of capital and, on the other hand, seen as responsible for not forcing employers to comply with legal standards (like the minimum wage or overtime regulations) and for the restrictive and discriminatory migration regime (such as the *hukou* regulations).

The demands (and the framing of the demands) changed repeatedly. Apart from a window of opportunity between the mid-2000s and the mid-2010s, when workers used high growth rates and regional labor shortages to put forward offensive or more ambitious demands for substantial improvements, before and after that their demands were quite defensive: for the payment of wage arrears or for compensation after lay-offs, for instance.

The new migrant working class and their struggles added to the social frictions produced by the growing social inequality and capitalist exploitation. The struggles did not lead to the formation of an organized labor movement with union or party representation, and, more important, workers could not build lasting organizational cores and resources for future struggles. However, workers accumulated important experiences and knowledge on how to organize labor protests that was passed on, and their struggles generated substantial pressure from below that produced changes in labor institutions and working conditions. They also "warped" the state, that is, they pushed the CCP regime slowly and gradually to transform its repressive and responsive capacities.[30]

The emergence of the migrant working class, its struggles and forms of organizing, impressed not just the CCP leadership and state authorities, but also different parts of the oppositional left as we shall see in the next section.

THE RECOMPOSED LEFT

> [W]hen the students pulled out the images of Chairman Mao, a lot of workers thought it was pretty weird, or said that they didn't understand the point of that. In our observation, most workers in the Pearl River Delta don't have any particular feelings about Mao. (Activist's comment on Maoist students' organizing effort, 2019)[31]

As discussed in the previous chapter, the changing class composition and growing social inequalities in the late transitional period and the early capitalist period found a reflection in the recomposition of the activist left-wing opposition and had an effect on leftist debates and initiatives inside and outside the CCP. While in the 1990s and early 2000s the main social confrontations involved peasants and urban state workers, from the mid-2000s the protests of migrant workers set the tone.

As in the 1990s, the majority among the oppositional left in the PRC continued to be influenced by Maoism. But while an old generation of Maoists kept their focus on the peasant situation and struggles, and even more so on the protests of urban state workers against the dismantling of state industries and welfare, a new generation of Maoists emerged that dealt with the situation of migrant workers or the new working class.

The recurrent struggles of urban workers, migrant workers, and peasants inspired left-wing debates and organizing that had an impact on forces inside the CCP as well. Towards the end of the 2000s, groups inside the party coopted leftist discourses and Maoist nostalgia. As we shall see, this deepened a split in the newly composed left between a Maoist Right and a Maoist Left—a split that defines the leftist landscape in the PRC up to the present day.

Labor NGOs' Interventions

In the 2000s and 2010s, oppositional leftist politics and positions critical of the CCP regime or social conditions were mainly discussed and used by particular leftist NGOs, online networks, student groups, and informal circles. In the PRC, the process of NGO-ization had already begun in the 1990s.[32] NGOs became popular as the regime retreated from certain social and welfare activities (e.g. in health care) following the slogan "small government, big society" or *xiaozhengfu, dashehui*. That created a certain space for the establishment of registered and informal private social organizations. Most NGOs engaged in some kind of social or aid work—and were not left-wing or oppositional in other ways. Only some followed an explicit left-wing political agenda in their support of social struggles from below. Among them were, for instance, environmental, feminist, LGBTIQ*, or labor NGOs.[33]

Witnessing the harsh conditions in world-market factories in Guangdong province in the early 1990s and the first waves of struggles of migrant factory workers, leftist activists from the PRC and Hong Kong began to discuss forms of labor support and solidarity, and set up labor NGOs from the mid-1990s on.[34] Urban intellectuals, as well as (former) migrant workers themselves, both from various leftist currents, were among the founders. Some of these labor NGOs enjoyed (financial) support from NGOs and foundations in Hong Kong and other countries, for instance, in Europe or North America, and most of them were active in Guangdong province in the south or in and around Beijing in the north.

Despite regime scrutiny and repression, especially from local state agencies who saw their interests threatened, labor NGOs found space for activity the regime regards as sensitive. For example, they supported migrant workers fighting for compensation after having suffered work accidents or work-related diseases. They also supported women* workers who needed legal advice and education in their struggle against harsh working conditions, or migrants who were dealing with discrimination due to their rural *hukou* status in the city. Many of these activities ran under the term *weiquan*, short for safeguarding legitimate rights and interests of, for instance, migrant workers.[35]

A range of more informal groups and individuals was also involved in *weiquan* activities and organized support for migrant workers and their individual or collective struggles. Among them were so-called citizen journalists and citizen lawyers, self-taught (former) workers who had turned activists and engaged in reporting, counseling, or other forms of support.

When migrant worker struggles became more widespread and militant in the late 2000s and early 2010s, several labor NGOs became "movement oriented" and recruited worker activists or trained workers in forms of collective action.[36] They supported workers' protest and strike organizing. In some instances, such NGOs helped to coordinate small, repeated protests from behind the scenes in the form of what has been called "disguised collective action" or "mobilizing without the masses," that is, launching publicity actions and campaigns on internet platforms while avoiding the formation of larger or formal organizations.[37] In other instances, NGOs got involved in collective bargaining, mobilizing and coaching workers on representation, negotiation, and protest action. "[L]abor NGOs found collective bargaining as the middle ground that they can pursue—a strategy that will not be seen as politically dangerous but that can contribute to substantial improvement of workers' welfare."[38] In that sense, they dared to go back to mobilization "with the masses." An example of such a changed role of a labor NGO is the successful strike actions for social insurance payments and more at Lide, a shoe factory in Guangzhou, in 2014 and 2015. A local labor NGO, the Panyu Migrant Workers Service Centre, played an important part by supporting the workers' actions and organizing attempts.[39]

As mentioned, many of those involved in labor NGOs were engaged in different leftist circles. These went through various changes in the 2000s and 2010s, the subject of the next subsection.

Grassroots Organizing

Labor NGOs and other initiatives supporting workers' struggles were mostly made up of intellectuals or (former) students with an urban or migrant background and (former) migrant workers. They had different leftist orientations that also determined their interventions.

More reformist, social democratic (or liberal) tendencies have been active in online debates and labor NGOs, most prominently in the China Labour Bulletin, an organization from Hong Kong with a network of contacts in the PRC that has pushed a social democratic agenda of independent unionism and collective bargaining.[40] Some initiatives involved people with Trotskyist positions aiming at workers' education and empowerment, or organizing solidarity inside and outside the PRC.[41] Another small tendency of unorthodox leftists mostly engaged in workplace interventions and solidarity, writing strike logs, and conducting and documenting worker interviews. And a few activists collected reports on worker struggles, in that way providing information for other supporters of labor unrest in the PRC and elsewhere.[42]

The strongest influence on labor activists continued to come from Maoism. The (oppositional) Maoist left experienced a generational change in the late 2000s and early 2010s, from an older generation that mainly referred to the old working class of urban state workers and had roots in the rebel struggles of the Cultural Revolution, to a new generation that grew out of an upsurge of leftist (mostly Maoist) discussions and focused on the wave of migrant workers' struggles.

Leftist debates were spurred on at this time by the spreading use of internet platforms (websites, message boards, chats, blogs) that gave room for exchanges (at least for a while, until state censorship caught up).[43] Young leftist (student) activists identifying as Marxists and/or Maoists organized in the early 2010s at several universities, for instance, in Beijing. From urban households and increasingly from migrant families themselves, these students formed so-called Marxist study groups. They read Mao's works and Maoist literature and applied it to the new realities of PRC capitalism, and some also began to visit the industrial zones in the south, learning about the conditions and organizing methods during summer schools.

Activities of Maoist and other leftist groups, supported by leftist NGOs and academic circles, included undercover inquiries in factories like those of the electronics supplier Foxconn[44] and the practice of "doing worker work" (*zuo gongren gongzuo*), "entering the factory" (*jin chang*), or *ronggong* (literally: mixing with workers), that is, working in factories, often in summer vacations or after graduation), to support organizing and strikes.[45] Some got involved not just in labor struggles but also in campus activism and feminist struggles. For instance, a group came together to support a sanitation workers' strike on campus for material improvements in Guangzhou in 2014.[46]

The most spectacular incident also marked the preliminary end of such (open) activity. Maoist students turned worker activists attempted to organize workers in the Jasic factory in Shenzhen, a producer of welding machines.[47] To fight against the harsh working conditions, they tried to set up a company union affiliated to the ACFTU. They had little support from other workers, but when the local police arrested some of the workers and activists, supporters organized demonstrations and mobilized dozens of students from Maoist groups to go to Shenzhen and stage protests. The police made more arrests, and state security agencies began a campaign to suppress the Maoist initiatives and study groups in the whole country afterwards.[48] The struggle was broken and a wave of repression hit not just those involved in the Jasic case itself but also other activist groups and labor NGOs. The defeat triggered debates among various leftist currents on the usability of Maoist strategies to educate and organize workers from the outside and through setting up a union in the ACFTU.[49]

Maoist Left and Right

Those on the left identifying as Maoist or having views close to Maoism include many of those involved in leftist labor NGOs, oppositional leftist debates, and leftist grassroots initiatives, as well as those close to the intellectual New Left and leftists inside the CCP as well. In the late 2000s and early 2010s, a political split widened between different currents of Maoism. Some Maoists welcomed the welfare reforms of Hu Jintao's Harmonious Society and the promise to solve the problems of peasants through the New Socialist Countryside program from the mid-2000s.

The so-called Chongqing Model stirred up even more excitement among some leftists. The CCP leader in the large city of Chongqing in western China, Bo Xilai, promoted social housing and other welfare measures, a campaign against organized crime, and a loosening of the *hukou* or migration regime. He supported Maoist folklore or a kind of "red" culture and socialist nostalgia. That earned him and the Chongqing Model the support of part of the New Left and other Maoist groups like some of those behind the websites Red China and Utopia. They hoped Bo Xilai would win influence in the CCP and push the party towards what they understood as a left-wing course.[50] However, Bo was seen as a competitor of designated party leader Xi Jinping. The CCP leadership decided against Bo's line and supported Xi Jinping as the next party leader. Bo was eventually arrested in 2012 and convicted of corruption, and that marked the end of the Chongqing Model.

The debate on the support or critique of the Chongqing Model deepened the split between what have been labeled a Maoist Left (*maozuo*) and a Maoist Right (*maoyou*).[51] These are descriptions for tendencies or debates, not for larger organizational entities. The Maoist Left distances itself from the CCP, which it sees as a capitalist or even right-wing force. It supports struggles from below, for instance of migrant workers, and advocates a revolutionary understanding of Maoism. While some favor a more democratic form of socialism, others hold on to authoritarian forms, and while some have an "internationalist" vision of class struggle, others support some kind of Chinese nationalism. Some Maoists from the "old" generation that came out of the Cultural Revolution rebel movement and later struggles, as well as the new generation of students and others who began to play a bigger role in the 2010s belong to the Maoist Left.

The Maoist Right continues to criticize the negative impact of the CCP regime's market reforms on the working class(es) in the PRC, the urban workers who lost their status and benefits, and the migrant workers who faced harsh working conditions in their urban jobs. However, it holds on to the Marxist-Leninist-Maoist ideology, supports party rule and a strong state, hopes to bring the CCP (leadership) back to a socialist course from within, and promotes Chinese nationalism, the pursuit of PRC economic and political interests abroad by the Chinese government. In recent years, it has even supported the CCP leadership under Xi Jinping for its promotion of (its own kind of) Marxism.

Regime Repression

The CCP regime, meanwhile, has developed a mix of different tools to limit left-wing oppositional activity since its upturn in the 1990s. Local authorities employed surveillance and other forms of control to restrict the activity of individuals or groups, especially where they supported social protests. Labor NGOs were threatened and forced to move out of certain districts or cities. Leftist websites and publications came under pressure or were shut down, as after Bo Xilai's fall.[52]

Oppositional activities were even more restricted under the new party leadership of Xi Jinping after 2012. The regime further tightened and adapted its censorship measures against leftist online activities and campaigns. Repression against different forms of organized opposition was intensified, targeting journalists, lawyers, and activists. However, while many of these oppositional figures are liberals who are not involved in left-wing organizing or activity, it was the crackdown on labor activists and NGOs in December 2015 which indicated that leftists were also increasingly in the crosshairs of the state security forces.

In the second half of the 2010s, the persecution of leftist oppositional groups became a task of the central state, with the central government setting the political line which local authorities had to follow. Earlier, local authorities had reacted to leftist activities in a more flexible and less consistent manner. Apparently, the CCP regime feared more organized connections between social protests and leftist mobilizations.

An example of the harsh response against, in this case Maoist, opposition was the aforementioned repression of the Jasic mobilization and, in its wake, of Maoist student groups, several NGOs, and more in 2018. This included threats, arrests, disappearances, and prison sentences. State repression of left-wing initiatives has clearly become preemptive, trying to prevent any meaningful collaboration of social protesters and left-wing activists. Neither labor NGOs backed by different leftist currents nor the Maoist (student) groups have been able to continue their engagement since the wave of repression began, and it seems that this generation of left-wing activism might have reached its end.

On the ideological front, the CCP regime has promoted a tamed and streamlined interpretations (or right-wing and nationalist versions) of Marxism, Maoism, and its own socialist legacy in an attempt to strengthen its legitimacy. The rejuvenation and redefinition of Marxism by the party leadership began already shortly after the CCP had allowed capitalists to join its ranks in the early 2000s. It feared losing legitimacy and support among workers and peasants. In 2004, for instance, it launched the "Marxist Theoretical Research and Development Project" (*makesi zhuyi lilun yanjiu he jianshe gongcheng*). "The goal of the project was to reexamine Marxism with a view to what Marxist classics had to say about socialist construction, rather than revolution, which had been the primary focus in the past." The CCP sought to "establish a new Marxist orthodoxy that leaves behind the revolutionary past" and ideologically justifies the reform course that has led the PRC into capitalism.[53]

Under Xi Jinping, the leadership tried to reinforce party rule through both institutional and ideological reforms. Faced with the slowdown of economic growth, widespread contradictions (like corruption) within the CCP and the state apparatus, and continuing social inequality and tensions, it decided to tighten its rule through campaigns, purges, and censorship. The CCP influence in many parts of society was bolstered through new guidelines and more party institutions with more power, for instance, in enterprises.

The repressive measures were complemented with the re-embrace of leftist rhetoric and Marxism in the official discourse.[54] The CCP leadership's "Marxism is a top-down attempt to unify the population behind a nationalist ideology, not to inspire class struggle."[55] The regime's promotion of anti-poverty or anti-corruption campaigns reminiscent of leftist demands are designed to diffuse social tensions and make the state more efficient (for governance from the center). Campaigns against "foreign" or "Western" influences are used to eliminate liberal and leftist opposition.[56] In 2021 and 2022, the CCP leadership pushed a discourse on "common prosperity" (*gongtong fuyu*), as well as measures to rein in private capitalists in the IT industry, and used this to underline the party's (alleged) concern for people's welfare.[57]

The tamed forms of Marxism and Maoism have a function in the CCP's political strategy. They can be used against domestic enemies, that is, liberals and their critique of the CCP regime or leftist opposition that betrays the CCP line. They also help to continually revive the myth of the CCP's "long march" or its role for national liberation and thereby strengthen party legitimacy.

Tough Times

In sum, the oppositional left that had reorganized in the course of the 1990s changed further in the following decades. Leftists engaged in (labor) NGOs supporting the struggles of migrant workers. They founded oppositional groups and engaged in online debates on the new class composition and leftist strategies throughout the 2010s. Maoism remained the main political ideology of leftist groups. Far fewer leftists supported other positions, such as Trotskyism and social democracy.

The Maoists organize in various circles and networks but have not managed to set up larger organizational cores. They are divided on various, often overlapping issues: some being preoccupied with the CCP's old socialist project vs. others who focus on the reform-period capitalism or so-called market socialism "with Chinese characteristics" (*zhongguo tese*); an old generation formerly involved in the Cultural Revolution and later struggles and focusing on the old socialist working class vs. a young generation of Maoists supporting the new migrant working class; reformist positions with a focus on gradual change of CCP politics vs. revolutionary positions for the development of power from below; and a majority supporting the CCP regime's nationalist global strategies vs. a minority holding on to the idea of a global left-wing or working-class movement. As a result, an oppositional Maoist Left promoting class struggle and change from below stands against a loyalist Maoist Right that supports the CCP regime and authoritarian governance.

Many from the Maoist Right or other groups claiming to be left-wing in some way support the party leadership for its strengthening of party rule; its pursuit of nationalist policies abroad; the repression in Xinjiang, Tibet, and Hong Kong to defend the country's territory; the attacks on liberals and on "Western influences"; or the more recent pressure on tech companies and the plan to introduce property taxes. Most of these policies are neither in the interest of the working class(es) nor left-wing per se.

The CCP regime has tolerated the Maoist Right and also managed to coopt leftist discourses and actors. The Maoist Left and other oppositional left-wing groups and circles have suffered from the repression of leftist activism in recent years. Today, most of these circles avoid public visibility and act very carefully when supporting social struggles.

Besides these left-wing circles and the ongoing workers' protests that inspired them, a second dialectic of social struggles and activist organizing shaped the past two decades in the PRC with women* and feminists as the main protagonists.

WOMEN*'S STRUGGLES AGAINST PATRIARCHAL REGIMES

> The birth of a baby is not only a matter of the family, but also a state affair. (From the editorial of the CCP's *People's Daily*, August 6, 2018)[58]

Women*'s struggles and feminism played an important but often under-rated role in the revolutionary struggle in China before 1949, in the trajectory of the CCP, and in the history of the PRC. In the last two decades, with the CCP's changed population and gender policies, women*'s struggles and various forms of (left-wing) feminism have begun to challenge the CCP's patriarchal regime and the development of capitalism in the PRC in a particular form. In this section, I look at the position of women* in society and their everyday resistance against the patriarchal order over past decades. In the next section, I discuss currents of feminism and recent feminist struggles.

After 1949, many women* supported the CCP and welcomed the establishment of socialism as early reforms brought them improvements. For instance, the Marriage Law gave them the right to make their own decisions on marriage and divorce, and in succeeding years up to 90 percent of women* were able to take on some form of wage labor. The latter was important for the regime. Its idea of women*'s liberation rested on Friedrich Engels's idea that this was accomplished through women*'s participation in wage labor (as that made women* part of the working class).[59]

Soon the liberating impetus was lost, though. The almost exclusively male CCP leadership made concessions to forces that defended the rural (and urban) patriarchal order under which women* were treated as second-class citizens and subject to sexist oppression and violence. Men* made use of patriarchal family rules and traditions to force women* into a subordinate position. Socialist managers often tied women* to low-skilled, auxiliary jobs and gave them fewer chances to get promoted. Women* had to deal with the double burden of wage labor and unwaged reproductive labor as most men* refused to share the latter. Few women* were able to reach higher levels in the CCP or state administration, which largely remained male* dominions.

For the CCP leaders, the prototype of a proletarian or peasant woman* was "the uncomplaining working mother, ready to retire or join the workforce as needed."[60] Women*'s liberation in the PRC was not only "unfinished," the CCP's gender policies also shaped the specific forms of a Maoist patriarchy.[61]

Social Feminism from Below

With the reforms in the late 1970s, the patriarchal order was reconfigured once again. On the one hand, the state increased its grip on society, for instance, by stepping up its control over women*'s bodies through the One-Child Policy.[62] The CCP leadership sought to limit population growth and the women*'s fertility rate as it saw that as a precondition for economic development. Especially in the 1980s and 1990s, the policy was often brutally implemented—

with high fines, forced abortions, and sterilizations. Meanwhile, the marketization of the economy brought with it the sexualization and commodification of the female* body, as well as an upsurge in concubinage and prostitution.[63] Traditional family roles were even strengthened, with further pressure on women* to submit to male relatives, to marry early, and to bear a son as that was seen as their duty in order to continue the family tradition. Meanwhile, unmarried ("left-over": *shengnü*) women*, divorced women* ("worn-out shoes": *po xie*), and single mothers faced discrimination from society or even the state.

On the other hand, the state retreated from parts of people's lives, for instance, in work units or communes. The market reforms opened spaces for (some) women*, who were able to migrate (leaving the patriarchal family behind) or engage in their own economic activities. However, most of them found themselves confronted with new forms of gendered division of labor, exploitation, and discrimination.[64] Many women* were pushed into low-skilled, dirty, dangerous, or boring factory or service work, with low wages and overtime, others into domestic care work where they were tightly controlled, faced violent attacks from the employers, and earned a low wage for never-ending workdays. They also suffered from the devaluation and discrimination of rural women* as "low" quality (*suzhi*).[65] When having a child or getting older, migrant women* were often faced with pressure from their families to go back to the countryside to bring up the child and take care of their or their husband's parents.

Those women* who remained in the countryside ("left-behind": *liushou funü*) had to take over farming work as many men* and youths migrated, leading to the "feminization" of agriculture. In addition, the migration of whole families or children was restricted and a large part of urban welfare was reserved for those with urban *hukou*. Reproductive labor, like taking care of migrants' children and the elderly, was done in the villages where the costs were lower and women* had to do the care work. Often older women* had to do this care work as their children had migrated.[66]

Urban women*, especially the older generation who had worked in the state sector, also faced new pressures. During the restructuring and partial privatization of state companies in the late 1990s and early 2000s, women* were the first to be sacked as they had done many of the low-skilled and auxiliary jobs. They were also the last to find new jobs in the private sector and either ended up unemployed, or entered the expanding informal sector of, for instance, street sellers, or became domestic care workers (*baomu*), a sector where they had to compete with rural migrant women*. In any case, it was very likely they ended up as part of the urban poor.[67] Overall, the "gender gap" widened in recent decades as women* earned less and less than men*,[68] were more likely to become landless, and found it harder to step up the career ladder in most sectors.

Ever since the founding of the PRC in 1949, women* have tried to gain more control over their lives through confronting the Maoist patriarchy. They continued to fight for more space and control in both the transitional period and the capitalist period. In their workplaces, women* resisted sexist managers and took part in labor struggles. Despite the One-Child Policy, some women* had more children than allowed. In their families, more women* refused to comply with traditions and did not give in to pressure to accept arranged marriages, to marry early, or to have a child soon after marriage. Women* also used migration to get away from such pressures and to find their own lives and loves. These often covert, sometimes open forms of resistance did not bring down the patriarchal order, but they prevented further deterioration of their life and work conditions in some cases, and in others slowly expanded the space of women* to decide their own fate.

Women*'s bargaining power improved as a result of the One-Child Policy, giving them more possibilities for personal life choices. Families with a daughter were forced to invest in her education and job training, which put more responsibility on her (for taking care of the parents when they retire) but also increased her leverage and possibilities. This raised bargaining power also played out on the marriage market, as the sexist preference of families for boys led to the abortion of female fetuses and a shortage of women*. And when women* migrated to urban areas and earned money, they improved their status in the family and generated resources they could use for their own education or the improvement of their lives.

Until the late 2000s and early 2010s, a substantial part of the younger generation of women* in the PRC had, indeed, changed their attitudes towards family, marriage, and children: many postponed marriage and bearing a child, and some even envisioned not marrying and not having children at all. As a result, the marriage rate fell, the fertility and the birth rate decreased, and the divorce rate increased.[69] Women* declared that they did not want to have (more) children because of the high costs of bringing up a child, the continuing discrimination of (would-be) mothers on the labor market, and the burden of reproductive labor. More and more women* also refused to take care of retired parents (theirs or their husband's).[70] What started slowly throughout the transitional years, the change of women*s attitudes and their pressure for more control, had, by the 2010s, become the obvious refusal to fulfill the family duties and perform reproductive labor as expected, in short: a kind of women*'s strike.[71]

New Attacks

The pressure had mixed effects. The CCP's developmental model is based on economic growth and expansion, which requires a steady supply of new labor power. Following industrialization, urbanization, and improvements in health care and education, most countries have seen lower fertility rates. In the PRC, the One-Child Policy accelerated this process and led to the rapid "overaging" of the population and the decrease of young people entering the labor market.

In the first half of the 2010s, the CCP regime realized that low fertility and birth rates could undermine the developmental model. In 2016, it introduced a Two-Child Policy and encouraged women* to have more than one child. However, the fertility rate fell further. In 2021, the regime even introduced a Three-Child Policy and it seems that the birth control measure will be abolished soon. It might be too late, though. All measures to encourage women* to have more children have failed so far and it is likely that the "overaging" of the population will continue and that the population will soon even begin to shrink.

In order to discipline women* and strengthen the family as the producer of necessary labor power, under Xi Jinping the CCP leadership has revived the image of a traditional family in which women* take responsibility for bringing up children. In recent years, women* were even asked to have children "for the nation," and in some regions local authorities have implemented natalist policies. The regime introduced monetary incentives for parents, promised to improve the protection of mothers at work, and introduced measures that make divorces more difficult. Whether any of these measures will work to increase the fertility rate and secure the supply of labor power for PRC capitalism in the future remains to be seen.

Increased Bargaining Power

In sum, during the socialist period, women* moved closer to legal equality. Their employment rate increased, but a high proportion were doing unskilled labor; they had to shoulder wage labor and reproductive labor; and they were largely excluded from higher ranks in management, the party, and state administration. They also kept their secondary status in the family and continued to suffer sexualized violence. Many of these problems persisted in the subsequent reform period and the capitalist period. In addition, birth control policies were implemented, women*'s bodies were sexualized and commodified, concubinage and prostitution saw an upsurge, and women* faced new forms of gendered divisions of labor.

Women* fought against new restrictions and for more control over their lives. The economic reforms opened up some spaces, and women* made use of opportunities given to them, for instance, trying to escape patriarchal control in the family through migration or setting up a business to gain economic independence. Women* with an urban status and middle-class background find it easier to gain control, as they have more legal and economic opportunities, while women* with a working-class, migrant, or rural background often lack resources to become more independent.

Overall, the women*'s struggle against discrimination and violence and for more space, opportunities, and happiness in family and society could not destroy patriarchal structures and practices.

It is often defensive in nature—holding a line against pressure from above. Still, women*'s bargaining power increased as an effect, for instance, of the One-Child Policy, and they could use that power and refuse to take on burdens like having more children. This refusal contributed to the demographic problems of low birth rates and an "overaging" population that the CCP regime is now facing. In the second half of the 2010s, it introduced natalist population policies, promoted traditional family values, and allowed a public sexist backlash against women*'s resistance—all means to discipline women* and to force them back into their role as producers of labor power.

The women*'s daily struggle was also accompanied by various currents of feminist or women*'s explicitly political struggle—as we shall see in the next section.

FEMINISTS (NOT) CHALLENGING THE PARTY-STATE

> Feminism has shown the potential to become a leading force in activist networking in China's fragmented world of social activism over the past decade. This has resulted in it being placed at the front line of suppression, accused of aiding foreign powers and of acting as a subversive force.[72]

In the course of the transition period, different currents of feminists tried to represent women*'s interests and struggles in the PRC, including the state feminists close to the CCP, new feminist NGOs that took up issues like domestic violence and sexual harassment, critical socialist feminists who tried to develop a left-wing approach on women*'s issues, and young feminists who used online campaigns and small-scale street actions to push for improvements for women*.

In China, feminist concepts and practices began to spread in the late nineteenth and early twentieth century, as in many other parts of the world. Mostly urban women*, some influenced by feminist and anarchist ideas, demanded an end to patriarchal Confucian practices and promoted education and self-empowerment of women*.[73] During the May 4 Movement in 1919, the promotion of women*'s rights was part of the demands for the modernization of the post-imperial Chinese state and society.[74]

In the 1920s, women* played an active role in labor struggles and in the CCP, and the liberation of women* became one of the projects and promises of the revolutionary movement. Inside the party, even the largely male* leadership accepted the necessity to liberate women* from patriarchal rule, but it saw feminist demands as secondary to class struggle and the fight against domestic reactionary enemies and colonial rule. CCP leaders tried to restrict women*'s demands and policies "that challenged patriarchal powerholders who were participating in their revolutionary coalition."[75] Nevertheless, many women* supported the CCP as they hoped to get rid of their chains through the revolutionary struggle.

After taking over power, the CCP regime facilitated the setting up of the All-China Women's Federation (ACWF). Formed in 1949 as a mass organization of the CCP, it represented a kind of state feminism for the promotion of women*'s interests inside party, state, and society.[76] The ACWF soon established organizational structures at every administrative level all over the country. Throughout the socialist period, it promoted women*'s rights and the participation of women in waged labor—often against the resistance of male CCP members or bureaucrats.

In the transitional period, the party-affiliated state feminists lost some of their influence due to the loosening of the party's grip on social spheres and people's personal lives. State feminists in and around the ACWF continued to be under the control of the CCP leadership and represented both women*'s and party interests.[77] The ACWF co-managed the adaptation of gender policies—including the (re-)feminization and sexualization of gender roles and the new gendered division of (waged and unwaged) labor.[78]

In the last few decades, the ACWF with its "women work" (*funü gongzuo*) activity continued to have a dual role: it is meant to "disseminate party policy to [...] the female population" as a government institution; and "it represents women in policy decisions and programs at all levels of administration" as a federation of women*'s organizations.[79] ACWF cadres confront discrimination and violence against women*, finding ways to push for women*'s interests within the authoritarian state institutions. But they have to tolerate or even justify conservative gender roles and support the (patriarchal) CCP order.[80] For instance, starting in the 1980s, the ACWF promoted the CCP's One-Child Policy while arguing against related coercive action against women*, and it also promoted the market reforms while "representing the interests of women workers who were the first to suffer the social and economic consequences of privatization and rationalization of enterprises."[81]

Feminist NGOs

Before the market reforms began, the ACWF was the only women*'s organization in the PRC. As it stayed closely connected to the party-state, starting in the 1980s, feminists (many of them professionals with an urban background) began looking for independent structures and spaces to organize women*. New forms of socialist and autonomous feminism developed, opening up more social opportunities and spaces for women*, opposing sexualized violence against women*, and undermining the (sexist) gender roles advocated by the CCP leadership. Around the time of the 1995 United Nations Fourth World Conference on Women in Beijing, many more women*'s groups or NGOs were set up which were independent of the ACWF and found other (often foreign) funding. Politically, they made use of the state feminist heritage and of newer (global) trends of feminist thought. Influenced by foreign debates on "gender," this cohort of feminists highlighted "difference," gender hierarchies, and the specific problems of discrimination and violence against women*.[82] Criticizing the limited perspective of the CCP (and ACWF feminists) who had seen the question of gender equality merely as one of equal rights and wage labor participation, it organized campaigns against sexual harassment, domestic violence, and related women*'s problems. It also provided, for instance, legal aid or medical assistance to women* in need, set up emergency hotlines for women*, or engaged in (academic) women*'s research.[83]

Many of the feminist projects involved collaboration at times with the ACWF and used its connections to organize feminist activities.[84] However, attempts by the ACWF itself "to establish partnerships" with new women's groups "have been met with suspicion and heavy critiques for their bureaucratic execution and hegemonic mentality."[85] So the relation between state feminists and the new generation of activists in feminist NGOs remained ambivalent.

The CCP regime set limitations to what feminist NGOs could do, and if these did not comply they came under pressure. Specific issues of sexualized violence and discrimination were tolerated, but drawing connections to "class" or "human rights" issues was too sensitive. Fearing more restrictions or repression, many feminists self-censored their discourses and did not address those issues.

Critical Socialist Feminists

In the late 2000s and early 2010s, a mainly academic current developed that has been called "critical socialist feminism."[86] Main protagonists include Song Shaogang and Dong Limin.[87] Although fairly small, I mention this current here as it fills a gap between state feminism and other oppositional feminist currents in the PRC in the past decades. Those connected to critical socialist feminism did not form a homogeneous group, but most of them criticized the strong influence of "Western" feminism and gender politics since the 1990s or the "aphasia" (*shiyu*) of Chinese feminism which took on many positions of "Western" feminism and gender politics.[88] Gender was seen as a middle-class concept that is individualist and culturalist, and largely ignores the accomplishments for women* in the socialist period. Proponents of this current spoke of "a threefold 'separation movement' (*fenli yundong*) executed in the post-1978 period, namely, the separation of women's theory from Marxist theory, the separation of the women's movement from the control of the state, and the separation of gender from class."[89]

But critical socialist feminists did not uncritically praise the socialist period under Mao Zedong. They argued *against* the complete rejection of the socialist past and *for* the recognition of the socialist experience and its heritage, which includes positive elements in their view. That sounds similar to positions from the New Left (see the section "Maoist Organizing and the New Left" in chapter 4). Yet, while there were some links between the two currents, the New Left continued to use class as the exclusive category, and most of its members remained "gender blind."[90]

Critical socialist feminists also clashed with the perspective of official state feminism which still promoted "equality between men and women" and, since the 2000s and Hu Jintao's Harmonious Society, also argued for a "harmonious development of the two sexes" (*liang xing hexie fazhan*) and paternalistic, traditional family concepts. Western left-wing feminist positions were rarely referred to in texts by critical socialist feminists, with the exception of Nancy Fraser and her argument for a reorientation of feminism towards "distributive justice" and less focus on "justice of recognition"—a critique of identity politics that neglects class issues.[91]

The critical socialist feminists' main focus was the socialist past, not the future, but they also analyzed the situation of women* after the start of the market reforms and the return to capitalism—the commercialization of women*'s bodies, the degrading and sacking of women* who worked in the (urban) state sector, and the discrimination against and exploitation of migrant women* working in the new factories or service jobs. In recent years, the protagonists have become more careful (and less outspoken or visible) as the CCP leadership attacks positions critical of its own vision of PRC and CCP history for alleged "historical nihilism" (*lishi xuwuzhuyi*) and increased the surveillance of and pressure on academics who are not strictly following the CCP line.

Activism by Young Feminists

Some of the women*'s NGOs set up since the 1990s were action-oriented and not formally registered (or they were registered as something other than what they actually did), and some groups had no consistent structure or stayed informal to avoid state control and repression.[92] These groups can be seen as the forerunners of groups and online projects of feminists set up since the late 2000s and 2010s.

The internet provided a new space for exchange and debate, and it was used to form "web-based organizations" in the late 2000s.[93] One of the first online magazines was Feminist Voices (*nüquan zhi sheng*), founded in 2009 by the feminist activist Lü

Pin and later turned into a Weibo microblog.[94] Influenced by the debates around Feminist Voices and similar publications, groups of young feminists began organizing small-scale street actions or performances and promoted them online since 2012. Many of the young feminists were students with an urban background, but "a substantial number" of them were "from rural and working-class backgrounds."[95] They attacked domestic violence and sexual harassment or demanded more public toilets for women*.[96] Their activities included the support of "people at the margins of society, including migrants, sex workers, domestic workers, and peasant women."[97]

After 2015, it became much harder for young feminists to act as groups or start campaigns due to repression (see the next subsection). However, many of them were involved in the support of women* who started a range of #Metoo (or *#mitu* in Chinese) campaigns against sexual harassment in the PRC beginning in 2018.[98] The #Metoo campaigns, launched by women* who accused teachers, managers, or state officials of sexual harassment or rape followed the example of similar campaigns elsewhere, but the protagonists in the PRC had to deal with the reactions of an authoritarian and repressive state machine.[99] As any organized protest provoked rapid retaliation from the state, they often applied "disguised collective actions," the online collaboration of women* who did not form organizational structures or did not even know each other personally, "to lower the cost of organizing contention."[100]

Regime Pressure

From the 1980s on, the feminist movement has been subject to state repression as the regime fears a destabilizing effect of uncontrolled women*'s struggles. Feminists from registered NGOs—or other official entities they chose as a legal structure (like companies) to campaign against domestic violence or sexual harassment—faced various forms of pressure. Those included bureaucratic procedures for the registration and recognition of social organizations on a local or regional level.[101] In the 2010s, the state introduced new regulations to put pressure on NGOs, like the Overseas NGO Law, the Charity Law, or the National Security Law that restricted (or even criminalized) forms of foreign funding or of collaboration with foreign individuals or entities. On a local level, feminist NGOs, like other NGOs, faced control and surveillance of local authorities as well as threats and orders to shut down and move.

The young feminists reacted to the pressure by avoiding setting up official organizations, engaging merely in small, flash-mob-like street actions, and moving campaigns online. That strategy was pretty successful until, in March 2015, five feminists were arrested for planning an anti-sexual harassment campaign on public transport.[102] This marked the moment when the central regime changed its policies towards grassroots protests and organizing. Subsequently, such protests were considered a politically sensitive issue, and those behind them were placed under surveillance (on- and offline), had to face police intervention, and were, in some cases, "disappeared" and imprisoned.

Subsequently, the pressure on feminist NGOs increased as well, and many closed down or moved their activities underground "as the leading feminists, persistently harassed by the police, found it too difficult and dangerous to continue with their activism."[103] The regime intensified the censorship and closed feminist blogs and websites, which some tried to prevent through self-censorship of their writings. The state, including state feminists from the ACWF, attacked feminists in the PRC for their alleged "Western feminism," which was linked to the often used category of "hostile foreign forces" (*jingwai didui shili*). Many feminists either left the PRC to continue their activity abroad, or they retreated from public campaigning and limited their support to individual cases or their feminist activities to forms accepted by the regime. Pressure on feminist activism, censorship, and attacks was accompanied by the state's tolerance (or support) of online sexist backlashes faced by feminist activists and women* criticizing sexist practices or supporting women* who raise their voice.

However, the pressure from below, from feminist NGOs as well as the young feminist groups and their actions, led to concessions to feminist demands—even though the CCP regime did not acknowledge that it had reacted to that pressure.[104] The most visible concessions were several laws that feminist organizations had long demanded and promoted and were finally implemented, including legal regulations against domestic violence and against sexual harassment in the PRC's Civil Code.[105]

Between Adaptation and Revolt

In sum, state feminists in the ACWF continued to closely collaborate with the CCP when trying to promote women*'s interests in the transitional and the capitalist periods. The UN Conference on Women opened a path for feminist activity in the form of NGOs and campaigns, but only as long as feminists restricted themselves to anti-violence or discrimination activities and did not link them to a more profound critique of patriarchal and capitalist structures under CCP rule. These NGOs organized concrete support of women* who had suffered discrimination or violence, and they campaigned for measures to contain sexual harassment and domestic violence against women* in the 1990s and 2000s.

In the late 2000s and early 2010s, a small group of critical socialist feminists developed a critique of "Western" feminism's influence on feminist debates and organizing in the PRC. They argued against the separation of women*'s theory and Marxist theory, criticized the commercialization of women*'s bodies as well as the degradation and exploitation of female* urban state workers and migrant workers, and asked for a new assessment of feminist activities during the socialist period.

A new generation of young activists organized feminist street actions and online campaigns in the early 2010s. Repression forced them to adapt and switch to the online support of women* behind #Metoo campaigns in a more decentralized or individualized form in the second half of the 2010s. Their activism mostly focused on discrimination and violence against women*, but locally some of them were also involved in other social protests, like labor struggles. For the regime, the activity of the young feminists was too much of a challenge as it expressed the profound dissatisfaction and "collective revenge" of many (young) women* in the PRC.

Overall, a (cooperative) part of feminism in the PRC learned to adapt to the authoritarian system by pushing for improvements for women* without directly confronting the CCP regime or questioning its rule. Another (confrontational) part was a "leading force in activist networking in China's fragmented world of social activism over the past decade."[106] The new feminist circles interacted with a wave of "social" feminism or women*'s resistance that has recently challenged the CCP's sexist gender and population policies. The rejection of marrying (early), having (more) children, and accepting the reactionary family ideology promoted by the CCP leadership might prove to be the biggest challenge for the CCP regime. As the party looks to overcome capitalist crises, environmental disasters, and social unrest (for instance, among migrant workers), the "birth strike" and the subsequent crisis of social reproduction of labor power threatens to exacerbate the shrinking of the labor force and undermine the further success of the party's China Model.

CONCLUSION: STRUGGLES FORCE THE REGIME TO ADAPT

In this chapter, I looked at two long-term social struggles that included left-wing demands and left-wing political initiatives or currents that addressed them. The rapid industrialization and urbanization of the PRC were carried out on the back of rural migrant labor. Migrant workers were only given a temporary status in the cities and suffered from low wages and bad living conditions. The number of migrant worker struggles increased substantially in the 2000s, and they remained widespread and frequent in the 2010s—with spatial, sectoral, and temporal variations and shifts. Despite the extra-legal nature of strikes and other forms of organized unrest, workers were able to organize protests and put pressure on capitalists and the state to improve conditions. The state set clear limits to what it would tolerate, though, as it tried to prevent the organization of cross-company or cross-regional protests. Protest leaders were usually sacked, activists who tried to set up unions arrested.

Left-wing labor activists formed NGOs in the 1990s and 2000s in order to support migrant worker struggles. A part of the (oppositional) left, consisting of left-wing Maoists and other currents' protagonists, was spurred on by the migrant social unrest and the possibility of a growing and powerful labor movement. Some even criticized the nationalist course of the CCP and its supporters, and placed the social struggles in the PRC in the global context of anti-capitalist and anti-patriarchal struggles. However, labor unrest seemed to lose energy and impact in the second half of the 2010s as a result of economic stagnation, factory closures and relocation, as well as regime measures like arbitration, repression, and censorship. While this disappointed left-wing activists, it was the harsh repression of labor NGOs starting in 2015, and of Maoist (student) activists and other left-wing initiatives in 2018, that led to a crisis of the oppositional left which has had to operate even more cautiously since.

Women*'s struggles continued after the founding of the PRC in 1949. While many women* had high hopes of the CCP when it took power in the late 1940s, expecting a substantial improvement of their conditions and an end to patriarchy, they were quickly disillusioned. Women* tried to improve their situation in a socialist system that combined Confucian discrimination and violence against women* with a kind of socialist (or Maoist) patriarchy that utilized female* labor for the socialist development model and still placed the burden of unwaged reproductive labor on women*'s backs. In the transitional and capitalist periods, women* faced new challenges like the state's attempt to control reproduction through the One-Child Policy, the sexualization of women*'s bodies, and a new sexist division of labor.

Women* resisted on all levels, struggling against birth control measures, against their renewed discrimination and sexualized violence, and against exploitation. It was the relaxation of the One-Child Policy after 2016 that revealed a decisive front line of the confrontation between the CCP and women* in the PRC. The virtual "birth strike" of the latter threatens the CCP's economic development model, as it undermines the steady supply of new labor power. The CCP leadership has begun to push traditional family roles and natalist policies to increase the number of births, but women* have resisted.

Political feminism reflected women*'s interests and struggles in various ways. State feminism and the CCP mass organization ACWF represented women*'s interests in the authoritarian state but without being able to change its patriarchal foundations and male* dominance. Feminist NGOs, inspired in part by Western debates on gender discrimination and sexualized violence, tried to push for women*'s interests independently of party and state. They were attacked by critical socialist feminists and others for largely ignoring the issue of class, and the legacy and accomplishments of feminism in the socialist period. Young feminists used the new possibilities of online activism for campaigns and organized street actions. Reacting to intensified repression from 2015 on, they supported #Metoo campaigns in a more decentralized and individualized way. The regime began to fight independent feminism, pushing it underground or abroad.

The CCP leadership reacted to migrant workers' struggles and women*'s struggles, as well as the political currents attached to them, not just with repression but also with concessions and cooptation. Besides criminalization and arrests, it conceded better material conditions as well as legal and institutional reforms without acknowledging them as reactions to the pressure from below. And it tried to coopt discourses around social issues, both on labor and women*'s issues. The regime revived its leftist rhetoric to strengthen its legitimacy. The first leader who did so in the city of Chongqing, Bo Xilai, was ousted and locked up as a competitor of Xi Jinping, who took over political leadership in 2012. But Xi Jinping had learned from Bo and coopted Maoist nostalgia, welfare concepts, and references to Marx and Marxism. The party's version of Marxism is domesticated, stripped of any subversive elements, and used to justify the authoritarian rule of the CCP and the capitalist exploitation of the workers. The regime also continued utilizing the state feminism of the ACWF as the official representation of women*'s interests and mixed it with nationalist discourses against foreign enemies and Western influences.

Neither migrant worker struggles and labor activism supporting them, nor women*'s struggles and feminist resistance have posed as much of a threat to the regime as, for instance, the workers' uprisings during the Cultural Revolution and the Tian'anmen Square Movement. However, the state still fears social instability and adopted repressive and responsive measures of counterinsurgency. These measures are only "fixes" and not sufficient to overcome the inherent contradictions of patriarchal capitalism and the social struggles it reproduces. They neither push the political system towards "democracy" (i.e. there is no transition to some kind of Western system) nor do they simply strengthen the authoritarian status quo. Rather there is some kind of "authoritarian evolution"—a dynamic transformation of the authoritarian regime pushed on by social pressures from below and political countermeasures from above.[107]

6

Conclusions: Social Discontent and Left Opposition in Socialism and Capitalism

In the previous four chapters, I looked at social discontent and unrest in the PRC in each decade since the 1950s that inspired left-wing debates or opposition. In these conclusions, I return to left-wing positions discussed in the introduction and the two parameters—exploitation and the distribution of wealth; repression and the distribution of power—that can be used to describe left-wing activities in the PRC during the socialist and the capitalist period.

In the *first* section, I review my findings on the social unrest and (oppositional) left in the past decades. In the *second* section, I discuss the dynamics of social unrest, left-wing organizing, and the regime's countermeasures. In the *third* section, I illustrate the results of this analysis in graphs of the left/right spectrum in the PRC in the socialist and in the capitalist period (see Figure 3 and Figure 4). In the *fourth* section, I put the results into the context of the ruptures and continuities in the history of the CCP itself; and in the *fifth* section, I sketch out in what way these results are relevant for the discussion on left-wing strategies and practices today—in the PRC and elsewhere.

HOW SOCIAL UNREST AND THE LEFT CHANGED SINCE 1949

Social movements from below and left-wing currents have changed with the transformation of class relations and the CCP regime itself. That becomes evident when we look at central features of each period of PRC history—economy and reforms, politics and the state, class relations and social actors, and leftist debate or critique in that period (see Table 2).

The socialist period from the mid-1950s to the mid-1970s (discussed in chapter 2) saw the implementation of the planned economy and the socialist industrialization project. The CCP established an authoritarian political regime under Mao Zedong as well as a new class hierarchy. This triggered new class struggles.

In both struggles discussed in chapter 2, workers, often with rather precarious status and conditions, fought against their discrimination and claimed unredeemed promises of improvements—during the strike wave 1956–57 and during the "economist" struggles of the Cultural Revolution (1966–1968). Oppositional left-wing activists formulated a political critique, in the mid-1950s asking the CCP regime to fulfill its promises of establishing equality and a society under the control of workers (and peasants). In the mid-1960s, radical rebel groups attacked the CCP regime for its hierarchical socialist class system and the formation of a "red bourgeoisie" of party and state cadres. It was this latest pressure from below, and especially the threat of mass mobilization, as well as radical movements and their (left-wing) attack on party rule that convinced a part of the CCP regime to initiate changes or what later would be called "reforms." These reforms, eventually started in the late 1970s, were meant to stabilize the socialist system and to keep the CCP in power, but they eventually led to the transition to capitalism.

In the first part of what turned out to be the transition period, that is, from the mid-1970s to the late-1980s (discussed in chapter 3), the CCP regime under Deng Xiaoping launched reforms that included the marketization of parts of the economy and the decentralization of economic decision making. Politically, the regime allowed a certain opening, but the CCP's authoritarian rule persisted and the socialist ruling class grabbed the new opportunities to accumulate power and wealth through appropriating public assets and through corruption.

The first two struggles discussed in chapter 3, the April 5 Movement in 1976 and the Democracy Wall Movement from 1978 to 1980, were made up of workers who were fed up with the record of the socialist project and particularly the arbitrary power

Table 2 Periodization of economy, politics, class relations, and leftist debates in the PRC since 1949

Period – chapter	*Economy*	*Politics*	*Class relations*	*Leftist debates*
Socialism (mid-1950s to mid-1970s) chapter 2	Socialist industrialization, planned economy	Development of the CCP's authoritarian rule	New class hierarchy and class struggle; workers against discrimination	Critique of new class hierarchy and "red bourgeoisie"
Transition (mid-1970s to late 1980s) chapter 3	Reform, marketization; decentralization	Certain political opening, continuity of CCP rule, corruption	Transformation of the socialist ruling class; workers against reform effects	Promotion of democratic socialism or alternative version of socialism
Transition/ Capitalism (early 1990s to early 2000s) chapter 4	Restructuring, privatization	Integration of reconfigured capitalist class, consolidation of CCP rule	Workers and peasants against effects of marketization and restructuring	Critique of (transition to) capitalism and neoliberalism; socialist nostalgia
Capitalism (since the mid-2000s) chapter 5	Rebalancing, upgrading; centralization, expansion	Harmonious Society; tightened repression, flexible authoritarianism	Welfare experiments; migrants and women* against capitalist and patriarchal conditions	Support of social struggles; moving underground to avoid harsh repression

of cadres and the poor working and living conditions. The workers involved in the third struggle discussed in chapter 3, the Tian'anmen Square Movement of 1989, were agitated about some of the reform effects, including inflation, job insecurity, and corruption. Among the participants were also many who had a permanent job and enjoyed welfare provisions. They feared (further) deterioration of their working and living conditions. All three movements included oppositional left-wing demands for political reforms towards more workers' rights and a more democratic form of socialism. The movement in 1989 and, especially, the workers with their demands for a different, more democratic socialism, posed such a serious threat to CCP rule that the regime began to consider even more radical reforms thereafter, reforms that included the attack on the core of the socialist economy and would take the country into capitalism.

From the late transition period in the early 1990s to the early capitalist period in the early 2000s (discussed in chapter 4), the CCP regime under Jiang Zemin restructured and privatized parts of the state sector while opening up the country to foreign investments. Politically, it consolidated its authoritarian rule to serve the reconfigured socialist (and now capitalist) ruling class.

The two social struggles discussed in chapter 4 were both directed against the effects of marketization and restructuring. The conditions of many peasants deteriorated substantially in the 1990s, especially through high taxation, cadre corruption, and land theft. Meanwhile, workers with permanent jobs and welfare provisions, who had been "inside the system" (*tizhinei*) of state employment, began to feel the effects of the restructuring in the late 1990s that brought them losses in status, welfare and wages, as well as unemployment and poverty. A nostalgia for Mao and Maoism spread among peasants and state workers, and showed not only their dissatisfaction with their current situation but also their longing for what they saw as a better, more just and egalitarian past. Different parts of the (oppositional) left were inspired by these struggles and the revival of Mao and Maoism. The New Left and grassroots Maoist groups formulated critiques of (the transition to) capitalism and neoliberalism, indulged in socialist nostalgia, and supported (in person or in writing) the wave of struggles of the state workers or old socialist working class in the late 1990s and early 2000s.

In the period since the mid-2000s (discussed in chapter 5), the CCP regime under Hu Jintao first initiated the rebalancing of the economy, with the aim of making it less export dependent and reducing regional differences by developing the hinterland. It also pushed for an industrial upgrading by investing in technological developments and sectors higher up the value chain. The CCP also changed its political rhetoric and introduced new limited welfare policies (under the banner "Harmonious Society") and new forms of conflict resolution. In the 2010s, when Xi Jinping came to power, state and private capital made increased efforts to expand globally, and the role of state and party in the economy was strengthened. The CCP tightened repression against oppositional groups, but it stayed on the course of a "flexible authoritarianism" it had developed in the previous decades, a course that included concessions when the regime considered them necessary to ensure social stability.

Both social struggles discussed in chapter 5—migrant workers' protests and women*'s everyday resistance—aimed at improving the conditions under capitalism. Migrant workers fought against exploitation and discrimination. Women* resisted the reconfigured patriarchal structures and sexist practices, tried to lessen the burden of reproductive labor, and fought for more control over their lives. Both social struggles challenged the CCP's capitalist and patriarchal model—though not to an extent that would make the model falter. Different parts of the oppositional left, including labor NGOs, Maoist grassroots groups, and left-wing feminists, supported the struggles of migrants or women*. Eventually, they suffered from state repression and had to move activities underground (or even abroad).

DYNAMICS OF STRUGGLES AND COUNTERMEASURES

Further analysis reveals the complex dynamics of struggles, movements, and countermeasures. The movements in the socialist and transition periods from the 1950s to the late 1980s were all triggered either by reforms carried out just before (nationalization, marketization) or by incisive events (e.g. death of a leader). These movements were quite short-term protests or upheavals—in the cases of the "economist" rebels and the Democracy Wall Movement lasting up to about two years. In most cases the state, the CCP leadership, or a particular party faction were the target of anger and critique while parts of the leadership initially showed some sympathy for the aims of the movements or offered concessions.

Oppositional and often left-wing circles or movements grew directly out of the social struggles. The shorter movements in 1957 or 1976 were not able to set up distinctive or even larger organizations, unlike during the Cultural Revolution from 1966 to 1968, the Democracy Wall Movement from 1978 to 1980, and, to a lesser extent, the Tian'anmen Square Movement 1989. In all cases, the CCP regime finally repressed the movements. The strong party and state influence on people's daily lives enabled the

CCP to regain control fairly quickly and punish dissidence. While the larger oppositional movements in the 1970s and 1980s discussed in this book came in shorter waves, workers' unrest seems to have occurred more frequently throughout this period—in the first half of the 1970s, the final years under Mao, in the early 1980s, just after the reforms had begun, and between 1985 and 1989 when the reforms showed negative effects on labor relations and conditions.[1]

The movements at the end of the transition period and during the capitalist period were triggered by effects of the reforms: restructuring and marketization in the cases of peasants and state workers who feared to lose the status they had enjoyed since the socialist period; harshness of living conditions, further undermining of working standards, and discrimination in the case of migrant workers; and reconfigured gender discrimination, sexualized violence, and the burden of reproductive labor in the case of women*. These movements were long-term ones, showing up in repeated single events (demonstrations), whole waves of events (strikes), or continuous practices (women*'s resistance to reproductive labor, a "birth strike") for at least several years.

Party and state control over many aspects of people's lives had loosened with the reforms, leaving more space for organizing and debate. Different compositions of (left-wing) activists supported the social protests. Their practices changed with the dynamics between struggles from below and countermeasures from above. The CCP regime still constituted the (eventual) addressee of most social protests and the actions of left-wing supporters, but the new capitalist relations produced more complex confrontations, and the immediate adversary could well be the local state or a private company. The regime used ever more sophisticated methods to weaken the protests or movements (concessions, cooptation) or to repress them.

Except for the peasant protests in the 1990s and 2000s, and the women*'s struggles in recent decades, most social movements discussed in this book were dominated by workers.[2] Disillusioned precarious workers were at the center of the protests in the mid-1950s and the mid-1960s, various groups of disappointed workers stood behind those in the mid- and late 1970s and the late 1980s.

Urban state workers still "inside the system" (*tizhinei*) and under attack led the protests in the late 1990s to early 2000s, and rural migrant workers "outside the system" (*tizhiwai*) have been the main force behind struggles since the mid-2000s.

In none of these events were workers led by any kind of "vanguard" of activists or intellectuals. Social unrest of workers and peasants or everyday struggles of women* inspired new compositions of left-wing activists, activists both from the ranks of the social protesters as well as from outside. Those would form informal groups, NGOs, networks, or online and offline media to support (and influence) the protagonists and their struggles—like in the case of labor NGOs and leftist groups supporting migrant workers and the feminist groups that took up the demands from women*'s struggles. In some events, worker activists with an oppositional left-wing background and experience in the Cultural Revolution rebel movement played a role in initiating or promoting unrest: this was the case in the Democracy Wall Movement of 1978–80 or in the urban state worker unrest in the late 1990s and early 2000s. And, in 1956–57, 1966–67 and 1989, movements of students or intellectuals overshadowed or preceded the workers' movements but were far from dominating workers' mobilization and involvement.[3]

The forms of social struggle included strikes, demonstrations, petitions, everyday (subversive) practices, and sometimes even uprisings and riots. The forms of left-wing debate and expression ranged from informal (sometimes underground) meetings and publications to semi-legal or registered organizations and media. In addition, in the past two decades, workers, labor activists, women*, and feminists alike have used online formats: chat-rooms, websites, blogs, discussion groups, and more. These formats enabled them to exchange information, coordinate protests, organize across long distances, include many more people in discussions and activities, and reach a bigger public. They also, however, made them vulnerable to new forms of censorship and to online abuse.

A changing combination of aims and motivations stood behind both the social discontent and struggles as well as the left-wing currents expressing them: first, the improvement of material conditions, second, the improvement of one's status or the fight against discrimination and repression, and, third, the general critique of the socialist or capitalist order and the struggle against the CCP ruling class. The latter was mostly promoted by oppositional left-wing groups that discussed or proposed continuous revolution (1966–68), alternative or democratic forms of socialism (late 1970s, 1989), or the return to a (mystified) version of socialism (late 1990s). More recently, oppositional left-wing groups seemed reluctant to present a general critique of the political order under the CCP, or to even discuss a revolutionary perspective, for fear of repression but also for lack of the power and influence that would make such a critique or perspective politically relevant.

The CCP regime developed a mix of tools used both by state institutions and party structures to diffuse social tensions as well as social or political protest. In many cases it made limited concessions (improvements of conditions or status) either during the protest or afterwards to prevent further tensions or escalations. For instance, in recent decades the protests of workers and of women* led to the implementation of new laws that improved their legal status. The cooptation of protesters or their demands was another tool the regime employed both to weaken the protest and to regain legitimacy. An example is the integration of the "ultra-left" into the CCP regime in the late 1960s, or the way the faction around Deng Xiaoping used the demands for reforms from below in the late 1970s to win the leadership struggle and implement market reforms.[4] Repression in various forms (police intervention, arrests, censorship, threats) was used in most cases, the extent depending on whether the regime felt that protests could spread and undermine its legitimacy. Participation in social protests like strikes or demonstrations was, at times, tolerated, but organizers or leaders faced serious punishments. In two cases, when the protests seriously challenged the CCP regime, it brought in the army to secure its rule (in 1967 and 1989).

Oppositional left-wing currents were not allowed or able to form (semi-)official organizations outside the CCP (except for a short time during the Cultural Revolution, and after the 1990s for small organizations like NGOs). Many informal left-wing groups and currents have faced repression or even elimination. Measures included censorship, threats and intimidation, reeducation in camps, prison sentences, rustication, and even killings. As a result, oppositional left-wing groups could often only persist informally or underground. In many cases they existed only for a relatively short period of time when, in reaction to social movements, they were able to temporarily use space for organizing and voicing dissent. However, some informal groups and networks survived over the life-span of a political generation, like the Cultural Revolution rebels who played a role in all the larger oppositional movements from the 1960s to the 2000s.[5]

Still, as oppositional left-wing groups with a certain political perspective could not establish lasting organizations, they were not able to form recognizable political currents as in countries with a wider space or repressive tolerance for such organizations like Germany, or countries with a history of decolonial struggle against a repressive regime like South Africa.[6] Ultimately, no social protest or political opposition brought about a regime change in the PRC. However, social movements, combined with left-wing currents, pressured the regime at various times so that it reacted with reforms. This dynamic of movements from below and countermeasures from above pushed the development of the PRC from socialism through a transition and finally to capitalism in the past seven decades.[7]

VISUALIZING THE PRC'S (OTHER) LEFT

One aim of this book is to provide an overview and categorization of social protests and oppositional left-wing currents they inspired. This can serve as a compass for those engaged in debates on the transition from socialism to capitalism, the role of the CCP, and the history of left-wing politics in the PRC. In this section, I discuss how left-wing groups and currents in the PRC fit into the two-dimensional left/right graph (see Figure 2) I introduced in chapter 1 to visualize the different political positions of participating actors. The groups and currents analyzed here represent different left-wing tendencies, ranging from a kind of moral economy and demands for equality in the socialist system to the fundamental critique of the CCP's "red bourgeoisie" and leftist or rather "loyalist" positions close to the CCP in the capitalist period.

Groups and currents often remained informal to avoid repression, they had blurred positions, changed their perspectives, or included wings with different opinions. All of this makes a categorization and clear visualization difficult.

In contrast to the example used in the introduction—post-World War II Germany—the PRC saw an incremental systemic transition in the past seventy years, from socialism to capitalism. While the CCP stayed in power, its composition as well as its political and economic strategies changed in the transitional period between the late 1970s and late 1990s. It was the central political organization in the socialist economy representing a socialist ruling class and became the central political organization in a capitalist economy representing a capitalist ruling class. In other words, as the product of left-wing movements and organizing in the first part of the twentieth century, it represented an authoritarian and exploitative socialist regime using left-wing rhetoric and strategies in the socialist period; and it represents a right-wing authoritarian and exploitative capitalist regime in the ongoing capitalist period similar to the regimes in other capitalist countries.

This transformation of the CCP regime, as well as the social struggles and left-wing currents before and after the transformation, cannot be expressed in one graph, so I suggest using two graphs (Figures 3 and 4). The first shows CCP forces as well as oppositional groups during the socialist period and the early transitional period (1950s–1980s; Figure 3). The two axes indicate diverging left-wing positions: left-collectivist vs. left-exploitative and egalitarian vs. authoritarian. Even though the mechanisms of exploitation are different in a socialist context than in a capitalist context, I still use the term exploitative for the socialist period and for the capitalist period. Collectivist, egalitarian, and authoritarian have similar meanings under socialism and capitalism.[8]

The positioning along the horizontal "wealth and exploitation" axis depends on the position of a group or current on social (in-)equality, relations of exploitation and appropriation, access to and supply of necessary goods, and the availability of support and welfare according to people's needs. The positioning along the vertical "power and repression" axis depends on a group's or current's critique or support of structures of power and repression, of (un)equal liberties, rights, and opportunities for all, and authoritarian or collective decision making and exercise of power.[9]

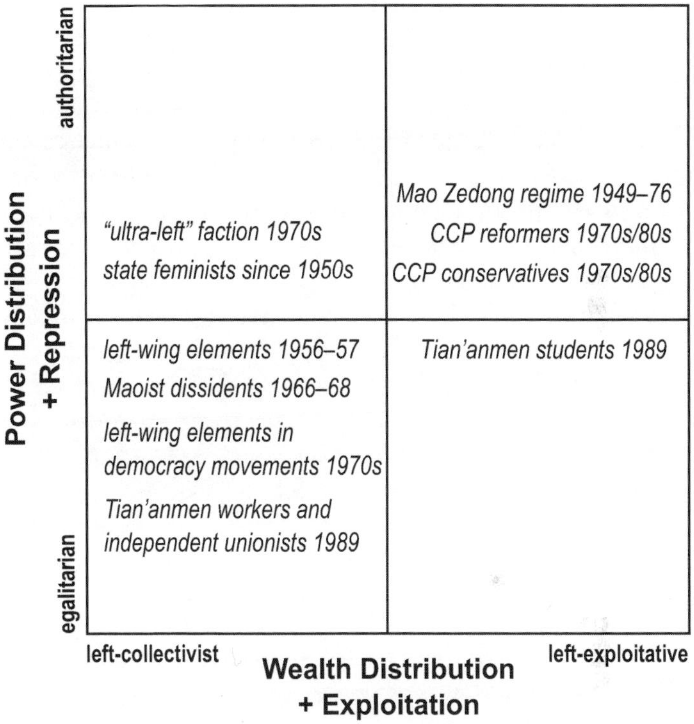

Figure 3 Left-wing groups and other political forces in the PRC during the socialist period and the early transitional period (1950s–1980s)

Most of the left-wing groups and currents chosen for analysis in this book stood in opposition to the CCP or, at least, implied or formulated a left-wing critique of the regime at the time regarding its authoritarian nature and its role within the exploitative socialist order. Therefore, they are placed in the bottom left square (*left-collectivist/egalitarian*): left-wing elements in the strike wave 1956–57, Maoist dissidents during the Cultural Revolution 1966–68, leftist worker activists in the democracy movements 1976 and 1978–80, and workers and independent unionists in the movement 1989.

Some leftist currents and groups discussed in this book supported the authoritarian rule of the CCP, even though they might have had political critiques regarding certain regime policies or were even competing for the domination of the party. They are placed in the top left square (*left-collectivist/authoritarian*): the "ultra-left" faction in the 1970s, and the state feminists in the ACWF since the 1950s.

The CCP regime under Mao Zedong, in power from 1949 until 1976, is placed in the top right square (*left-exploitative/authoritarian*), so are the main competing factions within the CCP, the "reformers" and the "conservatives" of the 1970s and 1980s who promoted authoritarian governance and different economic models—both of which were exploitative, however.[10] The sole entry in the bottom right square (*left-exploitative/egalitarian*) is those student leaders of the Tian'anmen Square Movement in 1989 that promoted some kind of political reforms and "democracy" but not the egalitarian version of socialism workers envisioned.[11]

The second graph shows CCP forces as well as oppositional groups during the late transitional period and the capitalist period (since the 1990s; Figure 4). Each of the two axes indicates the difference between left-wing and right-wing positions: left-collectivist vs. right-exploitative and egalitarian vs. authoritarian. The positioning along the horizontal "wealth and exploitation" axis and along the vertical "power and repression" axis is analogous to that in Figure 3.

Most of the left-wing groups and currents discussed in this book also formulated a left-wing critique of the regime regarding its authoritarian nature and its role within the exploitative (now) capitalist order. They are placed in the bottom left square (*left-collectivist/egalitarian*): Maoist grassroots groups supporting state workers in the 1990s, labor NGOs supporting migrant workers since the 1990s, Maoist and other leftist groups (including social democrats and Trotskyists) in the 2010s, NGOs promoting feminist issues since the 1990s, critical socialist feminists in the 2000s and 2010s, and young feminist activists in the 2010s.

Some leftist currents and groups supported the authoritarian rule of the CCP, even though they criticized the regime's turn towards capitalism. They are placed in the top left square (*left-*

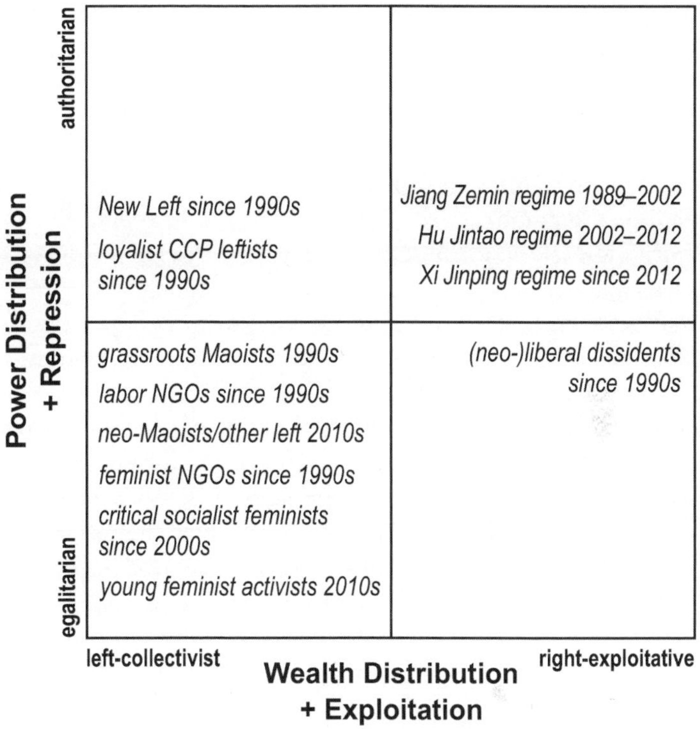

Figure 4 Left-wing groups and other political forces in the PRC during the late transitional period and the capitalist period (since the 1990s)

collectivist/authoritarian): the New Left intellectuals since the 1990s, and the various loyalist groupings in and around the CCP since the 1990s (who have supported, for instance, CCP leaders Bo Xilai or Xi Jinping).

The CCP regimes under Jiang Zemin (1989–2002), Hu Jintao (2002–12), and Xi Jinping (since 2012) are placed in the top right square (*right-exploitative/authoritarian*). The sole entry in the bottom right square (*right-exploitative/egalitarian*) are (neo-) liberal dissident groups or intellectuals that have appeared since the 1990s and have promoted some kind of "democracy" but, at the same time, a reformed capitalist system.[12]

In sum, the graphs visualize the distinction between different left-wing (and right-wing) groups in the PRC in the socialist period and their changed composition in the capitalist period. The categorization remains rough, based on two political features (wealth distribution and power distribution) with two attributes each (egalitarian vs. authoritarian and collectivist vs. exploitative). A more complex differentiation would increase the use-value but demand more features and attributes.

As it is, the graphs reflect a clear separation of egalitarian and authoritarian left-collectivist positions in the PRC in the socialist and the capitalist period. In my view, this distinction is as important as that between a Marxist-Leninist ("revolutionary") and a social democratic (reformist) left-wing strategy.[13] The sober analysis of the failure of authoritarian socialism, the acknowledgement of the capitalist nature of the current CCP regime, and the recognition of oppositional left-wing groups and currents throughout PRC history are necessary parts of a global left-wing debate. They not only enable us to learn from past mistakes when engaging in our own attempts to overcome exploitation and repression, they also help us to organize solidarity and support for the oppositional left in the PRC. That oppositional left has been suffering from CCP attacks for a long time, as we shall see in the next section.

THE CCP'S ANTI-LEFTIST RECORD

This book's focus lies on oppositional left-wing tendencies, social movements from below with left-wing demands, practices, and perspectives, or political groups or currents with left-wing agendas. The positions of the CCP, its leaderships, and its changing frictions and factions appear here and there in the narrative but deserve more attention than could be given in this book. In this section, I confine myself to addressing one characteristic of CCP policies in the past decades: the attitude of the party leaderships towards left-wing opposition.

The CCP changed from a leftist force during the socialist period and the early transitional period to a rightist force during the late transitional and the capitalist period. Still, several elements defined the party's rule over all the past decades and have survived historical shifts and changes: first, the aim of economic development and expansion through industrialization and infrastructure construction (development, productivism); second, the promotion of the interests of the country in the world-system (nationalism); third, one-party rule as the condition for accomplishing development goals (authoritarianism); fourth, the strategy to weaken, repress, or coopt powerful (left-wing) opposition from below (anti-leftism).

I will focus on the last point here. In the socialist period, the CCP used Maoism, an adapted form of Marxism-Leninism, to explain and justify its economic, political, and social course. This included rhetoric of class struggle and revolution. The CCP leadership defined the political line all other parts of society were supposed to follow—and it defined what it saw as deviation(s). Mao Zedong himself used the left/right spectrum in this respect in a 1955 speech before the Central Committee: "When the right time comes for something to be done, it has to be done. If you don't allow it, that is a Right deviation. If the right time has not come for something and yet you try to force it through, that is a 'left' deviation."[14]

It seems obvious that the CCP regime, with its revolutionary roots and socialist rhetoric, tried to deal with right deviation (of monarchists, KMT, or capitalist forces) during the socialist and the transitional period. Immediately after 1949, some of these forces were still quite strong, but after several anti-rightist purges in the early 1950s, and especially after the Anti-Rightist Campaign in 1957, most of them were severely weakened or exterminated.

Leftist forces inspired by social discontent or upheavals, however, persisted, as shown in this book. The CCP leaderships reacted with repeated anti-leftist campaigns and purges as left-wing critique and opposition are seen by the CCP leaders as undermining the party's legitimacy and rule (more than any re-emerging right-wing opposition). This began with conflicts on the party line and anti-leftist party cleansing purges in the 1940s and continued with crackdowns on strike waves and leftist critique around the Hundred Flowers Movement in the mid-1950s, attacks on the "economist wind" and left-wing rebels or Maoist dissidents during the Cultural Revolution in the second half of the 1960s, repression of movements for a democratic socialism in the mid- and late 1970s, the anti-leftist campaign in the second half of the 1970s formally against the Gang of Four, the crackdown against the workers' protests during the Tian'anmen Square Movement in 1989, the repression of various generations of Maoist grassroots activism, and attacks on left-wing grassroots labor activists and feminist activists in every decade since the 1990s.

The CCP leadership also changed its self-presentation and legitimizing strategy. During the socialist period, it merged two lines or political positions that were both necessary parts of the CCP's socialist project and its Marxist-Leninist-Maoist agenda: a developmental line focusing on socialist modernization and a mobilizational line focusing on social engineering and ideological guidance. At times, those who represented these lines harmonized in the attempt to build up socialism, at other times they merely coexisted to avoid conflict, and sometimes they openly competed, as after the GLF or during and after the Cultural Revolution. From the 1960s on, the CCP used the description of left and right (or variations of it) when referring to this antagonism or dialectic between the "right-wing" developmental line, for instance of the "capitalist roaders" Liu Shaoqi and Deng Xiaoping and the "left-wing" mobilizational line of Mao Zedong or the "ultra-left" faction and Gang of Four.

In the 1980s, that is, after the socialist period, the CCP leadership gave up using revolutionary or class struggle rhetoric. Economic development without social liberation or revolution became the main goal. In the 1990s, the CCP finally dismantled the socialist planned economy, and in the early 2000s, under party leader Jiang Zemin, it formally allowed capitalists to join its ranks. Socialism in the PRC form, which had already failed to accomplish revolution in the first place, was thereby further de-revolutionized. For many observers, "left" now stood for the "conservative" part of the leadership, that is, cadres who hung on to the socialist model and were reluctant to support the market reforms.

However, the CCP has still been promoting its own version of (what it calls) socialism. On the one hand, it wants to claim the historical "success" of "national liberation," utilize the symbolic value of party founder, leader, and icon Mao Zedong, and justify its description as a "communist party." On the other hand, the party's legitimacy is built upon socialist narratives of "serving the people" or "welfare for all"—or, at least, the myth that everyone will eventually benefit from the economic rise of the country. This is what makes left deviation or left-wing oppositional critique potentially explosive. Social or political issues raised by workers, peasants, women*, or leftist activists threaten the plausibility of the CCP's definition of socialism.

> [A]s long as "socialism" remains symbolically important for the party's political legitimacy, the CCP has to bear the burden of justifying its current practices in socialist terms, which will therefore involve a protracted ideological battle with the leftists over what is authentic socialism and who represents it.[15]

That ideological battle is fought on several fronts. First, since the 1990s, scholars at party schools and universities discuss and develop an adapted form of Marxism that is stripped of its subversive elements and presented as a science of how to run a ("market socialist") economy. In practice, what the CCP promotes is the control of capitalist forces by the state and a quasi-Keynesian version of welfare policies (anti-poverty, "common prosperity") that pretends to aim at wealth distribution but, in reality, does not touch the structural conditions for exploitation and social inequality.[16]

Second, in the past two decades, the socialist narratives of welfare and development have been maintained but also complemented, for instance by Confucian concepts and references to China's imperial history and legacy. The CCP adds to all its political and ideological terms, including its domesticated Marxism, the notorious "with Chinese characteristics" (*zhongguo tese*). Its references to Confucianism and imperial tradition enabled it to create a "Western" (hostile, dangerous) "other" versus the (good, benevolent) "Chinese." It makes use of Confucianism and (alleged) imperial tradition to stress the central role of the state or obedience to the rulers, and CCP policies even imply the superiority of the Han (the dominant ethnic group) vs "minorities" as the Uyghurs and other Muslim groups in Xinjiang.[17]

Third, since the 2000s, the party has re-emphasized its adapted (and depoliticized) Marxism. Local CCP leader Bo Xilai used

Maoist folklore, anti-corruption rhetoric, and limited welfare measures for the so-called Chongqing Model in the late 2000s, winning support from leftists loyal to the CCP. As mentioned in the previous chapter, Bo was seen as competition for the then would-be party leader Xi Jinping and was eventually disempowered and arrested for corruption in 2012. However, the new party leadership under Xi Jinping learned from his methods and also began referencing Marxism and Maoist symbolism more. The CCP still invests energy and resources in Marxist scholarship and ideology to legitimize its rule. That earns it the support of certain loyalist leftists, for instance, from the New Left, or other actors who sympathize with certain egalitarian leftist ideas while defending authoritarian party rule.[18] In some cases, this includes pressuring, attacking, censoring, and silencing people who oppose or simply do not follow the official party line.[19]

LESSONS FOR LEFT-WING STRATEGIES

The CCP was part of the left-wing (revolutionary) movement in China in the 1920s, and today's left (in the PRC and elsewhere) has to deal with the CCP's leftist legacy, as well as that of other political forces that came out of left-wing revolutionary movements before establishing different versions of actually existing socialism. However, these Communist Party regimes should be measured according to their political record (and not their pseudo-radical or pseudo-Marxist rhetoric, for instance).

For decades, the CCP has been an anti-leftist force or, more precisely, a force against left-collective and left-egalitarian ideas and practices. It has undermined and repressed social struggles and oppositional left-wing movements in the socialist period and ever since, as we have seen in the chapters of this book. Social conflicts and struggles in the PRC continue. While the country has intensified its economic and political engagement around the world, leftists should make up their mind and take a stand. Today's CCP is no ally in the struggle against capitalist exploitation, racism, gender discrimination, nationalism, imperialism, and environmental destruction.

The left in the PRC and elsewhere needs to find an answer to the global confrontation between what is presented as China vs U.S., Chinese socialism vs universalist Western capitalism, or authoritarianism vs liberal democracy. This presumed dichotomy serves both Western governments and the CCP regime. In reality, we see interconnected powers of capitalist exploitation with a more or less authoritarian governmental structure. Despite many differences, the political forces in power in the U.S., in European Union states, in the PRC, and in other countries all oppose left-wing movements demanding an end to capitalism, patriarchy, nationalism, imperialism, and more.

Realizing the egalitarian redistribution of wealth and power globally can hardly be accomplished without a revolution in the PRC and in the rest of the world. Currently, we are not seeing a revolutionary moment in the PRC, a moment in which such an egalitarian redistribution could be won. When such a moment emerges again, the revolution needs to be orchestrated by social actors from below. The experience of the CCP (and similar parties behind actually existing socialisms) teaches us that the revolutionary transformation of a society by a privileged class and its party in power is not just "a contradiction in terms" but simply no viable way to overcome exploitation, patriarchy, and authoritarian rule.[20]

What role can today's left in the PRC play? The loyalist leftists (or Maoist Right) in or close to the CCP will not get involved in social unrest or organizing that is openly oppositional. The New Left intellectuals will not "leave the ivory tower and appeal to the masses directly."[21] Many of them have supported PRC nationalism or even the regime under Xi Jinping after 2012.[22] That leaves the oppositional left, and mainly left-wing feminists and various currents of the Maoist Left. We will have to see whether feminists will attack both the structural gender discrimination and violence against women* and the capitalist structures and practices that define the CCP regime. Maoists have persistently invoked Cultural Revolution rhetoric, engaged in more confrontational debates and criticisms of the market reforms, and some of them were involved in the actual struggles of state workers (and later migrant workers). However, some of them are nationalist and statist, and most of them still believe in the Marxist-Leninist narrative and that a vanguard party, democratic centralism, and the dictatorship of the proletariat are necessary to carry out a revolution—the recipe that has failed. Meanwhile, most other left-wing currents are too small to exert any substantial influence.

In addition, the CCP regime and its repressive forces are currently too strong, and the oppositional left is too weak for it to play a bigger role in PRC politics. Even the question of whether there is a left-wing alternative is not discussed much with regard to the PRC, not only because the CCP holds on to its self-description as socialist, but also because the party has successfully prevented any leftist structure or group from developing enough strength even to be considered an alternative. The oppositional left in the PRC seems to face a difficult time when we look at the intensified repression and the arsenal of tools the CCP regime uses to counter discontent and protest. Most of the Maoist Left activists are keeping a low profile and avoid publicly appearing in the support of social struggles or in political debates on online platforms controlled by the state.

However, if there is any hope for fundamental change in the PRC for the better, the overcoming of capitalist exploitation, patriarchy, and social discrimination, it has to come through struggles of workers, peasants, migrants, and women*. The left could use such struggles to recompose and reinvent itself, overcome the socialist (or Cultural Revolution) nostalgia, and formulate a new left-wing strategy that goes beyond nationalism or national liberation and socialism.[23]

The chances for larger and more powerful social protests are not that small. The regime's situation is not as stable as it might appear (especially in fashionable leftist accounts of the CCP's almightiness, its technological potency, and its allegedly crisis-proof economic strategy): the economy is crisis-prone, the state's surveillance is less potent than described, the central state has difficulties controlling lower state levels, and environmental crises loom.[24] Social discontent continues, labor shortages could further increase workers' bargaining power, women*'s struggles could lead to more empowerment, and the harsh repression of protests in the past few years indicates that the regime might lose its capability of responding flexibly to social discontent.

Throughout PRC history, social movements from below have proven that, in certain moments, they are capable of collective action and cross-regional coordination, even without any complex organizational nexus. As the CCP leadership and the state combine economic and political power, they take on the responsibility for anything that goes wrong, and every protest potentially becomes a protest "against the government."[25] If the regime's tools to defuse or repress such movements do not work, then these movements could, indeed, change history.

What does that mean for the left outside of the PRC? Similarly to Maoists in the PRC, Maoists outside the PRC need to overcome their Cultural Revolution nostalgia and find a new leftist strategy beyond national liberation and authoritarian socialism. Regarding the current CCP regime, they and other leftists need to get a clear view of what is going on and then decide on which side of the barricade they want to be. In effect, the CCP uses a socialist or leftist costume to cover up capitalist, nationalist, racist, and patriarchal policies that characterize any rightist regime. Some leftists understand and still endorse the CCP's rightist policies and should be called out for that. Other leftists still fall for the costuming, or simply do not know enough about the PRC's past and present and the transformations of the CCP. This book is meant to provide the necessary information and analysis for them to make up their mind.

Ultimately, the question is whether the global left wants to hang on to authoritarian leftist strategies and support the exploitative CCP regime in its attempt to expand its global influence. If, by contrast, the plan is still to overcome capitalism and patriarchy globally, then the tasks are clear: follow and support the social struggles of workers, peasants, migrants, and women* in the PRC, connect to the oppositional left there and defend them against the attacks of the rightist regime.

Epilogue

In 2019, the year before the Covid-19 pandemic started, a wave of popular protests rolled over different parts of the world, from Chile to Hong Kong, challenging regimes and demanding social improvements and political freedoms.[1] In the following years, the Covid-19 pandemic restricted social and left-wing mobilizations in their attempts to gather or protest, and governments have used anti-pandemic measures to exert additional pressure. All the more astonishing, then, that protests continued, for instance, with the Black Lives Matter movement in the U.S. in 2020.

Now, in the second half of 2022, the global economic effects of the Covid-19 pandemic, of the countermeasures, for instance, in the PRC, of the war in Ukraine, and of the consequent sanctions against Russia are being felt and include rising inflation and debt crises. Rising energy and food prices threaten the livelihood especially of populations with tight budgets and limited access to resources. Countries spanning from Chile to Sri Lanka have seen a new upsurge of social protests in the recent months.[2] It remains to be seen whether these protests will spread further and culminate in a global wave of social conflicts and uprisings similar to the last big cycle of crisis and revolt between 2008 and 2012.

The left could facilitate the spread of these struggles against different faces of capitalism around the world, and help with the empowerment of their protagonists, but it must avoid mistakes of the past. Yet, just when the pandemic seems to slowly be fading out, giving more room again for protests and activism, the war in Ukraine has, once more, shed light on a weak spot of many left-wing groups: their support of or unclear position towards the post-socialist authoritarian regimes such as that of Vladimir Putin in Russia, which started the military attack on Ukraine, and that of Xi Jinping in the PRC, which confirmed its partnership with the Russian government.

Leftist support of contemporary authoritarian capitalist regimes as anti-imperialist or even socialist is one part of the problem.

Another part is the leftist mystification of the socialist past of these regimes, and leftist ignorance regarding deviant social struggles and oppositional left-wing currents during that socialist past. Only if the left in different parts of the world faces and criticizes the legacies of socialist regimes like those in the former Soviet Union or Russia, and in the PRC, will it be able to develop a credible alternative left-wing agenda that offers a perspective of global solidarity and change.

This demands an open debate among the left, and left-wing groups and currents in and from the PRC need to have a voice and position in the process. Yet, currently, they are at a weak point, and it is difficult for them to organize openly and get involved due to the harsh censorship and repression by the CCP—unless they defy regime pressure or leave the country.

This book attempts to shed light on the history of social struggles and left-wing movements in the PRC but is not meant to speak for or instead of left-wing activists from the PRC. It is meant to provide references and analysis for left-wing movements elsewhere that not only want to develop a critique of the CCP regime but also forms of solidarity and support for social struggles and oppositional left-wing currents in the PRC.

I wrote this from a particular political angle that puts the experiences of social struggles in the center of the analysis and tries to understand how left-wing currents developed out of these struggles and/or tried to intervene in them. I hope this book will provoke critical debate and more research that can fill the gaps left by my inquiry.

The revolutionary attempt once carried out prominently by the CCP led to the foundation of the PRC as a socialist state and the establishment of a new, socialist class society. That society later drifted into capitalism under the leadership of the CCP. This is an important part of the failure of the global left in the twentieth century—especially the failure of the revolutionary part of the left. Why and how the revolution in the PRC failed is closely linked to the class struggles and left-wing oppositional movements in the PRC. Therefore, these struggles and movements need to be studied and analyzed in order to learn from them—for future revolutionary attempts.

Chinese Terms and Characters

an chou fu lao 按酬付劳 work according to the wage
bagong 罢工 strike
baihua qifang 百花齐放 Hundred Flowers Movement
baomu 保姆 domestic care worker
baoshoupai 保守派 conservative group or faction
baowei ganbu 包围干部 forcible surrounding of cadres
beidouxing xueshe 北斗星学社 Big Dipper Society
Beijing zhi chun 北京之春 *Beijing Spring* (journal)
changzhang fuze zhi 厂长负责制 Factory Director Responsibility System
da bianlun 大辩论 holding big debates
da chuanlian 大串联 big linking up
da yue jin 大跃进 Great Leap Forward
dagongmei/dagongzai 打工妹/打工仔 working girl/working boy
daigong 怠工 slowdown
dalianhe 大联合 big alliance
daming dafang 大鸣大放 big speaking out, big opening up
danwei 单位 work unit
dazibao 大字报 big-character poster
dixia kanwu 地下刊物 underground journals
duoquan 夺权 power seizures
dusheng zinü zhengce 独生子女政策 One-Child Policy
ernai 二奶 mistress (literally: second wife)
fan fubi xuehui 反复辟学会 Anti-Restoration Society
fan zuo 反坐 anti-leftism
fang zuo 防左 preventing leftism
fanyoupai yundong 反右派运动 Anti-Rightist Campaign
feixinwen 非新闻 Wickedonna blog (literally: no news)
fenli yundong 分离运动 separation movement
funü gongzuo 妇女工作 women work
geming weiyuanhui 革命委员会 Revolutionary Committee
gongren 工人 worker
gongren zongbu 工人总部 Workers' General Headquarters
gongsi heying qiye 公司合营企业 joint-ownership enterprises
gongtong fuyu 共同富裕 common prosperity
gongzilian 工自联 short for 北京工人自治联合会 Beijing Workers' Autonomous Federation
guanliaozhuyi 官僚主义 bureaucratism
guomindang 国民党 Kuomintang, Nationalist Party

hefa quanyi 合法权益 lawful rights and interests
hexie shehui 和谐社会 Harmonious Society
hongse kongbu 红色恐怖 Red Terror
hongse zhongguo 红色中国 Red China (website)
hongweibing 红卫兵 Red Guards
hukou 户口 household registration (system)
hunan sheng wuchan jieji gemingpai da lianhe weiyuanhui 湖南无产阶级革命派大联合委员会, see *shengwulian*
jiage shuangguizhi 价格双轨制 dual-track pricing system
jianjiao buluo 尖椒部落 Pepper Tribe
jianshe shehuizhuyi xin nongcun 建设社会主义新农村 Building the New Socialist Countryside
jiating lianchan chengbao zeren zhi 家庭联产承包责任制 Household Contract Responsibility System
jieceng 阶层 social strata
jieji 阶级 class
jieji douzheng 阶级斗争 class struggle
jin chang 进厂 enter the factory
jingjizhuyi 经济主义 economism
jingwai didui shili 境外敌对势力 hostile foreign forces
jintian 今天 *Today* (journal)
jiti qingyuan 集体请愿 collective petition (for action to be taken)
jiti shangfang 集体上访 collective petition (to present grievances)
jizuo 极左 ultra-left
ku'er gongyou 酷兒工友 Queer Workers
kuomintang, see *guomindang*
liang xing hexie fazhan 两性和谐发展 harmonious development of the two sexes
lishi xuwuzhuyi 历史虚无主义 historical nihilism
liushou funü 留守妇女 left-behind women*
makesi zhuyi lilun yanjiu he jianshe gongcheng 马克思主义理论研究和建设工程 Marxist Theoretical Research and Development Project
maoyan 冒烟 giving off smoke
maoyou 毛右 Maoist Right
maozedong qizhi wang 毛泽东旗帜网 Maoflag (website)
maozuo 毛左 Maoist Left
minglingzhuyi 命令主义 commandism
minkan 民刊 people's literature
minzhu gaige yundong 民主改革运动 Democratic Reform Movement
minzhu qiang yundong 民主墙运动 Democracy Wall Movement
#mitu 米兔 #MeToo (in the PRC)
naoshi 闹事 cause disturbances (or trouble)
nongmingong 农民工 peasant worker
nüquan zhi sheng 女权之声 Feminist Voices

pi lin pi kong yundong 批林批孔运动 Campaign to Criticize Lin Biao and Confucius
pingnan hui 平难会 redress grievances societies, autonomous unions
po xie 破鞋 worn-out shoes
qimengshe 启蒙社 Enlightenment Society
qingli jieji duiwu 清理阶级队伍 Cleansing the Class Ranks campaign
qunzhong cankao xiaoxi 群众参考消息 Masses' Reference News
ronggong 融工 mix with workers
san bu gan 三不干 dirty work, hard work, night shifts
san fan 三反 Three Antis Campaign
san gao yi di 三高一低 three highs and one low
sanxian jianshe 三线建设 Third Front Construction
shandong bohai zhantuan 山东渤海战团 Shandong Bohai Battle Regiment
shangfang 上访 petitioning
Shanghai renmin gongshe 上海人民公社 Shanghai People's Commune
shaoshu minzu 少数民族 ethnic minorities
shehuizhuyi jiaoyu yundong 社会主义教育运动 or *she jiao* 社教 Socialist Education Movement
shengnü 剩女 "left-over" women*
shengwulian 省无联 Provincial Proletarian Alliance, short for *hunan sheng wuchan jieji gemingpai da lianhe weiyuanhui* 湖南无产阶级革命派大联合委员会 Hunan Provincial Proletarian Revolutionary Big Alliance Committee
shiyu 失语 aphasia
shiyue geming xiaozu 十月革命小组 October Revolution Group
shourong qiansong zhidu 收容遣送制度 Custody and Repatriation system (C&R)
si da ziyou 四大自由 four big freedoms
sige xiandaihua 四个现代化 or *sihua* 四化 Four Modernizations
siqing yundong 四清运动 Four Cleanups Movement
sirenbang 四人帮 Gang of Four
sisan pai 四三派 April 3 Faction
siwu luntan 四五论坛 April 5 Forum
siwu yundong 四五运动 April 5 Movement
suzhi 素质 quality
tansuo 探索 *Exploration* (journal)
tian'anmen guangchang yundong 天安门广场运动 Tian'anmen Square Movement
tie fanwan 铁饭碗 iron rice-bowl
tizhinei 体制内 inside the system
tizhiwai 体制外 outside the system
tonggou tongxiao 统购统销 unified purchasing and marketing
tongmenghui 同盟会 Revolutionary Alliance
tongzhi 同志 comrade, also used for/by gays, lesbians, and queers
wanyanshu 万言书 10,000-word articles

weiquan 维权 rights defense
wenhua dageming 文化大革命 or *wenge* 文革 Cultural Revolution
wu fan 五反 Five Antis Campaign
wumao dang 五毛党 50 Cent Army
wusi yundong 五四运动 May 4 movement
wu you zhi xiang 乌有之乡 Utopia (website)
xiagang 下岗 laid-off urban state worker
xiaofenhong 小粉红 Little Pink
xiaozhengfu, dashehui 小政府大社会 small government, big society
xin gongren wang 新工人网 New Workers (website)
xin zuopai 新左派 New Left
xin zuoyi 新左翼 New Left
xuetong lun 血统论 blood-line theory
xunxin zishi 寻衅滋事 picking quarrels and provoking trouble
yi da, san fan 一打三反 One Strike, Three Antis Campaign
yi gong yi nong 亦工亦农 worker-peasant system
zaofan 造反 rebel
zaofanpai 造反派 rebel group or faction
zhenya fangeming 镇压反革命 Campaign to Suppress Counter-revolutionaries
zhigong daibiao dahui 职工代表大会 Staff and Workers Congresses
zhiqing 知青or *zhishi qingnian* 知识青年 (urban) educated youth
zhongguo gongchanzhuyi qingnian tuan 中国共产主义青年团 Chinese Communist Youth League
zhongguo gongren wang 中国工人网 China Workers Net (website)
zhongguo honge hui 中国红歌会 Red Song Society (website)
zhongguo renquan tongmeng 中国人权同盟 Chinese Human Rights Alliance
zhongguo tese 中国特色 “with Chinese characteristics”
zhonghua quanguo funü lianhehui 中华全国妇女联合会 All-China Women’s Federation (ACWF)
zhonghua quanguo zonggonghui 中华全国总工会 All-China Federation of Trade Unions (ACFTU)
zhongyang wenge xiaozu 中央文革小组 Central Cultural Revolution Group (CCRG)
zhua geming, cu shengchan 抓革命, 促生产 grasping revolution and promoting production
zouzipai 走资派 capitalist roader
zuo an 左岸 Left Bank (website)
zuo gongren gongzuo 做工人工作 doing worker work

Notes

PREFACE

1. The gender asterisk (*) following the word "women" serves as a reference to the constructed character of gender. Going beyond binary and heterosexual gender concepts, women* refers to all who are described as women and all (trans*, inter*, or queer*) who intentionally choose a femme gender expression. "Men" with an asterisk (*) is used for a similar reason, while keeping in mind that cis men are not to the same extent subjected to patriarchal violence and oppression in capitalist (and socialist) countries as women* are.
2. These books can be found here: https://www.mandelbaum.at/reihen/kritik-und-utopie.
3. https://www.gongchao.org/en/the-communist-road-to-capitalism.
4. See my comments on that struggle in the second section of chapter 5. More details are provided by Zhang Yueran, "Leninists in a Chinese Factory: Reflections on the Jasic Labour Organising Strategy." *Made in China Journal*, vol. 5, no. 2 (May–August 2020), pp. 82–88. https://tinyurl.com/2s49czxy (accessed April 20, 2022), and Kevin Lin, "State Repression in the Jasic Aftermath: From Punishment to Preemption." *Made in China Journal*, vol. 4, no. 1 (January–March 2019), pp. 16–19. https://tinyurl.com/36zcc55c (accessed April 22, 2022).
5. On the situation in Xinjiang, see the author's interview with Darren Byler, "Standing with the Oppressed: On Colonialism and Terror Capitalism in Xinjiang," nqch.org, March 17, 2021. https://tinyurl.com/4yr2tm2v (accessed August 13, 2022) and the book by Darren Byler, *Terror Capitalism: Uyghur Dispossession and Masculinity in a Chinese City* (Durham: Duke University Press, 2021).

1 INTRODUCTION

1. A narrow definition, for instance, based on the subjective interpretation of what leftists should think or do, would neglect or ignore the ambivalent legacy of left-wing activity that today's left needs to face up to and deal with, and it would prevent a debate within a larger framework of left-wing politics on current or future projects of (left-wing) revolutionary change.
2. The forms of class rule, patriarchal discrimination, and racist oppression of internal migrants will be discussed in later chapters. The CCP's policies on what it defined as ethnic minorities (*shaoshu minzu*), the problems these groups faced, and their struggles against discrimination or for autonomy in

peripheral regions like Yunnan, Inner Mongolia, Xinjiang, or Tibet, cannot be covered here although they surely deserve a closer analysis.

3. Some of these social struggles also inspired liberal or right-wing reactions, but I do not explore those here.
4. In the conclusions, I look at one continuity in the history of the CCP and its leaderships: anti-leftism.
5. An example is the 2019 movement in Hong Kong; see Ralf Ruckus, "Out of Control—Hong Kong's Rebellious Movement and the Left," nqch.org, September 10, 2019. https://tinyurl.com/2p8tm2x8 (accessed September 11, 2019).
6. That does not mean I necessarily agree with them. As mentioned earlier, under the concept of "left-wing" I subsume tendencies that claim to be left-wing or express left-wing aims, whether they live up to those aims or not.
7. This is not to say that all who identified as anarchists or as communists shared the same ideas on left-wing strategies, organization, and goals. In fact, the described currents had their own disagreements and splits around organizational and strategic questions.
8. For an early example of the feminist struggle in left-wing social movements, see Carolyn Eichner's historiography of feminist activists during the Paris Commune in 1871: Carolyn J. Eichner, *Surmounting the Barricades: Women in the Paris Commune* (Bloomington/Indianapolis: Indiana University Press, 2004). The term "feminism" was not used before the 1880s, but feminist issues played a role in left-wing discussions as early as the French Revolution in 1789, and the struggle over feminist demands has continued to shape left-wing politics since.
9. Among the few examples of a strong anarchist influence in oppositional movements are the Makhnovshchina (1918–21) in what is today Ukraine and Revolutionary Catalonia (1936–39) in Spain.
10. While left and right appear mutually exclusive and complementary, they are better understood as part of a continuous spectrum, with an additional center and moderate or extreme forms of left and right. The way the left/right and other metaphors or descriptions are defined and used in political analyses or campaigns also depends on the position of the user. Engaged left-wing and right-wing actors have often used them in an evaluative manner, but while the former use the term "left" and push it to join forces and attack the existing order, the latter often do not claim to form a right but pretend to be moderate or at the center. More neutral observers use "left" and "right" more descriptively but, again, what counts as left or right might differ depending on the region. For instance, "liberal" positions are considered quite right-wing in Italy and France, fairly centrist in Germany and Britain, and somewhat left-wing in the US.
11. See, for instance, Hans Jürgen Eysenck, *The Psychology of Politics* (London: Routledge and Kegan Paul, 1963), and Maurice C. Bryson and William R. McDill, "The Political Spectrum: A Bi-dimensional Approach." *Rampart*

Journal of Individualist Thought, vol. IV, no. 2 (1968), pp. 19–26. https://tinyurl.com/2p8d6zbr (accessed April 20, 2022). Apologists of the capitalist democratic system also used the horseshoe model that merely indicates that the extreme left (communists) and the extreme right (fascists) were both "totalitarian" and therefore similar or closely related.

12. In other political contexts, these terms are filled with different meanings, and in some cases liberal or right-wing forces also claim to have egalitarian or collectivist positions, but there is no space to discuss that here.
13. For a similar graph to visualize political forces, see the website https://www.politicalcompass.org. The graph there is merely used as a tool for the illustration of political differences but not as a tool for the systematic analysis of political forces and their relation to social movements or changes.
14. A more precise (graded) positioning, not just in the four boxes but along both axes (scales), would be possible when analyzing the particular positions of each listed group or current.
15. In the standard Pinyin-transcription the party's name is *guomindang*.
16. The Comintern or Third International existed from 1919 to 1943.
17. The KMT's program included socialist elements, and the party had a left wing that promoted socialism and sympathized with the politics of the Soviet Union where many KMT cadres were trained. The right wing of the KMT under Chiang Kai-shek eventually prevailed, though, and cleansed the party of left-wing elements after 1927.
18. For a more detailed account, see Ralf Ruckus, *The Communist Road to Capitalism: How Social Unrest and Containment Have Pushed China's (R)evolution since 1949* (Oakland: PM Press, 2021), chapter 1.
19. The fault lines the CCP drew between cadres and urban workers or peasants, between urban workers and peasants, and between men* and women* were part of the conflicts between the party and left-wing oppositional forces. These class or gender confrontations could be framed in a left-wing form, the confrontation between "minorities" and Han Chinese rather not. The national self-determination or liberation struggle, for instance, in Xinjiang and Tibet in the 1950s, included theocratic, feudal, and other elements that were neither progressive nor left-wing.
20. For an explanation of this historical dynamic produced by struggles from below and countermeasures from above in the PRC since 1949, see Ruckus, *The Communist Road to Capitalism*, pp. 168ff.
21. It is important to note that the groups or currents listed in the right column were not alone in expressing the discontent described in the center column, that they were not just expressing the discontent but also had their own political agendas, and that some of them originated as a reaction to the mentioned social discontent and struggles but continued to exist and transform thereafter.
22. Another interesting example of social struggles that triggered left-wing debates (and influenced later protests) was left out here: the struggle of

peasants in the face of starvation during the Great Leap Forward (1958–61), for instance, against the state's procurement policies and the confiscation of grain.

2 AGAINST BROKEN PROMISES

1. Chen Feng, "Against the State: Labor Protests in China in the 1950s." *Modern China*, vol. 40, no. 5 (2014), p. 504.
2. Wu Yiching, *The Cultural Revolution at the Margins: Chinese Socialism in Crisis* (Cambridge/London: Harvard University Press, 2014), p. 23.
3. See the section "Squeezing the Peasants," in Ralf Ruckus, *The Communist Road to Capitalism: How Social Unrest and Containment Have Pushed China's (R)evolution since 1949* (Oakland: PM Press, 2021), pp. 28ff.
4. See the section "Class as Classification," in Wu Yiching, *The Cultural Revolution at the Margins*, pp. 38ff.
5. See the section "Maoist Patriarchy," in Ruckus, *The Communist Road to Capitalism*, pp. 34ff.
6. On this early confrontation and the role of the union, see Paul Harper, "The Party and the Unions in Communist China." *The China Quarterly* 37 (March 1969), pp. 84–119.
7. Elizabeth J. Perry, "Masters of the Country? Shanghai Workers in the Early People's Republic," in Jeremy Brown and Paul G. Pickowicz, eds., *Dilemmas of Victory: The Early Years of the People's Republic of China* (Cambridge/London: Harvard University Press, 2007), p. 60.
8. Jackie Sheehan, *Chinese Workers: A New History* (London: Routledge, 1998), p. 27.
9. On the One-Man Regiment, formally adopted in the first Five-Year Plan (1953–57), see, for instance, Franz Schurmann, *Ideology and Organization in Communist China* (Berkeley: University of California Press, 1968), pp. 253ff.
10. Joel Andreas, *Disenfranchised: The Rise and Fall of Industrial Citizenship in China* (Oxford: Oxford University Press, 2019), pp. 38–39.
11. On workers' strikes in 1956 and 1957, see especially François Gipouloux, *Les Cent Fleurs à l'usine: Agitation ouvrière et crise du modèle soviétique en China, 1956–1957* (Paris: Éditions de l'École des Hautes Études en Sciences Sociales, 1986), and Sheehan, *Chinese Workers*, chapter 2.
12. Chen Feng, "Against the State," p. 497.
13. Ibid., p. 495.
14. Ibid.
15. On wage differentials between different types of workers, see Michael Korzec and Martin K. Whyte, "Reading Notes: The Chinese Wage System." *The China Quarterly* 86 (June 1981), pp. 248–273.
16. Sheehan, *Chinese Workers*, p. 86, and Elizabeth J. Perry, "Shanghai's Strike Wave of 1957." *The China Quarterly* 137 (March 1994), p. 1.

17. Gipouloux, *Les Cent Fleurs*, pp. 164–5; Sheehan, *Chinese Workers*, p. 52. This refers to:

> "so-called joint-ownership enterprises (*gongsi heying qiye*). Under this arrangement, the former owners [of private firms] became state employees, receiving interest on the value of their shares in the enterprise. The capitalists no longer enjoyed profits, nor did they exercise any real managerial initiative. Except for the fact that the former owners clipped coupons, the joint-owned companies were in effect wholly state-run entities" (Perry, "Shanghai's Strike Wave," p. 7, referring to Carl Riskin, *China's Political Economy: The Quest for Development since 1949* [Oxford: Oxford University Press, 1987], pp. 96–7).

18. "The wages were meager, the rhythm of work was exhausting, and the housing conditions deplorable. Not to speak about the exclusion of workers from the decision-making processes" (Gipouloux, *Les Cent Fleurs*, p. 270; translated by R.R.).
19. Korzec and Whyte, "Reading Notes," pp. 255–256.
20. Gipouloux, *Les Cent Fleurs*, p. 87.
21. Perry, "Shanghai's Strike Wave," p. 12; Gipouloux, *Les Cent Fleurs*, p. 73; Sheehan, *Chinese Workers*, p. 79.
22. Nara Dillon, *Radical Inequalities: China's Evolutionary Welfare State in Comparative Perspective* (Cambridge/London: Harvard University Press, 2015), p. 215.
23. Perry, "Shanghai's Strike Wave," p. 10.
24. On the forms of resistance, see Gipouloux, *Les Cent Fleurs*, pp. 83, 86, 160, 172f., 190. Some of these forms are similar to what James Scott described as everyday forms of struggle or "weapons of the weak." See James C. Scott, *Weapons of the Weak: Everyday Forms of Peasant Resistance*. New Haven/London: Yale University Press, 1985.
25. Perry, "Shanghai's Strike Wave," p. 11.
26. Sheehan, *Chinese Workers*, p. 68; also see Gipouloux, *Les Cent Fleurs*, pp. 210–211.
27. Chen Feng, "Against the State," pp. 507–508.
28. Gipouloux, *Les Cent Fleurs*, pp. 209–210.
29. Chen Feng, "Against the State," p. 508.
30. Sheehan, *Chinese Workers*, p. 71.
31. The name of the movement goes back to a slogan Mao used in May 1956. "Flowers" refers to writers and cultural workers; see Göran Leijonhufvud, *Going Against the Tide: On Dissenter and Big-character Posters in China* (Copenhagen: Curzon Press, 1990), p. 16. *Daming dafang* stands for "big speaking out, big opening up" in the sense of freely airing one's views.
32. Andreas, *Disenfranchised*, p. 47.
33. Sheehan, *Chinese Workers*, p. 77.
34. Andreas, *Disenfranchised*, p. 50.

35. Perry, "Shanghai's Strike Wave," p. 21. "Labor reform" refers to re-education (or reform through labor) in labor camps.
36. Sheehan, *Chinese Workers*, p. 78.
37. Perry, "Shanghai's Strike Wave," p. 26. Perry points out that in this case the fragmentation (not the unity) of the working class led to militancy. Workers who were "subject to neither the [welfare] subsidies nor the [paternalistic] controls experienced by their counterparts at state enterprises [...] stood at the forefront of labor protests under the command economy" (Perry, "Shanghai's Strike Wave," p. 20–21).
38. Chen Feng, "Against the State," p. 488.
39. Perry, "Shanghai's Strike Wave," p. 15.
40. Sheehan, *Chinese Workers*, pp. 48–49.
41. Chen Feng, "Against the State," p. 493–494.
42. Sheehan, *Chinese Workers*, p. 83.
43. Chen Feng, "Against the State," p. 509.
44. Liu Guokai, *A Brief Analysis of the Cultural Revolution* (Armonk: M.E. Sharpe, 1987), p. 45.
45. "The infamous *hukou* (household registration) regulations introduced by the CCP leadership in the late 1950s classified every PRC citizen as 'agricultural' or 'nonagricultural' and, additionally, bound them to certain locations (cities or villages) that had diverging levels of development and living standards depending on the province or county. They were employed to curb migration and social mobility and to maintain a majority rural population with relatively poor conditions and a minority urban population with a certain set of welfare rights and better conditions" (Ruckus, *The Communist Road to Capitalism*, p. 11).
46. Kjeld Erik Brodsgaard, "Paradigmatic Change: Readjustment and Reform in the Chinese Economy, 1953–1981, Part I." *Modern China*, vol. 9, no. 1 (1983), pp. 55–56, and Stephen Andors, *China's Industrial Revolution: Politics, Planning, and Management, 1949 to the Present* (New York: Pantheon Books, 1977), p. 129.
47. For a comparison of the invitation to criticize CCP leaders in 1957, and again during the Cultural Revolution ten years later, see Joel Andreas and Dong Yige, "The Brief, Tumultuous History of 'Big Democracy' in China's Factories." *Modern China*, vol. 44, no. 5 (2018), pp. 455–496.
48. Chinese Communist Party, *Decision of the Central Committee of the Chinese Communist Party Concerning the Great Proletarian Cultural Revolution* (Beijing: Foreign Languages Press, 1966). https://tinyurl.com/3ubakryn (accessed April 20, 2022).
49. On the workers' involvement in the Cultural Revolution, see especially Wu Yiching, *The Cultural Revolution at the Margins*, chapters 4 and 5, and Sheehan, *Chinese Workers*, chapter 4.
50. Wu Yiching, *The Cultural Revolution at the Margins*, p. 101. For a more detailed explanation of the inequalities and divisions between workers, see

Wang Feng, *Boundaries and Categories: Rising Inequality in Post-Socialist Urban China* (Stanford: Stanford University Press, 2008), chapter 2.

51. Sheehan, *Chinese Workers*, p. 97.
52. Andrew G. Walder, *Chang Ch'un-Ch'iao and Shanghai's January Revolution* (Ann Arbor: Center for Chinese Studies, University of Michigan, 1978), p. 46.
53. Ibid., pp. 43–44.
54. Wu Yiching, *The Cultural Revolution at the Margins*, p. 103.
55. Walder, *Chang Ch'un-Ch'iao*, p. 45. Also see Lin Weiran, "An Abortive Chinese Enlightenment: The Cultural Revolution and Class Theory" (PhD diss., University of Wisconsin-Madison, 1996), pp. 272–273.
56. Sheehan, *Chinese Workers*, p. 116.
57. Walder, *Chang Ch'un-Ch'iao*, p. 52, and Wu Yiching, *The Cultural Revolution at the Margins*, p. 125.
58. Sheehan, *Chinese Workers*, p. 116; also see Liu Guokai, *A Brief Analysis*, p. 48.
59. Sheehan, *Chinese Workers*, p. 133.
60. The "One Strike" was meant to hit "counter-revolutionaries," the "Three Antis" were meant to counter graft/embezzlement, profiteering, and extravagance/waste.
61. Lin Weiran, "An Abortive Chinese Enlightenment," p. 295. Also see Lauri Paltemaa, "The Democracy Wall Movement, Marxist Revisionism, and the Variations on Socialist Democracy." *Journal of Contemporary China*, vol. 16, no. 53 (2007), p. 607.
62. Yu Luoke was a young factory apprentice from Beijing who produced a series of critical essays that circulated widely in China and led to his arrest and, eventually, his execution in 1970. One of the best-known essays is "On Family Background," in which he criticized the "blood-line theory." See Yu Luoke, "On Family Background." *Contemporary Chinese Thought*, vol. 32, no. 4 (Summer 2001), pp. 17–36.
63. Lin Weiran, "An Abortive Chinese Enlightenment," p. 301.
64. Ibid., p. 275.
65. Sheehan, *Chinese Workers*, p. 126.
66. Wu Yiching, *The Cultural Revolution at the Margins*, pp. 190–191.
67. Lin Weiran, "An Abortive Chinese Enlightenment," p. 319.
68. The three syllables *sheng*, *wu*, and *lian* stand for the characters for province, proletariat, and alliance, the short form for Hunan Provincial Proletarian Revolutionary Big Alliance Committee (*hunan sheng wuchan jieji gemingpai da lianhe weiyuanhui*). On Shengwulian and the "ultra-left," also see Klaus Mehnert, *Peking and the New Left: At Home and Abroad* (Berkeley: University of California Press, 1969); Shengwulian, "Whither China?" [1968], in Klaus Mehnert, *Peking and the New Left*, pp. 82–100; That Faint Light, "A People's History of the Cultural Revolution." That Faint Light Blog, July 14, 2012. https://tinyurl.com/37dx4cts (accessed April 20, 2022); and Wu Yiching, "The Great Retreat and its Discontents: Re-examining the Sheng-

wulian Episode in the Cultural Revolution." *The China Journal* 72 (July 2014), pp. 1–28.

69. Lin Weiran, "An Abortive Chinese Enlightenment," p. 324.
70. Kjeld Erik Brodsgaard, "The Democracy Movement in China, 1978–1979: Opposition Movements, Wall Poster Campaigns, and Underground Journals." *Asian Survey*, vol. 21, no. 7 (July 1981), p. 750.
71. Lin Weiran, "An Abortive Chinese Enlightenment," p. 330. Also see Wu Yiching, *The Cultural Revolution at the Margins*, pp. 175, 179.
72. For instance, the CCP regime decided in 1971 to make many temporary workers permanent. See Andreas, *Disenfranchised*, p. 148.
73. "To be sure, fierce struggles—often violent ones—were made against individual bureaucrats. But few attempts were made to situate socioeconomic struggles explicitly in the broader context of the distribution of political power under the state-socialist regime, and rebel workers did not address more general political issues with respect to the relationship of labor to the state or the vital issue of class relations in Chinese socialism" (Wu Yiching, *The Cultural Revolution at the Margins*, p. 106).
74. Lin Weiran, "An Abortive Chinese Enlightenment," p. 7. The ideas expressed had an impact on later movements in the 1970s and 1980s, but since the focus was on "socialist" class relations the critique was not further developed once the transition to capitalism was well under way in the 1990s. That is unfortunate, as the critique touched on some of the most important contradictions of "actually existing socialism" and of Maoism as a political concept.
75. Like granting migrants urban *hukou* or giving temporary workers permanent status as in the late 1950s and the early 1970s.

3 FOR A BETTER FUTURE

1. Sebastian Heilmann, *Nanking 1976: Spontane Massenbewegungen im Gefolge der Kulturrevolution. Eine Regionalstudie* (Bochum: Brockmeyer, 1990), p. 109 (translated by R.R.).
2. On these campaigns see, for instance, Peter R. Moody, "The New Anti-Confucian Campaign in China: The First Round." *Asian Survey*, vol. 14, no. 4 (April 1974), pp. 307–324; Parris H. Chang, "The Anti-Lin Piao and Confucius Campaign: Its Meaning and Purposes." *Asian Survey*, vol. 14, no. 10 (October 1974), pp. 871–886; Merle Goldman, "China's Anti-Confucian Campaign, 1973–74." *The China Quarterly* 63 (September 1975), pp. 435–462; and Dong Guoqiang and Andrew G. Walder, "Nanjing's 'Second Cultural Revolution' of 1974." *The China Quarterly* 212 (December 2012), pp. 893–918.
3. The Four Modernizations were first mentioned by Zhou Enlai in 1963, but were not implemented before and during the Cultural Revolution. The term stands for the modernization of agriculture, industry, national defense, and science and technology.

4. Maurice Meisner, "Marx, Mao and Deng on the Division of Labour in History," in Arif Dirlik and Maurice Meisner, eds., *Marxism and the Chinese Experience* (Armonk: M.E. Sharpe, 1989), p. 104.
5. On the Li Yi Zhe debates, see Anita Chan, Stanley Rosen, and Jonathan Unger, eds., *On Socialist Democracy and the Chinese Legal System: The Li Yizhe Debates* (Armonk: M.E. Sharpe, 1985).
6. Kjeld Erik Brodsgaard, "The Democracy Movement in China, 1978–1979: Opposition Movements, Wall Poster Campaigns, and Underground Journals." *Asian Survey*, vol. 21, no. 7 (July 1981), p. 752, 755.
7. For detailed information on the trajectory and composition of the April 5 Movement, see, for instance, Heilmann, *Nanking 1976* and Sebastian Heilmann, *Sozialer Protest in der VR China: Die Bewegung vom 5. April 1976 und die Gegen-Kulturrevolution der siebziger Jahre* (Hamburg: Institut für Asienkunde, 1994).
8. Heilmann, *Sozialer Protest*, pp. 128–129.
9. See a personal description of the events in Roger Garside, *Coming Alive: China after Mao* (New York: McGraw-Hill, 1981), pp. 129ff.
10. Sebastian Heilmann, "The Social Context of Mobilization in China: Factions, Work Units and Activists during the 1976 April Fifth Movement." *China Information*, vol. VIII, no. 3 (Winter 1993), p. 11.
11. Jackie Sheehan, *Chinese Workers: A New History* (London: Routledge, 1998), p. 147.
12. Jeffrey N. Wasserstrom, "Student Protests and the Chinese Tradition, 1919–1989," in Tony Saich, ed., *The Chinese People's Movement: Perspectives on Spring 1989* (Armonk: M.E. Sharpe, 1990), p. 6.
13. Philip S. Williams, "Some Provincial Precursors of Popular Dissent Movements in Beijing." *China Information*, vol. 6, no. 1 (June 1991), p. 3.
14. Heilmann, "The Social Context," p. 6–7, 16–17.
15. Heilmann, *Nanking 1976*, p. 80.
16. Heilmann, "The Social Context," p. 17.
17. Brodsgaard, "The Democracy Movement," p. 758.
18. Quoted in Sheehan, *Chinese Workers*, p. 162.
19. Frederick C. Teiwes and Warren Sun, "China's New Economic Policy under Hua Guofeng: Party Consensus and Party Myths." *The China Journal* 66 (2011), p. 7.
20. Isabella Weber, *How China Escaped Shock Therapy: The Market Reform Debate* (London/New York: Routledge, 2021), p. 106.
21. For more details on the DWM, see, for instance, Flemming Christiansen, Susanne Posborg, and Anne Wedell-Wedellsborg, *Die demokratische Bewegung in China: Revolution im Sozialismus?* (München: Verlag Simon and Magiera, 1981) and Helmut Opletal, "Der 'Pekinger Frühling'—Erinnerungen an die chinesische Demokratiebewegung 1978 bis 1981." University of Vienna Website, 2020. https://tinyurl.com/yckwn66z (accessed on April 20, 2022). For documents of the movement, see Gregor Benton and Alan Hunter, eds., *Wild Lily, Prairie Fire: China's Road to Democracy, Yan'an to Tian'anmen,*

1942–1989 (Princeton: Princeton University Press, 1995), chapter 4, and Claude Widor, ed., *Documents on the Chinese Democratic Movement, 1978–1980: Unofficial Magazines and Wall Posters*, vol. 2 (Paris: Éditions de l'École des Hautes Études en Sciences Sociales, 1984).

22. Chen Ruoxi, *Democracy Wall and the Unofficial Journals* (Berkeley: University of California Press, 1982), pp. 107–115. Also see Garside, *Coming Alive*, p. 200–201.
23. For more information on these journals, see Brodsgaard, "The Democracy Movement," pp. 764–768.
24. Ibid., pp. 747–748.
25. Lauri Paltemaa, "The Democracy Wall Movement, Marxist Revisionism, and the Variations on Socialist Democracy." *Journal of Contemporary China*, vol. 16, no. 53 (2007), p. 610.
26. Brodsgaard, "The Democracy Movement," p. 762.
27. Ibid., pp. 762–763. That is different from the dissident groups in socialist countries in Eastern Europe. In the PRC, the intelligentsia had suffered in the Anti-Rightist Campaign and during the Cultural Revolution and after, and many intellectuals were not prepared to take the risks connected to political activism. They expected an improvement from Deng's faction. As the reforms offered new opportunities to increase their "social prestige and status," they were willingly coopted (ibid., p. 763).
28. Gregor Benton and Alan Hunter, "Introduction," in Benton and Hunter, eds., *Wild Lily, Prairie Fire*, p. 21.
29. Brodsgaard, "The Democracy Movement," p. 763.
30. Sheehan, *Chinese Workers*, p. 158.
31. This followed the line of Li Yi Zhe and people like Chen Erjin, a former rebel Red Guard who wrote essays on a "proletarian democratic" revolution or system. For Chen Erjin's critique of the rise of a bureaucratic privileged class see Chen Erjin, *China—Crossroads Socialism: An Unofficial Manifesto for Proletarian Democracy* (London: Verso, 1984).
32. Sheehan, *Chinese Workers*, p. 162.
33. Brodsgaard, "The Democracy Movement," p. 770.
34. Stanley Rosen, "Guangzhou's Democracy Movement in Cultural Revolution Perspective." *The China Quarterly* 101 (March 1985), p. 16; Benton and Hunter, "Introduction," pp. 24–25.
35. Sheehan, *Chinese Workers*, p. 167.
36. Wei Jingsheng was one of the most prominent liberal, anti-Marxist activists in the DWM. For more information, see He Baogang, "Democracy as Viewed by Three Chinese Liberals: Wei Jingsheng, Hu Ping and Yan Jiaqi." *China Information*, vol. 6, no. 2 (Autumn 1991), pp. 23–43.
37. Sheehan, *Chinese Workers*, p. 167.
38. Tony Saich, "Workers in the Workers' State: Urban Workers in the PRC," in David S.G. Goodman, ed., *Groups and Politics in the People's Republic of China* (Cardiff: University College Cardiff Press, 1984), p. 164.

39. Chinese Communist Party, "Resolution on Certain Questions in the History of Our Party Since the Founding of the People's Republic of China (Adopted by the Sixth Plenary Session of the Eleventh Central Committee of the Chinese Communist Party on June 27, 1981)." marxists.org. https://tinyurl.com/ym8mafjt (accessed April 20, 2022).
40. Paltemaa, "The Democracy Wall Movement," pp. 607–608.
41. Benton and Hunter, "Introduction," p. 26.
42. Documented in Benton and Hunter, *Wild Lily, Prairie Fire*, pp. 280–281.
43. Kathleen Hartford, "The Political Economy behind Beijing Spring," in Saich, *The Chinese People's Movement*, p. 58.
44. Pat Howard, "Rice Bowls and Job Security: The Urban Contract Labour System." *Australian Journal of Chinese Affairs* 25 (January 1991), p. 99. In fact, contract labor had existed in the socialist period, for instance, for rural temporary workers. Under the new system, new regular or permanent workers were also meant to have a labor contract (instead of lifelong employment in one work unit). For more information on the contract labor system, see Michael Korzec, *Labour and the Failure of Reform in China* (New York: St. Martin's Press, 1992).
45. "[O]ver 50 percent of urban families were likely to have suffered a decline in real income in 1988 with 25–30 percent of workers in China only able to live a life of subsistence" (Jeanne L. Wilson, "'The Polish Lesson': China and Poland 1980–1990." *Studies in Comparative Communism*, vol. XXIII, No. 3/4 [Autumn/Winter 1990], p. 270). Also see Andrew G. Walder, "Workers, Managers and the State: The Reform Era and the Political Crisis of 1989." *The China Quarterly* 127 (September 1991), pp. 470–471.
46. Wilson, "The Polish Lesson," p. 270. On the negative effects of the reforms, see Mark Selden, "The Social Origins and Limits of the Democratic Movement," in Roger V. Des Forges, Luo Ning, and Wu Yen-Bo, eds., *Chinese Democracy and the Crisis of 1989: Chinese and American Reflections* (Albany: State University of New York Press, 1993), pp. 118–120.
47. According to Leung Wing-yue:

    "[w]orkers' participation in the demonstrations received little public coverage, but there were reports that the top leadership only became really alarmed when they learned that workers were participating in the protests and organizing strikes. Reports say circulars were sent to all factories and enterprises, sternly warning workers against participating in the protests and stating that any attempt to call strikes would be severely reprimanded" (Leung Wing-Yue, *Smashing the Iron Rice Pot: Workers and Unions in China's Market Socialism* [Hong Kong: Asia Monitor Resource Center, 1988], p. 119).

48. Zhang Yueran, "Workers on Tian'anmen Square," in Ivan Franceschini and Christian Sorace, eds., *Proletarian China: A Century of Chinese Labour* (London/New York: Verso, 2022), p. 151.

49. For more detailed information on the Tian'anmen Square Movement, see, for instance, Tony Saich, ed., *The Chinese People's Movement: Perspectives on Spring 1989* (Armonk: M.E. Sharpe, 1990) and Theodore Han and John Li, *Tian'anmen Square Spring 1989: A Chronology of the Chinese Democracy Movement* (Berkeley: Institute of East Asian Studies, 1992); on the workers' involvement, see the articles in Lu Ping, ed., *A Moment of Truth: Workers' Participation in China's 1989 Democracy Movement and the Emergence of Independent Unions* (Hong Kong: Hong Kong Trade Union Education Center/Asia Monitor Resource Center, 1990). For documents of the movement, see Benton and Hunter, *Wild Lily, Prairie Fire*, chapter 5.
50. Zhang Yueran, "Workers on Tian'anmen Square," p. 152.
51. Andrew G. Walder and Gong Xiaoxia, "Workers in the Tian'anmen Protests: The Politics of the Beijing Workers' Autonomous Federation." *Australian Journal of Chinese Affairs*, 29 (January 1993), pp. 2–3. For a detailed account of Gongzilian/BWAF, see Leung Wing-Yue, "The Politics of Labour Rebellions in China, 1989–1994" (PhD diss., University of Hong Kong, 1998), pp. 233ff.
52. Wang Shaoguang, "From a Pillar of Continuity to a Force for Change: Chinese Workers in the Movement," in Des Forges et al. eds., *Chinese Democracy and the Crisis of 1989*, p. 179; Lu Ping, "A Brief History of the Workers' Autonomous Federation," in Lu Ping, *A Moment of Truth*, p. 17. See more on the activity of other WAFs in Mary S. Erbaugh and Richard C. Kraus, "The 1989 Democracy Movement in Fujian and its Aftermath," in Jonathan Unger, ed., *The Pro-democracy Protests in China: Reports from the Provinces* (Armonk: M.E. Sharpe, 1991), pp. 150–165; Leung Wing-Yue, "The Politics of Labour Rebellions," pp. 244ff.; and Anita Chan and Jonathan Unger, "Voices from the Protest Movement, Chongqing, Sichuan." *Australian Journal of Chinese Affairs* 24 (July 1990), pp. 259–279.
53. Gongzilian activists claimed that number, see Walder and Gong, "Workers in the Tian'anmen Protests," p. 9.
54. Lu Ping, "A Brief History," p. 13.
55. Chan and Unger, "Voices from the Protest Movement," p. 274.
56. Walder and Gong, "Workers in the Tian'anmen Protests," p. 15.
57. Merle Goldman, "The Potential for Instability among Alienated Intellectuals and Students in Post-Mao China," in David Shambaugh, ed., *Is China Unstable? Assessing the Factors* (Armonk/London: M.E. Sharpe, 2000), pp. 122–123.
58. Sheehan, *Chinese Workers*, p. 213.
59. Walder and Gong, "Workers in the Tian'anmen Protests," p. 3; Wang Shaoguang, "Deng Xiaoping's Reforms and the Chinese Workers' Participation in the Protest Movement of 1989," in Paul Zarembka, ed., *Research in Political Economy*, vol. 13 (London: JAI Press, 1992), pp. 178–179.
60. Walder and Gong, "Workers in the Tian'anmen Protests," p. 7.
61. Wang Shaoguang, "From a Pillar of Continuity," p. 179.

62. Walder and Gong, "Workers in the Tian'anmen Protests," p. 8.
63. Ibid., p. 9.
64. Zhang Yueran, "Workers on Tian'anmen Square," p. 152.
65. Walder and Gong, "Workers in the Tian'anmen Protests," p. 10.
66. Zhang Yueran, "Workers on Tian'anmen Square," p. 153.
67. On the disconnect between students and workers, see, for instance, Walder and Gong, "Workers in the Tian'anmen Protests," pp. 23–24; Maurice Meisner, *Mao's China and After: A History of the People's Republic*, 3rd edn (New York: The Free Press, 1999), p. 508; and Zhang Yueran, "Workers on Tian'anmen Square," pp. 156–157.
68. Walder and Gong, "Workers in the Tian'anmen Protests," p. 25.
69. Lu Ping, "A Brief History," p. 19.
70. Sheehan, *Chinese Workers*, p. 219. See the reports on Xi'an, Hangzhou, and Shenyang: Joseph W. Esherick, "Xi'an Spring." *Australian Journal of Chinese Affairs* 24 (July 1990), p. 230; Keith Forster, "The Popular Protest in Hangzhou," in Unger, *The Pro-Democracy Protests in China*, p. 183; Anne Gunn, "'Tell the World About Us': The Student Movement in Shenyang, 1989," in Unger, *The Pro-Democracy Protests in China*, p. 77.
71. Wang Shaoguang, "From a Pillar of Continuity," p. 178.
72. See, for instance, Anita Chan, "Protest in a Hunan County Town: The Profile of a Democracy Movement Activist in China's Backwaters," in Unger, *The Pro-Democracy Protests in China*, pp. 137–149.
73. Wang Shaoguang, "Deng Xiaoping's Reforms," p. 22.
74. Leung Wing-Yue, "The Politics of Labour Rebellions," p. 224.
75. For more on historical connections between the Cultural Revolution and the movement in 1989, see Craig Calhoun and Jeffrey N. Wasserstrom, "The Cultural Revolution and the Democracy Movement of 1989: Complexity in Historical Connections," in Law Kam-yee, ed., *The Chinese Cultural Revolution Reconsidered: Beyond Purge and Holocaust* (Basingstoke/New York: Palgrave Macmillan, 2003), pp. 241–261; and Yang Guobin, "The Liminal Effects of Social Movements: Red Guards and the Transformation of Identity." *Sociological Forum*, vol. 15, no. 3 (September 2000), pp. 379–406.
76. Walder and Gong, "Workers in the Tian'anmen Protests," p. 28.
77. Zhang Yueran has a different interpretation. For him, workers understood that "the only way to eradicate inflation and inequality was to overthrow the bureaucracy as a whole and restore to the workers the power to control the production and circulation of goods." Their understanding of democracy "entailed the replacement of bureaucracy with workers' self-management, and the first step towards this goal was to establish democratic and independent workplace organizations. This vision of democracy clearly had a class character, premised as it was on the agency of the working class" (Zhang Yueran, "Workers on Tian'anmen Square," p. 156).
78. Anita Chan, "China's Long Winter." *Monthly Review*, vol. 41, no. 8 (January 1990), p. 10.

79. In fact, Zhang Yueran argues that, after the crackdown and repression, "many student participants in the 1989 movement transformed into the new urban middle class [...] In a sense, the economic reforms of the 1990s were a way for the CCP to absorb and coopt the generation of students who participated in 1989" (Zhang Yueran, "Workers on Tian'anmen Square," p. 158).

4 DEFENSE AND NOSTALGIA

1. Cited in Elizabeth J. Perry, "'To Rebel is Justified': Cultural Revolution Influences on Contemporary Chinese Protest," in Law Kam-yee, ed., *The Chinese Cultural Revolution Reconsidered: Beyond Purge and Holocaust* (Basingstoke/New York: Palgrave Macmillan, 2003), p. 271.
2. Alexander F. Day and Mindi Schneider, "The End of Alternatives? Capitalist Transformation, Rural Activism and the Politics of Possibility in China." *Journal of Peasant Studies*, vol. 45, no. 7 (November 2017), p. 1123.
3. For a detailed account, see Barry Naughton, *The Chinese Economy: Adaptation and Growth*, 2nd edn (Cambridge/London: MIT Press, 2018), pp. 268ff.
4. Most TVEs were set up during the dissolution of the rural collectives in the early 1980s as collectively or privately owned small- and medium-sized enterprises. They expanded massively in the 1980s and early 1990s. For a detailed account, see Naughton, *The Chinese Economy*, chapter 13.
5. For more detailed information on the situation and struggles of peasants in the past few decades, see, for instance, Thomas P. Bernstein and Lü Xiaobo, *Taxation without Representation in Contemporary Rural China* (Cambridge/New York: Cambridge University Press, 2003); Chen Guidi and Wu Chuntao, *Will the Boat Sink the Water? The Life of China's Peasants* (New York: Public Affairs, 2006); Kevin J. O'Brien and Li Lianjiang, *Rightful Resistance in Rural China* (Cambridge: Cambridge University Press, 2006); and Alexander F. Day, *The Peasant in Post-socialist China: History, Politics, and Capitalism* (Cambridge: Cambridge University Press, 2013).
6. Thomas P. Bernstein, "Instability in Rural China," in David Shambaugh, ed., *Is China Unstable? Assessing the Factors* (Armonk/London: M.E. Sharpe, 2000), p. 95.
7. Ibid., p. 96. On IOUs, see Andrew Wedeman, "Stealing from the Farmers: Institutional Corruption and the 1992 IOU Crisis." *The China Quarterly* 152 (December 1997), pp. 805–831, and Kathy L. Walker, "'Gangster Capitalism' and Peasant Protest in China: The Last Twenty Years." *Journal of Peasant Studies*, vol. 33, no. 1 (January 2006), p. 7. IOU ("I owe you") slips were issued by local officials for crops instead of cash.
8. Day and Schneider, "The End of Alternatives?", p. 4.
9. Ibid.
10. Bernstein, "Instability in Rural China," p. 97. For more on the One-Child Policy see chapter 5.
11. Bernstein, "Instability in Rural China," p. 97.

12. Kathy L. Walker, "From Covert to Overt: Everyday Peasant Politics in China and the Implications for Transnational Agrarian Movements." *Journal of Agrarian Change*, vol. 8, no. 2 and 3 (April and July 2008), p. 467.
13. Bernstein, "Instability in Rural China," pp. 103–104; Li Lianjiang and Kevin J. O'Brien, "Protest Leadership in Rural China," in Peter Hays Gries and Stanley Rosen, eds., *Chinese Politics: State, Society and the Market* (London/New York: Routledge, 2010), pp. 90–91.
14. Bernstein, "Instability in Rural China," pp. 97–98. Also see Walker, "From Covert to Overt," p. 470.
15. O'Brien and Li Lianjiang give examples of how "villagers frame their claims around Communist Party policies, state laws, and official values; solicit assistance from influential allies; and combine legal tactics with collective action to defend their 'lawful rights and interests' (*hefa quanyi*)" (O'Brien and Li, *Rightful Resistance*, p. 5). See the description of "everyday forms" of peasant resistance against state measures as well as "coping behaviors" since the 1950s in Gao Wangling, "A Study of Chinese Peasant 'Counter-action,'" in Kimberley Ens Manning and Felix Wemheuer, eds., *Eating Bitterness: New Perspectives on China's Great Leap Forward and Famine* (Vancouver/Toronto: UBC Press, 2011), p. 276.
16. Perry, "To Rebel is Justified," p. 271.
17. Bernstein, "Instability in Rural China," pp. 103–104.
18. Walker, "Gangster Capitalism," p. 19. For more on the Mao revival, see the third section of this chapter.
19. Kevin J. O'Brien and Li Lianjiang, "Campaign Nostalgia in the Chinese Countryside." *Asian Survey*, vol. 39, no. 3 (May–June 1999), p. 377.
20. See the first section of chapter 3 for similar claims for the "big freedoms" in the 1970s.
21. O'Brien and Li, "Campaign Nostalgia," p. 387.
22. Walker, "From Covert to Overt," p. 474.
23. On the repression against rural protest leaders, see Li and O'Brien, "Protest Leadership," pp. 96–100.
24. Walker, "Gangster Capitalism," p. 10; Day and Schneider, "The End of Alternatives?" p. 6; and Bernstein, "Instability in Rural China," p. 96.
25. Day and Schneider, "The End of Alternatives?" p. 8. Also see Walker, "Gangster Capitalism," p. 15; and Walker, "From Covert to Overt," p. 470.
26. For a detailed account on this policy, see Anna L. Ahlers, *Rural Policy Implementation in Contemporary China. New Socialist Countryside* (London/New York: Routledge, 2014).
27. Day and Schneider, "The End of Alternatives?" p. 10.
28. The urbanization rate in the PRC grew from about 20 percent in 1980 to about 50 percent in 2010 and close to 65 percent in 2021, see Statista, "Degree of Urbanization in China from 1980 to 2021." statista.com, 2022. https://tinyurl.com/2p8c9rr7 (accessed April 20, 2022).
29. Day and Schneider, "The End of Alternatives?" p. 13.

30. Jay Chen Chih-Jou, "Peasant Protests over Land Seizures in Rural China." *Journal of Peasant Studies*, vol. 47, no. 6 (October 2020), pp. 1328, 1330. Also see the reports on peasant struggles against (illegal) land seizures and "land taking compensation" in Zhejiang in Christopher Heurlin, "Land Protests in Rural China," in Teresa Wright, ed., *Handbook of Protests and Resistance in China* (Cheltenham/Northampton: Edward Elgar, 2019), pp. 184–202. On the effects of land requisitioning for the development of rural unemployment and "no wage and no land" peasants, see Rachel Murphy and Tao Ran, "No Wage and No Land: New Forms of Unemployment in Rural China," in Grace O.M. Lee and Malcolm Warner, eds., *Unemployment in China: Economy, Human Resources and Labour Markets* (London/New York: Routledge, 2007), pp. 128–148. On the most prominent case of resistance to land seizure, in Wukan, Guangdong, see Johan Lagerkvist, "The Wukan Uprising and Chinese State–Society Relations: Toward 'Shadow Civil Society'?" *International Journal of China Studies*, vol. 3, no. 3 (December 2012), pp. 345–361, and Sally Sargeson, "Violence as Development: Land Expropriation and China's Urbanization." *Journal of Peasant Studies*, vol. 40, no. 6 (2013), pp. 1063–1085.
31. Chen Chih-Jou, "Peasant Protests," pp. 1341–1342. Chen also mentions that "strict censorship has also reduced the number of reported protests" (ibid., p. 1343) so we might just not hear about as many protests as before and the number might not have fallen (that much) after all.
32. Ibid., p. 1342.
33. Ibid.
34. Quoted in Antoine Kernen, "The Reemergence of Street Protests: State Workers Challenge the Chinese State," in Thomas B. Gold, William Hurst, Won Jaeyoun, and Li Qiang, eds., *Laid-off Workers in a Workers' State: Unemployment with Chinese Characteristics* (New York: Palgrave Macmillan, 2009), p. 234.
35. For detailed information on the situation and struggles of urban workers in the state sector, see, for instance, Cai Yongshun, *State and Laid-off Workers in Reform China: The Silence and Collective Action of the Retrenched* (London/New York: Routledge, 2006); John Hassard, Jackie Sheehan, Zhou Meixiang, Jane Terpstra-Tong, and Jonathan Morris, *China's State Enterprise Reform: From Marx to the Market* (London/New York: Routledge, 2007); and the articles in Gold et al., eds., *Laid-off Workers in a Workers' State.*
36. On the restructuring and its effects, see, for instance, Ross Garnaut, Song Ligang, and Yao Yang, "Impact and Significance of State-owned Enterprise Restructuring in China." *The China Journal* 55 (January 2006), pp. 35–63, and Hassard et al., *China's State Enterprise Reform.*
37. Numbers range from about 30 to 50 million in the second half of the 1990s. See Dorothy J. Solinger, "Labour Market Reform and the Plight of the Laid-off Proletariat." *The China Quarterly* 170 (June 2002), p. 304; Cai Yongshun, "State Policies and Chinese Laid-off Workers' Limited Resistance,"

in Gold et al., *Laid-off Workers in a Workers' State*, p. 203; Mary E. Gallagher, "China's Older Workers: Between Law and Policy, Between Laid-off and Unemployed," in Gold et al., *Laid-off Workers in a Workers' State*, p. 138; and Human Rights Watch, *Paying the Price: Worker Unrest in Northeast China*. Refworld, UNHCR, August 2, 2002. https://tinyurl.com/f4kbrdnh (accessed April 20, 2022).

38. "Officially, a *xiagang* worker is one who meets all three of the following conditions: s/he began working before the contract system was instituted in 1986 and had a formal, permanent job in the state sector (plus those contract laborers whose contract term is not yet concluded); because of his/her firm's problems in business and operations, has been let go, but has not yet cut off relations with the original firm; and has not yet found other work in society" (Solinger, "Labour Market Reform," p. 304).
39. Kernen, "The Reemergence of Street Protests," p. 226.
40. Li Ju, "Victory and Defeat: The Contentious Politics of One Generation of State Workers in China since the 1960s." *International Review of Social History*, vol. 61, no. 2 (August 2016), p. 213.
41. See, for instance, Marc Blecher, "Hegemony and Workers' Politics in China." *The China Quarterly* 170 (June 2002), pp. 283–303, and Cai Yongshun, "State Policies."
42. See the examples of "foot-dragging," "indifference," and more in Li Ju, "Fight Silently: Everyday Resistance in Surviving State-owned Enterprises in Contemporary China." *Global Labour Journal*, vol. 3, issue 2 (September 2012), pp. 194–216.
43. Kernen, "The Reemergence of Street Protests," p. 225.
44. Ibid., p. 227.
45. Ibid., p. 234.
46. William Hurst, "The Power of the Past: Nostalgia and Popular Discontent in Contemporary China," in Gold et al., *Laid-off Workers in a Workers' State*, pp. 120–121; William Hurst and Kevin O'Brien, "China's Contentious Pensioners." *The China Quarterly* 170 (June 2002), p. 356.
47. Ching-Kwan Lee, "Pathways of Labour Insurgency," in Elizabeth J. Perry and Mark Selden, eds., *Chinese Society: Change, Conflict and Resistance*, 2nd edn (London/New York: RoutledgeCurzon, 2003), p. 82.
48. For a description of these events, see, for instance, Human Rights Watch, "Paying the Price," and *China Labour Bulletin*, "The Liaoyang Workers' Struggle: Portrait of a Movement." China Labour Bulletin website, July 2003. https://tinyurl.com/bdewzx9b (accessed April 20, 2022).
49. Solinger, "Labour Market Reform," pp. 315ff.
50. Cai Yongshun, "State Policies," pp. 204, 211ff.
51. Li Ju, "Victory and Defeat," p. 216.
52. "The 'harmonious society,' or *hexie shehui* […] was raised as a strategic goal of the Chinese Communist Party under Hu Jintao in 2004 in order to respond to rising social discontent stemming from the economic and social

development of the previous two decades as well as increasing globalization" (China Media Project, "The CMP Dictionary: Harmonious Society." China Media Project, May 14, 2021. https://tinyurl.com/yckzhvrx [accessed April 20, 2022]).

53. Cited in Wang Shaoguang, "Deng Xiaoping's Reforms and the Chinese Workers' Participation in the Protest Movement of 1989," in Paul Zarembka, ed., *Research in Political Economy*, vol. 13 (London: JAI Press, 1992), pp. 163–197.
54. Books on the reinvention and modification of Maoism since the 1990s in the PRC often lack depth and consistency. Examples are Kerry Brown and Simone van Nieuwenhuizen, *China and the New Maoists* (London: Zed Books, 2016) and Jude Blanchette, *China's New Red Guards: The Return of Radicalism and the Rebirth of Mao Zedong* (Oxford: Oxford University Press, 2019).
55. Wang Shaoguang, "Deng Xiaoping's Reforms." See also Geremie R. Barmé, "The Irresistible Fall and Rise of Chairman Mao," in Geremie R. Barmé, ed., *Shades of Mao: The Posthumous Cult of the Great Leader* (New York/London: M.E. Sharpe, 1996), p. 4.
56. Ibid., p. 5.
57. This part of the book focuses on the political references to and usage of Maoism or Mao Zedong and not on the cultural, fashion, or religious aspects. For those, see the various texts in Barmé, *Shades of Mao*.
58. Zhang Weihong, "A Typology of the Mao Craze," in Barmé, *Shades of Mao*, p. 158.
59. Yang Guobin, "China's Zhiqing Generation: Nostalgia, Identity, and Cultural Resistance in the 1990s." *Modern China*, vol. 29, no. 3 (July 2003), pp. 267–268.
60. Ibid., p. 268.
61. Ibid., p. 285.
62. Chen Feng, "An Unfinished Battle in China: The Leftist Criticism of the Reform and the Third Thought Emancipation." *The China Quarterly* 158 (June 1999), pp. 454–455.
63. Ibid., p. 447.
64. Rightists, in contrast, supported the economic reforms but opposed some of the policies regarding CCP rule, the state, and ideology. "What the Party was opposing, in fact, was leftists' economic views, which were inimical to many current policy practices. As far as political issues were concerned, the leftists held similar views to those the Party asserted, such as absolute Party leadership, restrictions on civil liberties, ideological control and so on" (ibid., p. 460).
65. Ibid., p. 450.
66. Blanchette, *China's New Red Guards*, p. 46.
67. Merle Goldman, "The Potential for Instability among Alienated Intellectuals and Students in Post-Mao China," in David Shambaugh, ed., *Is China*

Unstable? Assessing the Factors (Armonk/London: M.E. Sharpe, 2000), p. 116.

68. Chen Feng, "An Unfinished Battle in China," p. 459.
69. "Che Guevara was performed 37 times, including 3 additional performances that had not been planned and a special performance free of charge for college students who couldn't afford the ticket price. The average theater attendance rate reached as high as 120 percent. A total of more than 10,000 people went to see the show" (Huang Jisu, "Che Guevara: Notes on the Play, Its Production, and Reception," in Zhong Xueping and Wang Ban, eds., *Debating the Socialist Legacy and Capitalist Globalization in China* [Basingstoke/New York: Palgrave Macmillan, 2014], p. 208).
70. Cheng Yinghong, "Che Guevara: Dramatizing China's Divided Intelligentsia at the Turn of the Century." *Modern Chinese Literature and Culture*, vol. 15, no. 2 (Fall 2003), pp. 14, 18, 19.
71. "Ultimately, we managed to drop a stone into the pond of 'end of history' and 'farewell to revolution,' causing a momentary displeasure to those who were ready to thoroughly enjoy their illusions" (Huang Jisu, *Che Guevara*, p. 209). For more on the play *Che Guevara* and its authors, see Claire Conceison, *Significant Other: Staging the American in China* (Honolulu: University of Hawai'i Press, 2004), pp. 177ff.
72. Robert Weil, "Conditions of the Working Classes in China." *Monthly Review*, vol. 58, issue 2 (June 2006). https://tinyurl.com/4xdtuv6b (accessed April 20, 2022).
73. Ibid.; *Monthly Review*, "On December 24, 2004, Maoists in China Get Three-year Prison Sentences for Leafleting." MR online, January 21, 2005. https://tinyurl.com/5bc36zu6 (accessed April 20, 2022).
74. For more on this, see Cheng Zhiming, "The Changing Pattern of State Workers' Labour Resistance in Shaanxi Province, China." *Communication, Politics and Culture*, vol. 45, no. 2 (2012), pp. 197–216.
75. On Utopia see Blanchette, *China's New Red Guards*, pp. 75ff., and Brown and Nieuwenhuizen, *China and the New Maoists*, chapter 6.
76. Andreas Møller Mulvad, "China's Ideological Spectrum: A Two-dimensional Model of Elite Intellectuals' Visions." *Theory and Society*, vol. 47 (2018), p. 643.
77. These liberal discourses of intellectuals continued in the 2000s and early 2010s, using the possibilities offered by the internet, before the censorship and repression under the CCP regime of Xi Jinping made it more difficult to publish liberal positions. For a detailed account of liberals and their debates and activities, see Li Junpeng, "The Making of Liberal Intellectuals in Post-Tiananmen China" (PhD diss., Graduate School of Arts and Sciences, Columbia University, New York, 2017). https://tinyurl.com/2wuc8vrn (accessed April 20, 2022). For English translations of texts written by Chinese liberals, see https://www.readingthechinadream.com/liberals.html.
78. Li Junpeng, "The Making of Liberal Intellectuals," p. 60. Shi Anshu et al. write:

> "From the perspective of an anti-modern modernity, Wang Hui re-examined the short twentieth century; Cui Zhiyuan imagined the distant future of liberal socialism, calling for a second thought liberation and institutional innovation; Wang Shaoguang focused on the relationship between the socialist state, society, and the market, searching for theories of representational democracy and people's society; and Gan Yang promoted the integration of the three traditions [Confucianism, Maoism, and Dengism] on the basis of his faith in the possibility of Confucian socialism. All are responses to the question of how to restore the effectiveness and legitimacy of Chinese socialism" (Shi Anshu, François Lachapelle, and Matthew Galway, "The Recasting of Chinese Socialism: The Chinese New Left since 2000." *China Information*, vol. 32, no. 1 [2018], p. 153).

For English translations of texts written by Chinese New Left authors, see https://www.readingthechinadream.com/new-left.html.

79. Li Junpeng, "The Making of Liberal Intellectuals," pp. 53–54.
80. Wen Dale, *China Copes with Globalization: A Mixed Review* (San Francisco: International Forum on Globalization, 2006), p. 39. https://www.yumpu.com/en/document/read/26201346/china-report-with-cover-international-forum-on-globalization (accessed April 20, 2022).
81. See, for instance, Zheng Yongnian, *Globalization and State Transformation in China* (Cambridge: Cambridge University Press, 2004), chapter 8, and Zhang Taisu, "What it Means to Be 'Liberal' or 'Conservative' in China: Putting the Country's Most Significant Political Divide in Context." China File, April 24, 2015. https://tinyurl.com/yv34sfn5 (accessed April 20, 2022).
82. Christopher Connery, "The Chinese Left: Contexts and Strategies." theasiadialogue.com, October 21, 2016. https://tinyurl.com/yckpypnf (accessed April 20, 2022).
83. Ibid. Also see Brian Hioe, "The Chinese New Left: Anti-capitalist within China, Imperialist outside of China?" New Bloom, December 3, 2016. https://tinyurl.com/3ruccvmm (accessed April 20, 2022).
84. The nationalism of leftist groups inside and outside the party spiked, for instance, during diplomatic confrontations around the (accidental) NATO bombing of the PRC embassy in Belgrade in 1999 or the territorial dispute about the Diaoyu/Senkaku Islands between the PRC and Japan in 2012.
85. Examples of small communist parties that were repressed are the Marxism-Leninism-Mao Zedong Thought Communist Party of China or Mamao Party, founded in 1991; the Mao Zedong Thought Communist Party of China, founded in 2008; the Central Committee of the Chinese Proletarian Revolution or so-called Genuine Communist Party, founded in 2010; and the Supreme Constitution Party founded in 2013 (Dui Hua, "Leftist Subversion in China: 1980 to Present." Dui Hua Reference Materials, October 29, 2013. https://tinyurl.com/ytyjfpc6 [accessed April 20, 2022]; Dui Hua, "Leftist Dissent under Xi: The Old Leftists, Part II." *Dui Hua, Human Rights*

Journal, October 23, 2019. https://tinyurl.com/bdda455f [accessed April 20, 2022]).

86. For more on migrant workers see the next chapter.
87. Beverly Silver calls these struggles "Polanyi-type": "By Polanyi-type labor unrest, we mean the backlash resistances to the spread of a global self-regulating market, particularly by working classes that are being unmade by global economic transformations as well as by those workers who had benefited from established social compacts that are being abandoned from above" (Beverly J. Silver, *Forces of Labor: Workers' Movements and Globalization since 1870* [Cambridge: Cambridge University Press, 2003], p. 20).

5 SOCIAL UNREST AND ORGANIZING

1. Quoted in Pun Ngai and Li Wanwei, *Dagongmei: Arbeiterinnen aus Chinas Weltmarktfabriken erzählen*—Übersetzt und herausgegeben von Ralf Ruckus (Berlin/Hamburg: Assoziation A, 2008), p. 149 (translated by R.R.).
2. See chapter 2, second section.
3. Recently, sociologist Doug Guthrie, formerly employed by Apple University, described how the CCP regime has used the migration regime to supply (global) capital with labor up to the present day:

   "There are 350 million people that are what we call 'float[ing]' around the country, but they're actually moved by the government. This batch labor system is a tremendously powerful system in which the government moves people. The Chinese government moves people around the country to be at whatever factory needs them for seasonal production. This is amazing. It's an amazing system" (Chris Marquis, "The China Story behind Apple's $3 trillion Valuation with Doug Guthrie." SupChina, January 7, 2022. https://tinyurl.com/2utpe8bc [accessed April 20, 2022]).

4. For information on Sun Zhigang, see China Digital Space, "Sun Zhigang," China Digital Space website, undated. https://tinyurl.com/2a95npra (accessed August 7, 2022).
5. Jenny Chan and Mark Selden, "China's Rural Migrant Workers and Labour Politics," in Guo Yingjie, ed., *Handbook on Class and Social Stratification in China* (Cheltenham/Northampton: Edward Elgar, 2016), p. 364; Pun Ngai, *Migrant Labor in China: Post-socialist Transformations* (Cambridge: Polity Press, 2016), p. 68.
6. See chapter 4, first section.
7. For more on the dormitory labor regime, see Pun Ngai and Chris Smith, "Putting Transnational Labour Process in its Place: The Dormitory Labour Regime in Post-socialist China." *Work, Employment and Society*, vol. 21, no. 1 (2007), pp. 27–45.
8. Ching-Kwan Lee, "Pathways of Labor Activism," in Elizabeth J. Perry and Mark Selden, eds., *Chinese Society: Change, Conflict and Resistance*, 3rd edn

(New York: Routledge, 2010), p. 65; Qin Ling, "Introduction: The Survival and Collective Struggles of Workers in China's Coastal Private Enterprises since the 1990s," in Hao Ren et al., *China on Strike: Narratives of Workers' Resistance* (Chicago: Haymarket Books, 2016), pp. 1–26.

9. James C. Scott, *Weapons of the Weak: Everyday Forms of Peasant Resistance* (New Haven/London: Yale University Press, 1985).
10. On migrant worker protests, see, for instance, Manfred Elfstrom, *Workers and Change in China: Resistance, Repression, Responsiveness* (Cambridge/New York: Cambridge University Press, 2021); Manfred Elfstrom and Sarosh Kuruvilla, "The Changing Nature of Labor Unrest in China." *ILR Review*, vol. 67, no. 2 (April 2014), pp. 453–480; Xu Zhun and Chen Ying, "Spatial Shift in China's Labor Struggles: Evidence and Implication." *Journal of Labor and Society*, vol. 22, no. 1 (March 2019), pp. 129–138; Daniel Fuchs, "Going West—Industrial Relocation and Migrant Labour Unrest in Chengdu and Chongqing" (PhD diss., Department of Development Studies, SOAS, University of London, 2019); Chan and Selden, "China's Rural Migrant Workers"; Pun Ngai, *Migrant Labor in China*; Rho Sungmin, "The Workers' Dilemma: Collective Action and Factory Workers in China" (PhD diss., Department of Political Science of Stanford University, 2015). https://tinyurl.com/3dtx5t8f (accessed April 20, 2022); Jeffrey Becker, *Social Ties, Resources, and Migrant Labor Contention in Contemporary China: From Peasants to Protesters* (Lanham/Boulder: Lexington Books, 2014); and Ching-Kwan Lee, "Pathways of Labor Activism."
11. Rho Sungmin, "The Workers' Dilemma," p. 55.
12. Elfstrom, *Workers and Change*, p. 33; Elfstrom and Kuruvilla, "The Changing Nature," pp. 457, 466.
13. Rho Sungmin, "The Workers' Dilemma," pp. 29, 31.
14. Beverly J. Silver and Zhang Lu, "China as an Emerging Epicenter of World Labor Unrest," in Hung Ho-fung, ed., *China and the Transformation of Global Capitalism* (Baltimore: Johns Hopkins University Press, 2009), pp. 174–187. https://tinyurl.com/47359s9u (accessed April 20, 2022).
15. Christian Göbel, "Social Unrest in China: A Bird's-eye View," in Teresa Wright, ed., *Handbook of Protests and Resistance in China* (Cheltenham/Northampton: Edward Elgar, 2019), pp. 27–45; Jay Chen Chih-Jou, "A Protest Society Evaluated: Popular Protests in China, 2000–2019." *Mobilization: An International Journal*, vol. 25, no. 5 (2020), pp. 641–660.
16. On industrial relocation see Fuchs, "Going West," chapter 5, and Xu Zhun and Chen Ying, "Spatial Shift," pp. 129–130; on relocation and wage arrears as causes of struggles in Shenzhen and Chongqing see Jake Lin, *Chinese Politics and Labor Movements* (Cham: Palgrave Macmillan, 2020), p. 172; on struggles moving west see Xu Zhun and Chen Ying, "Spatial Shift," pp. 134–135.
17. China Labour Bulletin, "Tower Crane Operators across China Organise Labour Day Strike over Low Pay." China Labour Bulletin website, May 2, 2018. https://tinyurl.com/yxnep823 (accessed April 20, 2022); Wang Jiang-

song, "The Significance of Crane Operators across China Going on Strike." China Change, May 7, 2018. https://tinyurl.com/s5fntx5a (accessed April 20, 2022); Tan Jiangying, "Truckers on Strike and the Structural Contradictions of China's Logistics Industry." China Change, June 15, 2018. https://tinyurl.com/mtpy37cz (accessed April 20, 2022).

18. For the different forms of migrant workers' protest and resistance, see Elfstrom, *Workers and Change*, pp. 27–31.
19. The overall number of arbitration, mediation, and labor court cases has steadily increased since the 1990s and plateaued at quite a high level in the second half of the 2010s; see China Labour Bulletin, "Beijing Court Tells Employers to Resolve Labour Disputes through Negotiation." China Labour Bulletin website, April 9, 2018. https://tinyurl.com/ypr3afj9 (accessed April 20, 2022); and Zhuang Wenjia and Chen Feng, "'Mediate First': The Revival of Mediation in Labour Dispute Resolution in China." *The China Quarterly* 222 (2015), pp. 380–402.
20. Pun Ngai, *Migrant Labor in China*, pp. 80–81.
21. The second generation was characterized as showing "three highs and one low" (*san gao yi di*): "high levels of education, career aspirations, and demands for material and psychological enjoyment, but low ability to endure hardship" (Rho Sungmin, "The Workers' Dilemma," p. 30).
22. Chris Chan King-Chi, "The Challenge of Labour in China: Strikes and the Changing Labour Regime in Global Factories" (PhD diss., Department of Sociology, University of Warwick, 2008). https://tinyurl.com/bdfvhbyd (accessed April 20, 2022), p. 30.
23. Chris Chan King-Chi and Pun Ngai, "The Making of a New Working Class? A Study of Collective Actions of Migrant Workers in South China." *The China Quarterly* 198 (June 2009), pp. 287–303.
24. Chan and Selden, "China's Rural Migrant Workers," p. 362; Pun Ngai and Chris Chan King-Chi, "The Subsumption of Class Discourse in China." *boundary 2*, vol. 35, no. 2 (2008), pp. 75–91; Ann Anagnost, "From 'Class' to 'Social Strata': Grasping the Social Totality in Reform-era China." *Third World Quarterly*, vol. 29, no. 3 (2008), pp. 497–519.
25. Pun Ngai, *Migrant Labor in China*, p. 60.
26. Xu Zhun and Chen Ying, "Spatial Shift," pp. 136–137.
27. Rho Sungmin calls this "atomized incorporation," which means: "the state institutionally incorporates workers as individuals via legal channels and, at the same time, tolerates isolated labor protests. Yet, the state has consistently demonstrated its resolve in eliminating any possibility for emergence of an organized labor movement" (Rho Sungmin, "The Workers' Dilemma," pp. 33–34).
28. Elfstrom, *Workers and Change*, p. 3.
29. Elfstrom differentiates an "orthodox" model, used against contained or smaller boundary-spanning forms of struggle (that were relatively easy to control), and a "high-risk" model, used against bigger boundary-spanning

and transgressive forms of struggle (that demanded more efforts by the state and measures that risked enabling or even provoking more struggles). See Elfstrom, *Workers and Change*, p. 9.

30. Ibid., p. 6.
31. Chuang, "Seeing through Muddied Waters, Part 2: An Interview on Jasic and Maoist Labor Activism." Chuang website, July 2, 2019. https://tinyurl.com/226ywhv6 (accessed April 20, 2022).
32. A phenomenon not restricted to the PRC; see Aziz Choudry and Dip Kapoor, eds., *NGOization: Complicity, Contradictions and Prospects* (London/New York: Zed Books, 2013).
33. The focus here lies on labor NGOs. Feminist NGOs will be discussed in the fourth section of the chapter. For a short history of LGBTIQ* NGOs in the PRC, see Stephanie Wang Yingyi, "Unfinished Revolution: An Overview of Three Decades of LGBT Activism in China." *Made in China Journal*, vol. 6, no. 1 (2021), pp. 90–95. https://tinyurl.com/56ej7u3d (accessed April 20, 2022).
34. Activists had more room in Hong Kong in these years, as the British colonial regime allowed the setting up of independent organizations. Even after the handover of Hong Kong to the PRC in 1997, NGOs could continue their activity in the PRC's new Special Administrative Region. They played a particular role, especially, in workers' organizing and struggles in the factory zone bordering on Hong Kong, until the CCP regime tightened its grip on labor activism in the PRC after 2015 and its control of social organizations in Hong Kong in 2020 and 2021.
35. Labor NGOs also filled a void. The CCP regime did not allow workers to organize independently. The state union ACFTU did not support workers' struggles and was not accepted by workers as a legitimate representative of their interests vis-à-vis state and private enterprises. Labor NGOs acted as mediators in areas of widespread protests like Guangdong province, organizing material support and "educating" migrant workers in using "legal rights" granted in state laws and regulations.
36. Chen Feng and Yang Xuehui, "Movement-oriented Labour NGOs in South China: Exit with Voice and Displaced Unionism." *China Information*, vol. 31, no. 2 (2017), pp. 155–175. Moderate labor NGOs were also criticized by activists and leftist observers for their paternalism and their focus on legal rights and education. See, for instance, Ching-Kwan Lee and Shen Yuan, "The Anti-Solidarity Machine? Labor Nongovernmental Organizations in China," in Sarosh Kuruvilla, Ching-Kwan Lee, and Mary E. Gallagher, eds., *From Iron Rice Bowl to Informalization: Markets, Workers, and the State in a Changing China* (Ithaca/London: ILR Press, 2011), pp. 173–187, and Eli Friedman, "External Pressure and Local Mobilization: Transnational Activism and the Emergence of the Chinese Labor Movement." *Mobilization*, vol. 14, no. 2 (June 2009), pp. 199–218.

37. Diana Fu, "Disguised Collective Action in China." *Comparative Political Studies*, vol. 50, no. 4 (2017), pp. 499–527; Diana Fu, *Mobilizing without the Masses. Control and Contention in China* (Cambridge/New York: Cambridge University Press, 2018).
38. Rho Sungmin, "The Workers' Dilemma," p. 41.
39. For more information, see Kevin Lin, "Workers on the Move—the Lide Strike." International Viewpoint, July 14, 2015. https://tinyurl.com/2n34ttec (accessed April 20, 2022); China Labour Bulletin, "The Lide Shoe Factory Workers' Campaign for Relocation Compensation." China Labour Bulletin website, June 22, 2015. https://tinyurl.com/5c8a54ph (accessed April 20, 2022); and Chen Feng and Yang Xuehui, "Movement-oriented Labour NGOs." The Panyu Migrant Workers Service Centre was among the groups targeted by police and state security during the crackdown in December 2015 (see the subsection "Regime Repression").
40. See the China Labour Bulletin website: https://clb.org.hk.
41. Today, Trotskyism has few followers in the PRC. It was different in the 1920s and 1930s, before campaigns and purges wiped them out in the 1940s.
42. A very useful resource was the blog "Wickedonna" (*feixinwen*, literally: no news) used by Lu Yuyu and Li Tingyu to compile a daily list of labor actions around the country by scanning through online resources. They collected about 70,000 incidents between 2013 and 2016 before they were arrested by the security forces and charged with "picking quarrels and provoking trouble" (*xunxin zishi*). For information see Chuang, "Picking Quarrels: Lu Yuyu, Li Tingyu and the Changing Cadence of Class Struggle in China." *Chuang Journal*, no. 2 (2019), pp. 361–422. https://tinyurl.com/bddrmzd5 (accessed April 20, 2022); Cao Yaxue, "Documenting Mass Protest Incidents: The Extraordinary Story of Two Ordinary Chinese." China Change, October 31, 2020. https://tinyurl.com/ya58sd7a (accessed April 20, 2022), and the Wickedonna blog: https://newsworthknowingcn.blogspot.com.
43. Websites included Utopia (*wu you zhi xiang*), China Workers Net (*zhongguo gongren wang*), New Workers (*xin gongren wang*), Red Song Society (*zhongguo honge hui*), Left Bank (*zuo an*), or Maoflag (*maozedong qizhi wang*).
44. Elfstrom, *Workers and Change*, p. 35; Pun Ngai, Lu Huilin, Guo Yuhua, and Shen Yuan, eds., *iSlaves: Ausbeutung und Widerstand in Chinas Weltmarktfabriken*—Übersetzt und herausgegeben von Ralf Ruckus (Vienna: Mandelbaum, 2013).
45. Shannon Lee, "'Doing Worker Work': Activist Workers and the Jasic Affair." Shannon Lee's China Blog, February 27, 2019. https://tinyurl.com/26zheydt (accessed April 20, 2022); Au Loong-Yu, "The Jasic Struggle in China's Political Context." *New Politics*, vol. XVII, no. 2 (2019). https://tinyurl.com/bddnnxds (accessed April 20, 2022).
46. Yi Xi, "New Foundations for Struggle and Solidarity: The Culmination of Development and Privatization on a Guangzhou Island." libcom.org, October

7, 2014. https://tinyurl.com/e5frz8jx (accessed April 20, 2022). Initiatives that tried to combine feminist or LGBTIQ* with labor issues or protests are *ku'er gongyou* (Queer Workers) and *jianjiao buluo* (Pepper Tribe); see Ian Tian Liujia, "Socialism from the Grassroots: New Directions of Leftist Organizing in Post-socialist China." *Upping the Anti*, issue 22 (January 30, 2022). https://tinyurl.com/2p9uvha8 (accessed April 20, 2022).

47. See the website of the support group: https://jiashigrsyt1.github.io/727oneyear

48. Wong Sue-Lin, "Chinese Students Assaulted at Pro-Marxist Society Protest." Reuters, November 2, 2018. https://tinyurl.com/2k2vew9z (accessed April 20, 2022); Yang Yuan, "Inside China's Crackdown on Young Marxists: Why Is the Communist Power Arresting and Detaining Leftist Students?" *Financial Times*, February 14, 2019. https://tinyurl.com/bdhwxrxd (accessed April 20, 2022).

49. For more on the Jasic case and the critique of the strategy used by Maoist groups, see Zhang Yueran, "The Jasic Struggle and the Future of the Chinese Labour Movement." *Made in China Journal*, vol. 3, no. 3 (July–September 2018), pp. 12–17. https://tinyurl.com/mvwbvpzz (accessed April 20, 2022); Shannon Lee, "Preliminary Thoughts on the Shenzhen Jasic Events." Shannon Lee's China Blog, September 17, 2018. https://tinyurl.com/mbkhad2c (accessed April 20, 2022); Chuang, "Seeing through Muddied Waters, Part 1: Jasic, Strikes and Unions." Chuang website, June 10, 2019. https://tinyurl.com/5n6wdemc (accessed April 20, 2022); Chuang, "Seeing through Muddied Waters, Part 2"; Qian Benli, "Jasic Struggle: Debate among Chinese Maoists." *Against the Current*, no. 200 (May–June 2019). https://tinyurl.com/89d84e8t (accessed April 20, 2022); and Ralf Ruckus, "Critical Perspectives on the 'Jasic Movement'—Suitable Tactics of Intervention?" nqch.org, January 18, 2020. https://tinyurl.com/yeycuts3 (accessed April 20, 2022), including a list of English and Chinese articles on the Jasic struggle.

50. On the Chongqing Model and support from Maoists and the New Left, see Cui Zhiyuan, "The Chongqing Experiment: The Way Forward for China?" in Mark Leonard, ed., *China 3.0* (London: European Council on Foreign Relations, 2012), pp. 26–31; Wang Hui, "The Rumour Machine: Wang Hui on the Dismissal of Bo Xilai." *London Review of Books*, vol. 34, no. 9 (2012), pp. 13–14; and Kerry Brown and Simone van Nieuwenhuizen, *China and the New Maoists* (London: Zed Books, 2016), chapter 4.

51. Chen Ziming, "Jian xi liang zhong Maopai: baohuangpai yu zaofanpai" (A Brief Analysis of the Two Types of Maoists: The Royalists and the Rebels). aisixiang.com, May 6, 2013. http://www.aisixiang.com/data/63649.html (accessed April 20, 2022).

52. Chris Buckley and Andrew Jacobs, "Maoists in China, Given New Life, Attack Dissent." *The New York Times*, January 4, 2015. http://nyti.ms/1KcSQiZ (accessed April 20, 2022).

53. Arif Dirlik, "Back to the Future: Contemporary China in the Perspective of Its Past, Circa 1980," in Wang Ban and Lu Jie, eds., *China and New Left Visions: Political and Cultural Interventions* (Lanham/Boulder: Lexington Books, 2012), pp. 33–34.
54. Zhao Suisheng, "Xi Jinping's Maoist Revival." *Journal of Democracy*, vol. 27, no. 3 (July 2016), pp. 83–97.
55. Timothy Cheek and David Ownby, "Make China Marxist Again: Under Xi Jinping, the Chinese Communist Party has reembraced Marx. But Xi's state Marxism is a top-down attempt to unify the population behind a nationalist ideology, not to inspire class struggle." *Dissent Magazine* (Fall 2018). https://tinyurl.com/4r9yzpe7 (accessed April 20, 2022).
56. These new campaigns draw on existing nationalist discourses the CCP leadership has been promoting, for instance, against the interests of or influences from regimes in the U.S. or Japan. In the past, mostly those from the Maoist Right have supported nationalist campaigns, for instance, the largely government-controlled anti-Japanese protests in 2012 about the Diaoyu/Senkaku Islands disputed by the regimes of the PRC and Japan; see Atsushi Okudera and Nozomu Hayashi, "Mao References in Anti-Japan Protests a Concern for Chinese Authorities." *Asahi Shimbun*, September 18, 2012. https://tinyurl.com/ms2b7aru (accessed July 31, 2022).
57. Ralf Ruckus, "Leitplanken für den Kapitalismus." *WOZ*, September 9, 2021. https://tinyurl.com/v3r7bupx (accessed April 20, 2022). In some ways, the promotion of "common prosperity" and the regime's interventions in labor conflicts (for instance, in the gig economy) resemble the Harmonious Society rhetoric and measures taken in the mid- and late 2000s under Hu Jintao. Both are limited state interventions into class relations with the aim of easing social tensions without changing the capitalist structures.
58. Zhang Yiqi, "Sheng wa shi jiashi yeshi guoshi" (Having a Child is Not Only a Family Affair but Also a State Affair). *Renmin Ribao* (*People's Daily*), August 6, 2018. http://politics.people.com.cn/n1/2018/0806/c1001-30210179.html (accessed April 13, 2022).
59. Friedrich Engels, "The Origin of the Family, Private Property and the State" [1884]. marxists.org, 2021. https://tinyurl.com/mpezjkme (accessed April 20, 2022).
60. Marilyn B. Young, "Chicken Little in China: Women after the Cultural Revolution," in Sonia Kruks, Rayna Rapp, and Marilyn B. Young, eds., *Promissory Notes: Women in the Transition to Socialism* (New York: Monthly Review Press, 1989), p. 236.
61. This position was contested in left-wing feminist circles, as some rather emphasized the improvements for women* in the PRC in the socialist period (e.g. in their legal status and their participation in the labor force). However, Phyllis Andors coined the term of the "unfinished liberation of Chinese women" under socialism (Phyllis Andors, *The Unfinished Liberation of Chinese Women, 1949–1980* [Bloomington: Indiana University Press, 1983]),

and Judith Stacey wrote that in the PRC, "[s]ocialism has not liberated women because a socialist mode of production has proven to be compatible with a patriarchal sex-gender system. [...] [S]ocialism can reform and reconstruct a besieged patriarchal order so that it comes to rest on new and firmer joists" (Judith Stacey, *Patriarchy and Socialist Revolution in China* [Berkeley/Los Angeles: University of California Press, 1983], p. 266).

62. This is, actually, connected: because the party had dissolved the communes on the countryside which had managed birth control measures (and controlled women* beforehand), it feared a higher birth rate and introduced the One-Child Policy to prevent that development.
63. On prostitution, see, for instance, Zheng Tiantian, *Red Lights: The Lives of Sex Workers in Postsocialist China* (Minneapolis/London: University of Minnesota Press, 2009); on forms of concubinage or "*ernai*" (mistress; literally: second wife) see Xiao Suowei, "Women's Work: How 'Ernai' Mistresses Bolster Fragile Masculinity (Part 1)." *Sixth Tone*, May 15, 2019. https://tinyurl.com/5c5xh8rd (accessed April 20, 2022), and Xiao Suowei, "For Love or Money: What Drives China's Migrant Mistresses? (Part 2)." *Sixth Tone*, May 21, 2019. https://tinyurl.com/6y96ph62 (accessed April 20, 2022).
64. Zhang Qin, "Negotiating Change: The Emergence and Development of the Women's Movement in Contemporary China" (PhD diss., Rutgers, State University of New Jersey, New Brunswick, 2008), p. 4.
65. Yan Hairong, *New Masters, New Servants: Migration, Development, and Women Workers in China* (Durham/London: Duke University Press, 2008), chapter 3.
66. Hannah Schling, "Gender, Temporality, and the Reproduction of Labour Power: Women Migrant Workers in South China." *Sozial.Geschichte Online* 14 (2014), pp. 42–61. https://tinyurl.com/5n6bd4wh (accessed April 20, 2022).
67. Liu Jieyu, *Gender and Work in Urban China: Women Workers of the Unlucky Generation* (London/New York: Routledge, 2007).
68. "Between 1990 to 2010, the average income of Chinese urban women relative to men had decreased from 78 to 67 percent, while for their rural counterparts this ratio had decreased from 79 to 60 percent" (Dong Yige, "Does China Have a Feminist Movement from the Left?" *Made in China Journal*, vol. 4, no. 1 [2019], p. 61 [quoting ACWF sources]. https://tinyurl.com/y795fjf7 [accessed April 20, 2022]).
69. Helen Davidson, "China's Birthrate Falls to 61-year Low Despite Moves to Stave Off Demographic Crisis." *The Guardian*, January 17, 2022. https://tinyurl.com/4k674p75 (accessed April 20, 2022).
70. Several factors play a role here, among them the "overaging" of the population, the fact that due to the One-Child Policy one child is solely responsible for the situation of their parents (or even grandparents), changing attitudes of younger people in the PRC towards their filial duties, and the increase in the cost of housing and health.

71. This includes not just the outright refusal of marriage or child-bearing, but also other forms of deviance, for instance, women* deciding to focus just on their career or on "marrying up" while refusing to be obedient to husbands or male relatives as expected. On "Made-in-China" feminism see Angela Wu Xiao and Dong Yige, "What is Made-in-China Feminism(s)? Gender Discontent and Class Friction in Post-socialist China." *Critical Asian Studies*, vol. 51, no. 4 (2019), pp. 1–22.
72. Zeng Jinyan, "Chinese Feminism under (Self-)Censorship: Practice and Knowledge Production." *Made in China Journal*, vol. 6, no. 2 (2021), p. 166. https://tinyurl.com/2p8y75kc (accessed April 20, 2022).
73. Peter Zarrow, "He Zhen and Anarcho-feminism in China." *Journal of Asian Studies*, vol. 47, no. 4 (November 1988), pp. 796–813; Amy Qin, "Qiu Jin (1875–1907)—A Feminist Poet and Revolutionary Who Became a Martyr Known as China's 'Joan of Arc.'" *The New York Times*, March 8, 2018. https://www.nytimes.com/interactive/2018/obituaries/overlooked-qiu-jin.html (accessed April 20, 2022); and Sharon R. Wesoky, "Bringing the Jia Back into Guojia: Engendering Chinese Intellectual Politics." *Signs: Journal of Women in Culture and Society*, vol. 40, no. 3 (2015), pp. 647–666.
74. Zhang Qin, "Negotiating Change," p. 126.
75. Christina Gilmartin, "Gender, Politics, and Patriarchy in China: The Experiences of Early Women Communists, 1920–27," in Kruks et al., *Promissory Notes*, p. 101. More on this in the following subsections.
76. Wang Zheng mentions "an early usage of 'state feminists,' referring to feminists employed as bureaucrats in positions of power or women politicians who promote gender equality policies" (Wang Zheng, "'State Feminism'? Gender and Socialist State Formation in Maoist China." *Feminist Studies*, vol. 31, no. 3 [2005], p. 519). For a discussion of the term "state feminism" see Dorothy McBride Stetson and Amy Mazur, eds., *Comparative State Feminism* (Thousand Oaks/London: Sage Publications, 1995). The ACWF runs its own English website: https://www.womenofchina.cn.
77. Jin Yihong, "The All-China Women's Federation: Challenges and Trends," in Hsiung Ping-Chun, Maria Jaschok, and Cecilia Milwertz, eds., *Chinese Women Organizing: Cadres, Feminists, Muslims, Queers* (Oxford/New York: Berg, 2001), pp. 125–126.
78. For instance, the ACWF actively promoted the reemployment of unemployed female* urban state workers as domestic care workers; see Astrid Lipinsky, *Der Chinesische Frauenverband: Eine kommunistische Massenorganisation unter marktwirtschaftlichen Bedingungen* (Berlin: LIT Verlag, 2006), pp. 230ff.
79. Maria Jaschok, Cecilia Milwertz, and Hsiung Ping-Chun, "Introduction," in Hsiung Ping-Chun et al., *Chinese Women Organizing*, p. 9.
80. Zhang Qin, "Negotiating Change," p. 4. According to Wang Zheng, it is still important to acknowledge women*'s agency in the PRC that finds spaces within the state structures to push for women*'s interests, despite the "patri-

archal centralized power structure" or the dominance of the "patriarchal state" (Wang Zheng, "State Feminism," p. 520).

81. Jaschok et al., "Introduction," p. 9.
82. The debate and different positions among feminists in the PRC were partly inspired and, therefore, show similarities with debates on "equality" and "difference" in the U.S. and other (Western) countries in the 1980s and 1990s. Criticisms of feminist positions focusing on gender and difference were later formulated by feminists in the PRC as well, for instance by critical socialist feminists (see the next subsection).
83. Zhang Qin, "Negotiating Change," p. 6. Besides pushing for improvements for women* and fighting against sexist violence, some of these activities also filled in the gaps left by the state's partial withdrawal from social welfare and education for women* in the reform period.
84. Elizabeth Croll, "New Spaces, New Voices: Women Organizing in Twentieth-century China," in Hsiung Ping-Chun et al., *Chinese Women Organizing*, p. 35; Zhang Qin, "Negotiating Change," pp. 5, 112, 119. The Global Feminisms Project conducted interviews with some ACWF cadres who were also involved in feminist NGOs in the 1990s and early 2000s; see Global Feminisms Project, "China Interviews." Global Feminisms Project website (2021). https://tinyurl.com/3br6rz3n (accessed April 20, 2022).
85. Jaschok et al., "Introduction," p. 13.
86. Nicola Spakowski uses that term; see Nicola Spakowski, "Socialist Feminism in Postsocialist China." *positions*, vol. 26, no. 4 (2018), pp. 561–592.
87. Others who played a role in discussions along the lines of critical socialist feminism include Yan Hairong, Pun Ngai, Zhong Xueping, Bai Di, Lü Xinyu, He Guimei, Gao Xiaoxian, and Zuo Jiping (Spakowski, "Socialist Feminism," pp. 562–563).
88. Ibid., p. 567; Dong Limin, "Nüxingzhuyi: Bentuhua ji qi weidu" (Feminism: Indigenization and Its Dimensions), *Nankai Xuebao*, no. 2 (2005), p. 11. The domination of theoretical debates and organizing by feminist actors from the U.S. and other "Western" countries could also be seen in Eastern Europe in the 1990s. It surely reflects the reproduction of unequal and neo-colonial relations in social and left-wing movements. What remains weak in this critique is the generalization of "Western" and the simple juxtaposition of "Western" feminism vs. "Eastern" (or Chinese) feminism. That understates the many-voiced debates on feminist issues within the "Western" world (North America, Europe, Australia/New Zealand) and, more importantly, it ignores other feminist currents that play a role in shaping the global debates, that is, the multitude of feminist positions rooted in local experiences in the "Eastern" worlds (Eastern Europe, East Asia) and the "Southern" worlds (Africa, South America, Middle East, South and Southeast Asia, Pacific).
89. Spakowski, "Socialist Feminism," pp. 578–579.
90. Ibid., p. 569; also see Wesoky, "Bringing the Jia Back into Guojia."
91. On Nancy Fraser's critique, see, for instance, Nancy Fraser, "Feminism, Capitalism and the Cunning of History." *New Left Review* 56 (2009), pp. 97–117.

92. This included groups that organized around issues (at that time) not recognized by some women*'s groups, like lesbian initiatives. See He Xiaopei, "Chinese Queer (Tongzhi) Women Organizing in the 1990s," in Hsiung Ping-Chun et al., *Chinese Women Organizing*, pp. 41–59.
93. Zhang Qin, "Negotiating Change," p. 102.
94. Lü Pin, "Finding a Voice. A Leading Chinese Feminist Tells Her Story." *Logic*, no. 7 (2019). https://tinyurl.com/4b8ambdj (accessed April 20, 2022).
95. Dong Yige, "Does China Have a Feminist Movement from the Left?", p. 59.
96. For more information about (and photos of) the street actions, see Mimiyana, "Zhongguo qingnian nüquan yundong jianshi—shang (2012–2013)" (Short History of China's Movement of Young Feminists, 1st part, 2012–2013). chinesefeminism.org (April 5, 2021). https://tinyurl.com/mv3upcrj (accessed April 20, 2022) and Mimiyana, "Zhongguo qingnian nüquan yundong jianshi—xia (2014–2019)" (Short History of China's Movement of Young Feminists, 2nd part, 2014–2019). chinesefeminism.org (April 5, 2021). https://tinyurl.com/yc7tck5h (accessed April 20, 2022).
97. Dong Yige, "Does China Have a Feminist Movement from the Left?", p. 60.
98. Feminists in (or from) the PRC adapted the #Metoo hashtag, partly in order to avoid censorship, and used the character for *mi* (for rice in Chinese) and *tu* (for rabbit).
99. "[T]hree central features of the #MeToo movement in China enabled it to form and spread in the context of an authoritarian, oppressive, highly controlled and surveilled party-state: (1) decentralized organizing by numerous nonprofessional activists [volunteer groups of members who often did not know each other well], (2) extensive use of social media [people who knew how to outsmart censorship temporarily], and (3) active domestic and overseas collaboration [including diaspora groups of feminists, some of whom had left China earlier due to repression]" (Xiong Jing and Dušica Ristivojević, "#MeToo in China: How Do the Voiceless Rise Up in an Authoritarian State?" *Politics & Gender*, vol. 17, no. 3 [2021], p. 490).
100. Xiong Jing and Ristivojević, "#MeToo in China," p. 494.
101. Zhang Qin, "Negotiating Change," p. 104.
102. Wang Zheng, "Detention of the Feminist Five in China." *Feminist Studies*, vol. 41, no. 2 (2015), pp. 476–482.
103. Xiong Jing and Ristivojević, "#MeToo in China," p. 492.
104. Feng Jiayun, "China Contemplates Better Laws to Promote Gender Equality, but Remains Hostile to 'Radical' Feminist Campaigns." SupChina, December 22, 2021. https://tinyurl.com/36t2f35f (accessed April 20, 2022).
105. Xiong Jing and Ristivojević, "#MeToo in China," p. 497, referencing the Civil Code of the People's Republic of China, Article 1010, that came into effect on January 1, 2021.
106. Zeng Jinyan, "Chinese Feminism under (Self-)Censorship," p. 166.
107. Elfstrom, *Workers and Change*, p. 13.

6 CONCLUSIONS

1. The continuity of labor unrest and strikes between the early 1970s and the late 1980s is not well documented, though, and needs more research.
2. The book does not cover all social protests since 1949 in the PRC. Not discussed, for instance, are peasant protests during the GLF in the late 1950s/early 1960s, nor, in recent years, against the capitalization of agriculture and land theft.
3. Elizabeth J. Perry, "Shanghai's Strike Wave of 1957." *The China Quarterly* 137 (March 1994), p. 25.
4. For a historical account of the CCP regime's usage of concession, cooptation, and repression to contain social movements and resistance from below in the PRC from 1949 up to today, as well as of the dynamic of struggles from below, see Ralf Ruckus, *The Communist Road to Capitalism: How Social Unrest and Containment Have Pushed China's (R)evolution since 1949* (Oakland: PM Press, 2021).
5. See Yang Guobin, *The Red Guard Generation and Political Activism in China* (New York: Columbia University Press, 2016).
6. The left in (West) Germany, the example cited in the introduction, has had different conditions in which to operate. Left-wing actors mostly had the possibility to organize openly both socially and politically, to publish political programs, and to voice critique and engage in public debates on exploitation, repression, and the role of the government. However, left-wing forces in Germany also faced repression. In West Germany (and the whole of Germany after reunification in 1990) this included, for instance, the banning of some political parties, the criminalization of left-wing mobilizations, police harassment of activists, or activists being banned from civil servant jobs. The extent, harshness, and duration of anti-leftist measures in the PRC led to the particular landscape of left-wing activity that changed over time. It is important to mention, that the anti-leftist measures left-wing dissenters faced in East Germany from the late 1940s until 1989 were similar to those used in the PRC.
7. For an elaborated version of this argument, see the Conclusion in Ruckus, *The Communist Road to Capitalism*.
8. For short definitions of these four terms, see the third section of chapter 1. On the term exploitation also see footnote 10 in this chapter.
9. As mentioned in chapter 1, further differentiating and placing each group or current not just in one of the four squares but at specific positions along the two scales would demand further investigation and more precise information on their position regarding the distribution of wealth and power. Such data would include particular positions on labor relations, gender politics, migration regimes, environmental policies, organizational hierarchies, (direct) democracy, and more. This exceeds the scope of this inquiry.

10. While the term "exploitative" is used here for the socialist and the capitalist period, the mechanisms of exploitation were, indeed, different in certain aspects. In both periods, women*'s labor, usually unwaged or low-waged, was exploited for the reproduction of labor power. Urban and rural workers had to work longer than needed for their reproduction, and the result of their surplus labor was appropriated, accumulated, and redistributed. During the socialist period, this was done through the state system of purchasing, pricing, taxation, and allocation. Most peasants and precarious workers lived in poor conditions, had low wages and little access to benefits, welfare, higher education, or positions of economic or political influence and power while certain sections of urban workers had better conditions and opportunities. Upper sections of state cadres used their status to gain higher remuneration and much better access to benefits, welfare, higher education, and positions of economic and political influence and power. During the capitalist period, private and state entrepreneurs appropriated surpluses, accumulated personal profits, and influenced political power, while state structures continued to play a central role in reproducing and securing the exploitative mechanisms.
11. Not listed here is the right-wing, liberal, or pro-"Western" capitalist opposition to the CCP regime that has formed at various times between 1949 and the late 1980s. This kind of opposition was voiced, for instance, during the Hundred Flowers Movement in 1957 and the Democracy Wall Movement 1978–80. It remained mostly small, isolated, and was harshly repressed (for instance, through anti-rightist campaigns that affected other political currents as well).
12. For a detailed account of the liberals in the PRC since the 1990s, see Li Junpeng, "The Making of Liberal Intellectuals in Post-Tiananmen China" (PhD diss., Graduate School of Arts and Sciences, Columbia University, New York, 2017). https://tinyurl.com/2wuc8vrn (accessed April 20, 2022). The liberals included "left" liberals who promote a more egalitarian distribution of wealth. They would hover somewhere on the edge between the bottom left and the bottom right square. Other right-wing tendencies sympathizing with nationalism, fascism, male supremacy, or Han supremacy existed inside and outside the CCP but are not analyzed here.
13. For a short discussion of the historical failure of Marxism-Leninism and social democracy, see the section "Failure of the Leftist Grand Narratives" in Ruckus, *The Communist Road to Capitalism*, pp. 182ff.
14. Mao Tse-Tung, "The Debate on the Co-operative Transformation of Agriculture and the Current Class Struggle (October 11, 1955)," in *Selected Works of Mao Tse-Tung*, vol. 5 (Oxford/New York: Pergamon Press, 1977), pp. 230–231.
15. Chen Feng, "An Unfinished Battle in China: The Leftist Criticism of the Reform and the Third Thought Emancipation." *The China Quarterly* 158 (1999), p. 466.

16. When, in 2021, the CCP regime under Xi Jinping began to promote "common prosperity" (*gongtong fuyu*) and call on private companies to contribute to society, commentators saw this as a sign of the socialist orientation of the regime. In reality, the CCP is promoting the limited redistribution of wealth in order to maintain social stability. Its programs of poverty relief or other welfare measures are part of quasi-Keynesian policies. See Ralf Ruckus, "Leitplanken für den Kapitalismus." *WOZ*, September 9, 2021. https://tinyurl.com/v3r7bupx (accessed April 20, 2022).
17. There are further influences not discussed here, like neoconservatism. Its propositions have "been crucial as theoretical fuel for the development of CCP ideology over the last three decades. The elevation of a former neoconservative intellectual, Wang Huning, to the Standing Committee of the Politburo, the highest body of the CCP, in 2017, is an indication of its lasting impact on successive leadership generations. Indeed, the articulation of the 'Chinese Dream' under Xi Jinping can be viewed as an amalgamate of a neo-Confucian appeal for meritocratic elite governance and a neo-Conservative defense of 'authoritarian modernity'" (Andreas Møller Mulvad, "China's Ideological Spectrum: A Two-dimensional Model of Elite Intellectuals' Visions." *Theory and Society*, vol. 47 [2018], p. 645).
18. The CCP's political intervention and monetary investment in Marxist scholarship also earns it the support of parts of the left in other corners of the world.
19. Those who do not follow the official line also face online attacks by CCP supporters such as those called Little Pink (*xiaofenhong*; young volunteers active, for instance, on Twitter or Instagram, who attack people who criticize the CCP regime) or the 50 Cent Army (*wumao dang*; online commentators paid by the state who support the CCP regime); see Fang Kecheng and Maria Repnikova, "Demystifying 'Little Pink': The Creation and Evolution of a Gendered Label for Nationalistic Activists in China." *New Media & Society*, vol. 20, no. 6 (2018), pp. 2062–2086; Han Rongbin, "Defending the Authoritarian Regime Online: China's 'Voluntary Fifty-cent Army'." *The China Quarterly* 224 (2015), pp. 1006–1025; and Jason Y. Wu, "Categorical Confusion: Ideological Labels in China." *Political Research Quarterly*, online first, September 9, 2020, p. 8. https://tinyurl.com/yskye96d (accessed April 20, 2022).
20. Arif Dirlik, "Back to the Future: Contemporary China in the Perspective of Its Past, Circa 1980," in Wang Ban and Lu Jie, eds., *China and New Left Visions: Political and Cultural Interventions* (Lanham/Boulder: Lexington Books, 2012), p. 18.
21. Cheng Yinghong, "Che Guevara: Dramatizing China's Divided Intelligentsia at the Turn of the Century." *Modern Chinese Literature and Culture*, vol. 15, no. 2 (Fall 2003), p. 27.
22. To be more precise, backing Chinese nationalism or the current CCP regime does not just mean endorsing the CCP's authoritarian policies in the PRC, including its neocolonial strategy in Xinjiang, but also its expansionist or

even imperialist strategy globally, and its support for capitalist and authoritarian regimes in other parts of the world.

23. For a list of key aspects of left-wing politics and a list of elements for a left-wing strategy, see Ruckus, *The Communist Road to Capitalism*, Conclusion, third section.
24. For a more detailed argument on the potential instability of the CCP regime, see ibid., pp. 173ff.
25. Manfred Elfstrom, *Workers and Change in China: Resistance, Repression, Responsiveness* (Cambridge/New York: Cambridge University Press, 2021), p. 161.

EPILOGUE

1. See, for instance, Jack Shenker, "This Wave of Global Protest Is Being Led by the Children of the Financial Crash." *Guardian*, October 29, 2019. https://tinyurl.com/yy76gfw8 (accessed July 31, 2022), and Joseph Choonara, "A New Cycle of Revolt." *International Socialism* no. 165, December 2019. https://tinyurl.com/yckztb8r (accessed July 31, 2022).
2. Nikhil Kumar, "War, Protest and Spiking Prices: How spiraling inflation is setting the world on fire. As the Ukraine war rages on, driving up the cost of fuel and food, high prices have sparked unrest around the world." *Grid*, July 6, 2022. https://tinyurl.com/24ynek9j (accessed July 31, 2022).

Works Cited

Ahlers, Anna L. *Rural Policy Implementation in Contemporary China: New Socialist Countryside*. London/New York: Routledge, 2014.

Anagnost, Ann. "From 'Class' to 'Social Strata': Grasping the Social Totality in Reform-era China." *Third World Quarterly*, vol. 29, no. 3 (2008), pp. 497–519.

Andors, Phyllis. *The Unfinished Liberation of Chinese Women, 1949–1980*. Bloomington: Indiana University Press, 1983.

Andors, Stephen. *China's Industrial Revolution: Politics, Planning, and Management, 1949 to the Present*. New York: Pantheon Books, 1977.

Andreas, Joel. *Disenfranchised: The Rise and Fall of Industrial Citizenship in China*. Oxford: Oxford University Press, 2019.

Andreas, Joel, and Dong Yige. "The Brief, Tumultuous History of 'Big Democracy' in China's Factories." *Modern China*, vol. 44, no. 5 (2018), pp. 455–496.

Au Loong-Yu. "The Jasic Struggle in China's Political Context." *New Politics*, vol. XVII, no. 2 (2019). https://tinyurl.com/bddnnxds (accessed April 20, 2022).

Barmé, Geremie R., ed. *Shades of Mao: The Posthumous Cult of the Great Leader*. New York/London: M.E. Sharpe, 1996.

Barmé, Geremie R. "The Irresistible Fall and Rise of Chairman Mao," in *Shades of Mao: The Posthumous Cult of the Great Leader*, edited by Geremie R. Barmé, pp. 3–73. New York/London: M.E. Sharpe, 1996.

Becker, Jeffrey. *Social Ties, Resources, and Migrant Labor Contention in Contemporary China: From Peasants to Protesters*. Lanham/Boulder: Lexington Books, 2014.

Benton, Gregor, and Alan Hunter, eds. *Wild Lily, Prairie Fire: China's Road to Democracy, Yan'an to Tian'anmen, 1942–1989*. Princeton: Princeton University Press, 1995.

Benton, Gregor, and Alan Hunter. "Introduction," in *Wild Lily, Prairie Fire: China's Road to Democracy, Yan'an to Tian'anmen, 1942–1989*, edited by Gregor Benton and Alan Hunter, pp. 3–68. Princeton: Princeton University Press, 1995.

Bernstein, Thomas P. "Instability in Rural China," in *Is China Unstable? Assessing the Factors*, edited by David Shambaugh, pp. 95–111. Armonk/London: M.E. Sharpe, 2000.

Bernstein, Thomas P., and Lü Xiaobo. *Taxation without Representation in Contemporary Rural China*. Cambridge/New York: Cambridge University Press, 2003.

Blanchette, Jude. *China's New Red Guards: The Return of Radicalism and the Rebirth of Mao Zedong*. Oxford: Oxford University Press, 2019.

Blecher, Marc. "Hegemony and Workers' Politics in China." *The China Quarterly* 170 (June 2002), pp. 283–303.

Brodsgaard, Kjeld Erik. "The Democracy Movement in China, 1978–1979: Opposition Movements, Wall Poster Campaigns, and Underground Journals." *Asian Survey*, vol. 21, no. 7 (July 1981), pp. 747–774.

Brodsgaard, Kjeld Erik. "Paradigmatic Change: Readjustment and Reform in the Chinese Economy, 1953-1981, Part I." *Modern China*, vol. 9, no. 1 (1983), pp. 37–83.

Brown, Kerry, and Simone van Nieuwenhuizen. *China and the New Maoists*. London: Zed Books, 2016.

Bryson, Maurice C., and William R. McDill. "The Political Spectrum: A Bi-dimensional Approach." *Rampart Journal of Individualist Thought*, vol. IV, no. 2 (1968), pp. 19–26. https://tinyurl.com/2p8d6zbr (accessed April 20, 2022).

Buckley, Chris, and Andrew Jacobs. "Maoists in China, Given New Life, Attack Dissent." *The New York Times*, January 4, 2015. http://nyti.ms/1KcSQiZ (accessed April 20, 2022).

Byler, Darren. *Terror Capitalism: Uyghur Dispossession and Masculinity in a Chinese City*. Durham: Duke University Press, 2021.

Byler, Darren. "Standing with the Oppressed: On Colonialism and Terror Capitalism in Xinjiang." nqch.org, March 17, 2021. https://tinyurl.com/4yr2tm2v (accessed August 13, 2022).

Cai Yongshun. *State and Laid-off Workers in Reform China: The Silence and Collective Action of the Retrenched*. London/New York: Routledge, 2006.

Cai Yongshun. "State Policies and Chinese Laid-off Workers' Limited Resistance," in *Laid-off Workers in a Workers' State: Unemployment with Chinese Characteristics*, edited by Thomas B. Gold, William Hurst, Won Jaeyoun, and Li Qiang, pp. 203–223. New York: Palgrave Macmillan, 2009.

Calhoun, Craig, and Jeffrey N. Wasserstrom. "The Cultural Revolution and the Democracy Movement of 1989: Complexity in Historical Connections," in *The Chinese Cultural Revolution Reconsidered: Beyond Purge and Holocaust*, edited by Law Kam-yee, pp. 241–261. Basingstoke/New York: Palgrave Macmillan, 2003.

Cao Yaxue. "Documenting Mass Protest Incidents: The Extraordinary Story of Two Ordinary Chinese." China Change, October 31, 2020. https://tinyurl.com/ya58sd7a (accessed April 20, 2022).

Chan, Anita. "China's Long Winter." *Monthly Review*, vol. 41, no. 8 (January 1990), pp. 1–14.

Chan, Anita. "Protest in a Hunan County Town: The Profile of a Democracy Movement Activist in China's Backwaters," in *The Pro-democracy Protests in China: Reports from the Provinces*, edited by Jonathan Unger, pp. 137–149. Armonk: M.E. Sharpe, 1991.

Chan, Anita, and Jonathan Unger. "Voices from the Protest Movement, Chongqing, Sichuan." *Australian Journal of Chinese Affairs* 24 (July 1990), pp. 259–279.

Chan, Anita, Stanley Rosen, and Jonathan Unger, eds. *On Socialist Democracy and the Chinese Legal System: The Li Yizhe Debates*. Armonk: M.E. Sharpe, 1985.

Chan, Jenny, and Mark Selden. "China's Rural Migrant Workers and Labour Politics," in *Handbook on Class and Social Stratification in China*, edited by Guo Yingjie, pp. 362–382. Cheltenham/Northampton: Edward Elgar, 2016.

Chan King-Chi, Chris. "The Challenge of Labour in China: Strikes and the Changing Labour Regime in Global Factories." PhD diss., Department of Sociology, University of Warwick, 2008. https://tinyurl.com/bdfvhbyd (accessed April 20, 2022).

Chan King-Chi, Chris, and Pun Ngai. "The Making of a New Working Class? A Study of Collective Actions of Migrant Workers in South China." *The China Quarterly* 198 (June 2009), pp. 287–303.

Chang, Parris H. "The Anti-Lin Piao and Confucius Campaign: Its Meaning and Purposes." *Asian Survey*, vol. 14, no. 10 (October 1974), pp. 871–886.

Cheek, Timothy, and David Ownby. "Make China Marxist Again: Under Xi Jinping, the Chinese Communist Party has reembraced Marx. But Xi's state Marxism is a top-down attempt to unify the population behind a nationalist ideology, not to inspire class struggle." *Dissent Magazine* (Fall 2018). https://tinyurl.com/4r9yzpe7 (accessed April 20, 2022).

Chen Chih-Jou, Jay. "A Protest Society Evaluated: Popular Protests in China, 2000–2019." *Mobilization: An International Journal*, vol. 25, no. 5 (2020), pp. 641–660.

Chen Chih-Jou, Jay. "Peasant Protests over Land Seizures in Rural China." *Journal of Peasant Studies*, vol. 47, no. 6 (October 2020), pp. 1327–1347.

Chen Erjin. *China—Crossroads Socialism: An Unofficial Manifesto for Proletarian Democracy*. London: Verso, 1984.

Chen Feng. "An Unfinished Battle in China: The Leftist Criticism of the Reform and the Third Thought Emancipation." *The China Quarterly* 158 (June 1999), pp. 447–467.

Chen Feng. "Against the State: Labor Protests in China in the 1950s." *Modern China*, vol. 40, no. 5 (2014), pp. 488–518.

Chen Feng and Yang Xuehui. "Movement-oriented Labour NGOs in South China: Exit with Voice and Displaced Unionism." *China Information*, vol. 31, no. 2 (2017), pp. 155–175.

Chen Guidi and Wu Chuntao. *Will the Boat Sink the Water? The Life of China's Peasants*. New York: Public Affairs, 2006.

Chen Ruoxi. *Democracy Wall and the Unofficial Journals*. Berkeley: University of California, 1982.

Chen Ziming. "Jian xi liang zhong Maopai: baohuangpai yu zaofanpai" (A Brief Analysis of the Two Types of Maoists: The Royalists and the Rebels), aisixiang.com, May 6, 2013. http://www.aisixiang.com/data/63649.html (accessed April 20, 2022).

Cheng Yinghong. "Che Guevara: Dramatizing China's Divided Intelligentsia at the Turn of the Century." *Modern Chinese Literature and Culture*, vol. 15, no. 2 (Fall 2003), pp. 1–43.

Cheng Zhiming. "The Changing Pattern of State Workers' Labour Resistance in Shaanxi Province, China." *Communication, Politics and Culture*, vol. 45, no. 2 (2012), pp. 197–216.

China Digital Space. "Sun Zhigang," China Digital Space website, undated. https://tinyurl.com/2a95npra (accessed August 7, 2022).

China Labour Bulletin. "Beijing Court Tells Employers to Resolve Labour Disputes through Negotiation." China Labour Bulletin website, April 9, 2018. https://tinyurl.com/ypr3afj9 (accessed April 20, 2022).

China Labour Bulletin. "The Liaoyang Workers' Struggle: Portrait of a Movement." China Labour Bulletin website, July 2003. https://tinyurl.com/bdewzx9b (accessed April 20, 2022).

China Labour Bulletin. "The Lide Shoe Factory Workers' Campaign for Relocation Compensation." China Labour Bulletin website, June 22, 2015. https://tinyurl.com/5c8a54ph (accessed April 20, 2022).

China Labour Bulletin. "Tower Crane Operators across China Organise Labour Day Strike over Low Pay." China Labour Bulletin website, May 2, 2018. https://tinyurl.com/yxnep823 (accessed April 20, 2022).

China Media Project (CMP). "The CMP Dictionary: Harmonious Society." China Media Project, May 14, 2021. https://tinyurl.com/yckzhvrx (accessed April 20, 2022).

Chinese Communist Party. *Decision of the Central Committee of the Chinese Communist Party Concerning the Great Proletarian Cultural Revolution*. Beijing: Foreign Languages Press, 1966. https://tinyurl.com/3ubakryn (accessed April 20, 2022).

Chinese Communist Party. "Resolution on Certain Questions in the History of Our Party Since the Founding of the People's Republic of China (Adopted by the Sixth Plenary Session of the Eleventh Central Committee of the Chinese Communist Party on June 27, 1981)." marxists.org. https://tinyurl.com/ym8mafjt (accessed April 20, 2022).

Choonara, Joseph. "A New Cycle of Revolt." *International Socialism*, no. 165 (December 2019). https://tinyurl.com/yckztb8r (accessed July 31, 2022).

Choudry, Aziz, and Dip Kapoor, eds. *NGOization: Complicity, Contradictions and Prospects*. London/New York: Zed Books, 2013.

Christiansen, Flemming, Susanne Posborg, and Anne Wedell-Wedellsborg. *Die demokratische Bewegung in China: Revolution im Sozialismus?* München: Verlag Simon and Magiera, 1981.

Chuang. "Picking Quarrels: Lu Yuyu, Li Tingyu and the Changing Cadence of Class Struggle in China." *Chuang Journal*, no. 2 (2019), pp. 361–422. https://tinyurl.com/bddrmzd5 (accessed April 20, 2022).

Chuang. "Seeing through Muddied Waters, Part 1: Jasic, Strikes and Unions." Chuang website, June 10, 2019. https://tinyurl.com/5n6wdemc (accessed April 20, 2022).

Chuang. "Seeing through Muddied Waters, Part 2: An Interview on Jasic and Maoist Labor Activism." Chuang website, July 2, 2019. https://tinyurl.com/226ywhv6 (accessed April 20, 2022).

Conceison, Claire. *Significant Other: Staging the American in China*. Honolulu: University of Hawai'i Press, 2004.

Connery, Christopher. "The Chinese Left: Contexts and Strategies." theasiadialogue.com, October 21, 2016. https://tinyurl.com/yckpypnf (accessed April 20, 2022).

Croll, Elizabeth. "New Spaces, New Voices: Women Organizing in Twentieth-century China," in *Chinese Women Organizing: Cadres, Feminists, Muslims, Queers*, edited by Hsiung Ping-Chun, Maria Jaschok, and Cecilia Milwertz, pp. 25–40. Oxford/New York: Berg, 2001.

Cui Zhiyuan. "The Chongqing Experiment: The Way Forward for China?" in *China 3.0*, edited by Mark Leonard, pp. 26–31. London: European Council on Foreign Relations, 2012.

Davidson, Helen. "China's Birthrate Falls to 61-year Low Despite Moves to Stave Off Demographic Crisis." *The Guardian*, January 17, 2022. https://tinyurl.com/4k674p75 (accessed April 20, 2022).

Day, Alexander F. *The Peasant in Post-socialist China: History, Politics, and Capitalism*. Cambridge: Cambridge University Press, 2013.

Day, Alexander F., and Mindi Schneider. "The End of Alternatives? Capitalist Transformation, Rural Activism and the Politics of Possibility in China." *Journal of Peasant Studies*, vol. 45, no. 7 (November 2017), pp. 1221–1246.

Dillon, Nara. *Radical Inequalities: China's Revolutionary Welfare State in Comparative Perspective*. Cambridge/London: Harvard University Press, 2015.

Dirlik, Arif. "Back to the Future: Contemporary China in the Perspective of Its Past, Circa 1980," in *China and New Left Visions: Political and Cultural Interventions*, edited by Wang Ban and Lu Jie, pp. 33–34. Lanham/Boulder: Lexington Books, 2012.

Dong Guoqiang and Andrew G. Walder. "Nanjing's 'Second Cultural Revolution' of 1974." *The China Quarterly* 212 (December 2012), pp. 893–918.

Dong Limin. "Nüxingzhuyi: Bentuhua ji qi weidu (Feminism: Indigenization and Its Dimensions)." *Nankai Xuebao*, no. 2 (2005), pp. 7–12.

Dong Yige. "Does China Have a Feminist Movement from the Left?" *Made in China Journal*, vol. 4, no. 1 (2019), pp. 58–63. https://tinyurl.com/y795fjf7 (accessed April 20, 2022).

Dui Hua. "Leftist Subversion in China: 1980 to Present." Dui Hua Reference Materials, October 29, 2013. https://tinyurl.com/ytyjfpc6 (accessed April 20, 2022).

Dui Hua. "Leftist Dissent under Xi: The Old Leftists, Part II." *Dui Hua, Human Rights Journal*, October 23, 2019. https://tinyurl.com/bdda455f (accessed April 20, 2022).

Eichner, Carolyn J. *Surmounting the Barricades: Women in the Paris Commune*. Bloomington/Indianapolis: Indiana University Press, 2004.

Elfstrom, Manfred. *Workers and Change in China: Resistance, Repression, Responsiveness*. Cambridge/New York: Cambridge University Press, 2021.

Elfstrom, Manfred, and Sarosh Kuruvilla. "The Changing Nature of Labor Unrest in China." *ILR Review*, vol. 67, no. 2 (April 2014), pp. 453–480.

Engels, Friedrich. "The Origin of the Family, Private Property and the State" [1884]. marxists.org, 2021. https://tinyurl.com/mpezjkme (accessed April 20, 2022).

Erbaugh, Mary S., and Richard C. Kraus. "The 1989 Democracy Movement in Fujian and its Aftermath," in *The Pro-democracy Protests in China: Reports from the Provinces*, edited by Jonathan Unger, pp. 150–165. Armonk: M.E. Sharpe, 1991.

Esherick, Joseph W. "Xi'an Spring." *Australian Journal of Chinese Affairs* 24 (July 1990), pp. 209–235.

Eysenck, Hans Jürgen. *The Psychology of Politics*. London: Routledge and Kegan Paul, 1963.

Fang Kecheng and Maria Repnikova. "Demystifying 'Little Pink': The Creation and Evolution of a Gendered Label for Nationalistic Activists in China." *New Media & Society*, vol. 20, no. 6 (2018), pp. 2062–2086.

Feng Jiayun. "China Contemplates Better Laws to Promote Gender Equality, but Remains Hostile to 'Radical' Feminist Campaigns." SupChina, December 22, 2021. https://tinyurl.com/36t2f35f (accessed April 20, 2022).

Forster, Keith. "The Popular Protest in Hangzhou," in *The Pro-democracy Protests in China: Reports from the Provinces*, edited by Jonathan Unger, pp. 166–186. Armonk: M.E. Sharpe, 1991.

Fraser, Nancy. "Feminism, Capitalism and the Cunning of History." *New Left Review* 56 (2009), pp. 97–117.

Friedman, Eli. "External Pressure and Local Mobilization: Transnational Activism and the Emergence of the Chinese Labor Movement," *Mobilization*, vol. 14, no. 2 (June 2009), pp. 199–218.

Fu, Diana. "Disguised Collective Action in China." *Comparative Political Studies*, vol. 50, no. 4 (2017), pp. 499–527.

Fu, Diana. *Mobilizing without the Masses: Control and Contention in China*. Cambridge/New York: Cambridge University Press, 2018.

Fuchs, Daniel. "Going West—Industrial Relocation and Migrant Labour Unrest in Chengdu and Chongqing." PhD diss., Department of Development Studies, SOAS, University of London, 2019.

Gallagher, Mary E. "China's Older Workers: Between Law and Policy, Between Laid-off and Unemployed," in *Laid-off Workers in a Workers' State: Unemployment with Chinese Characteristics*, edited by Thomas B. Gold, William Hurst, Won Jaeyoun, and Li Qiang, pp. 135–158. New York: Palgrave Macmillan, 2009.

Gao Wangling. "A Study of Chinese Peasant 'Counter-action.'" *Eating Bitterness: New Perspectives on China's Great Leap Forward and Famine*, edited by Kimberley Ens Manning and Felix Wemheuer, pp. 272–294. Vancouver/Toronto: UBC Press, 2011.

Garnaut, Ross, Song Ligang, and Yao Yang. "Impact and Significance of State-owned Enterprise Restructuring in China." *The China Journal* 55 (January 2006), pp. 35–63.

Garside, Roger. *Coming Alive: China after Mao*. New York: McGraw-Hill, 1981.

Gilmartin, Christina. "Gender, Politics, and Patriarchy in China: The Experiences of Early Women Communists, 1920–27," in *Promissory Notes: Women in the Transition to Socialism*, edited by Sonia Kruks, Rayna Rapp, and Marilyn B. Young, pp. 82–105. New York: Monthly Review Press, 1989.

Gipouloux, François. *Les Cent Fleurs à l'usine: Agitation ouvrière et crise du modèle soviétique en China, 1956–1957*. Paris: Éditions de l'École des Hautes Études en Sciences Sociales, 1986.

Global Feminisms Project. "China Interviews." Global Feminisms Project website (2021). https://tinyurl.com/3br6rz3n (accessed April 20, 2022).

Göbel, Christian. "Social Unrest in China: A Bird's-eye View," in *Handbook of Protests and Resistance in China*, edited by Teresa Wright, pp. 27–45. Cheltenham/Northampton: Edward Elgar, 2019.

Gold, Thomas B., William Hurst, Won Jaeyoun, and Li Qiang, eds. *Laid-off Workers in a Workers' State: Unemployment with Chinese Characteristics*. New York: Palgrave Macmillan, 2009.

Goldman, Merle. "China's Anti-Confucian Campaign, 1973–74." *The China Quarterly* 63 (September 1975), pp. 435–462.

Goldman, Merle. "The Potential for Instability among Alienated Intellectuals and Students in Post-Mao China," in *Is China Unstable? Assessing the Factors*, edited by David Shambaugh, pp. 112–124. Armonk/London: M.E. Sharpe, 2000.

Gunn, Anne. "'Tell the World About Us': The Student Movement in Shenyang, 1989," in *The Pro-democracy Protests in China: Reports from the Provinces*, edited by Jonathan Unger, pp. 64–78. Armonk: M.E. Sharpe, 1991.

Han Rongbin. "Defending the Authoritarian Regime Online: China's 'Voluntary Fifty-cent Army.'" *The China Quarterly* 224 (2015), pp. 1006–1025.

Han, Theodore, and John Li. *Tiananmen Square Spring 1989: A Chronology of the Chinese Democracy Movement*. Berkeley: Institute of East Asian Studies, 1992.

Harper, Paul. "The Party and the Unions in Communist China." *The China Quarterly* 37 (March 1969), pp. 84–119.

Hartford, Kathleen. "The Political Economy Behind Beijing Spring," in *The Chinese People's Movement: Perspectives on Spring 1989*, edited by Tony Saich, pp. 50–82. Armonk/New York: M.E. Sharpe, 1990.

Hassard, John, Jackie Sheehan, Zhou Meixiang, Jane Terpstra-Tong, and Jonathan Morris. *China's State Enterprise Reform: From Marx to the Market*. London/New York: Routledge, 2007.

He Baogang. "Democracy as Viewed by Three Chinese Liberals: Wei Jingsheng, Hu Ping and Yan Jiaqi." *China Information*, vol. 6, no. 2 (Autumn 1991), pp. 23–43.

He Xiaopei. "Chinese Queer (Tongzhi) Women Organizing in the 1990s," in *Chinese Women Organizing: Cadres, Feminists, Muslims, Queers*, edited by

Hsiung Ping-Chun, Maria Jaschok, and Cecilia Milwertz, pp. 41–59. Oxford/New York: Berg, 2001.

Heilmann, Sebastian. *Nanking 1976: Spontane Massenbewegungen im Gefolge der Kulturrevolution. Eine Regionalstudie*. Bochum: Brockmeyer, 1990.

Heilmann, Sebastian. "The Social Context of Mobilization in China: Factions, Work Units and Activists during the 1976 April Fifth Movement." *China Information*, vol. VIII, no. 3 (Winter 1993), pp. 1–19.

Heilmann, Sebastian. *Sozialer Protest in der VR China: Die Bewegung vom 5. April 1976 und die Gegen-Kulturrevolution der siebziger Jahre*. Hamburg: Institut für Asienkunde, 1994.

Heurlin, Christopher. "Land Protests in Rural China," in *Handbook of Protests and Resistance in China*, edited by Teresa Wright, pp. 184–202. Cheltenham/Northampton: Edward Elgar, 2019.

Hioe, Brian. "The Chinese New Left: Anti-capitalist within China, Imperialist outside of China?" New Bloom, December 3, 2016. https://tinyurl.com/3ruccvmm (accessed April 20, 2022).

Howard, Pat. "Rice Bowls and Job Security: The Urban Contract Labour System." *Australian Journal of Chinese Affairs* 25 (January 1991), pp. 93–114.

Huang Jisu. "Che Guevara: Notes on the Play, Its Production, and Reception," in *Debating the Socialist Legacy and Capitalist Globalization in China*, edited by Zhong Xueping and Wang Ban, pp. 205–216. Basingstoke/New York: Palgrave Macmillan, 2014.

Human Rights Watch. *Paying the Price: Worker Unrest in Northeast China*. Refworld, UNHCR, August 2, 2002. https://tinyurl.com/f4kbrdnh (accessed April 20, 2022).

Hurst, William. "The Power of the Past: Nostalgia and Popular Discontent in Contemporary China," in *Laid-off Workers in a Workers' State: Unemployment with Chinese Characteristics*, edited by Thomas B. Gold, William Hurst, Won Jaeyoun, and Li Qiang, pp. 115–132. New York: Palgrave Macmillan, 2009.

Hurst, William, and Kevin O'Brien. "China's Contentious Pensioners." *The China Quarterly* 170 (June 2002), pp. 345–360.

Jaschok, Maria, Cecilia Milwertz, and Hsiung Ping-Chun. "Introduction," in *Chinese Women Organizing: Cadres, Feminists, Muslims, Queers*, edited by Hsiung Ping-Chun, Maria Jaschok, and Cecilia Milwertz, pp. 3–21. Oxford/New York: Berg, 2001.

Jin Yihong. "The All-China Women's Federation: Challenges and Trends," in *Chinese Women Organizing: Cadres, Feminists, Muslims, Queers*, edited by Hsiung Ping-Chun, Maria Jaschok, and Cecilia Milwertz, pp. 123–140. Oxford/New York: Berg, 2001.

Kernen, Antoine. "The Reemergence of Street Protests: State Workers Challenge the Chinese State," in *Laid-off Workers in a Workers' State: Unemployment with Chinese Characteristics*, edited by Thomas B. Gold, William Hurst, Won Jaeyoun, and Li Qiang, pp. 225–244. New York: Palgrave Macmillan, 2009.

Korzec, Michael. *Labour and the Failure of Reform in China*. New York: St Martin's Press, 1992.

Korzec, Michael, and Martin K. Whyte. "Reading Notes: The Chinese Wage System." *The China Quarterly* 86 (June 1981), pp. 248–273.

Kumar, Nikhil. "War, Protest and Spiking Prices: How spiraling inflation is setting the world on fire. As the Ukraine rages on, driving up the cost of fuel and food, high prices have sparked unrest around the world." *Grid*, July 6, 2022. https://tinyurl.com/24ynek9j (accessed July 31, 2022).

Lagerkvist, Johan. "The Wukan Uprising and Chinese State-Society Relations: Toward 'Shadow Civil Society'?" *International Journal of China Studies*, vol. 3, no. 3. (December 2012), pp. 345–361.

Lee, Ching-Kwan. "Pathways of Labour Insurgency," in *Chinese Society: Change, Conflict and Resistance*, 2nd edn, edited by Elizabeth J. Perry and Mark Selden, pp. 71–92. London/New York: RoutledgeCurzon, 2003.

Lee, Ching-Kwan. "Pathways of Labor Activism," in *Chinese Society: Change, Conflict and Resistance*, 3rd edn, edited by Elizabeth J. Perry and Mark Selden, pp. 57–79. New York: Routledge, 2010.

Lee, Ching-Kwan, and Shen Yuan. "The Anti-Solidarity Machine? Labor Nongovernmental Organizations in China," in *From Iron Rice Bowl to Informalization: Markets, Workers, and the State in a Changing China*, edited by Sarosh Kuruvilla, Ching-Kwan Lee, and Mary E. Gallagher, pp. 173–187. Ithaca/London: ILR Press, 2011.

Lee, Shannon. "Preliminary Thoughts on the Shenzhen Jasic Events." Shannon Lee's China Blog, September 17, 2018. https://tinyurl.com/mbkhad2c (accessed April 20, 2022).

Lee, Shannon. "'Doing Worker Work': Activist Workers and the Jasic Affair." Shannon Lee's China Blog, February 27, 2019. https://tinyurl.com/26zheydt (accessed April 20, 2022).

Leijonhufvud, Göran. *Going Against the Tide: On Dissenter and Big-character Posters in China*. Copenhagen: Curzon Press, 1990.

Leung Wing-Yue. *Smashing the Iron Rice Pot: Workers and Unions in China's Market Socialism*. Hong Kong: Asia Monitor Resource Center, 1988.

Leung Wing-Yue. "The Politics of Labour Rebellions in China, 1989–1994." PhD diss., University of Hong Kong, 1998.

Li Junpeng. "The Making of Liberal Intellectuals in Post-Tiananmen China." PhD diss., Graduate School of Arts and Sciences, Columbia University, New York, 2017. https://tinyurl.com/2wuc8vrn (accessed April 20, 2022).

Li Ju. "Fight Silently: Everyday Resistance in Surviving State-owned Enterprises in Contemporary China." *Global Labour Journal*, vol. 3, issue 2 (September 2012), pp. 194–216.

Li Ju. "Victory and Defeat: The Contentious Politics of One Generation of State Workers in China since the 1960s." *International Review of Social History*, vol. 61, no. 2 (August 2016), pp. 197–222.

Li Lianjiang and Kevin J. O'Brien. "Protest Leadership in Rural China," in *Chinese Politics: State, Society and the Market*, edited by Peter Hays Gries and Stanley Rosen, pp. 85–108. London/New York: Routledge, 2010.

Lin, Jake. *Chinese Politics and Labor Movements*. Cham: Palgrave Macmillan, 2020.

Lin, Kevin. "Workers on the Move—the Lide Strike." International Viewpoint, July 14, 2015. https://tinyurl.com/2n34ttec (accessed April 20, 2022).

Lin, Kevin. "State Repression in the Jasic Aftermath: From Punishment to Preemption." *Made in China Journal*, vol. 4, no. 1 (January–March 2019), pp. 16–19. https://tinyurl.com/36zcc55c (accessed April 22, 2022).

Lin Weiran. "An Abortive Chinese Enlightenment: The Revolution and Class Theory." PhD diss., University of Wisconsin-Madison, 1996.

Lipinsky, Astrid. *Der Chinesische Frauenverband: Eine kommunistische Massenorganisation unter marktwirtschaftlichen Bedingungen*. Berlin: LIT Verlag, 2006.

Liu Guokai. *A Brief Analysis of the Cultural Revolution*. Armonk: M.E. Sharpe, 1987.

Liu Jieyu. *Gender and Work in Urban China: Women Workers of the Unlucky Generation*. London/New York: Routledge, 2007.

Lü Pin. "Finding a Voice: A Leading Chinese Feminist Tells Her Story." *Logic*, no. 7 (2019). https://tinyurl.com/4b8ambdj (accessed April 20, 2022).

Lu Ping, ed. *A Moment of Truth: Workers' Participation in China's 1989 Democracy Movement and the Emergence of Independent Unions*. Hong Kong: Hong Kong Trade Union Education Center/Asia Monitor Resource Center, 1990.

Lu Ping. "A Brief History of the Workers' Autonomous Federation," in *A Moment of Truth: Workers' Participation in China's 1989 Democracy Movement and the Emergence of Independent Unions*, edited by Lu Ping, pp. 13–20. Hong Kong: Hong Kong Trade Union Education Center/Asia Monitor Resource Center, 1990.

Mao Tse-Tung. "The Debate on the Co-operative Transformation of Agriculture and the Current Class Struggle (October 11, 1955)," in *Selected Works of Mao Tse-Tung*, vol. 5 (Oxford/New York: Pergamon Press, 1977), pp. 211–234.

Marquis, Chris. "The China Story Behind Apple's $3 trillion Valuation with Doug Guthrie." SupChina, January 7, 2022. https://tinyurl.com/2utpe8bc (accessed April 20, 2022).

McBride Stetson, Dorothy, and Amy Mazur, eds. *Comparative State Feminism*. Thousand Oaks/London: Sage Publications, 1995.

Mehnert, Klaus. *Peking and the New Left: At Home and Abroad*. Berkeley: University of California Press, 1969.

Meisner, Maurice. "Marx, Mao and Deng on the Division of Labour in History," in *Marxism and the Chinese Experience*, edited by Arif Dirlik and Maurice Meisner, pp. 79–116. Armonk: M.E. Sharpe, 1989.

Meisner, Maurice. *Mao's China and After: A History of the People's Republic*, 3rd edn. New York: The Free Press, 1999.

Mimiyana. "Zhongguo qingnian nüquan yundong jianshi—shang (2012–2013)" (Short History of China's Movement of Young Feminists, 1st part, 2012–2013). chinesefeminism.org (April 5, 2021). https://tinyurl.com/mv3upcrj (accessed April 20, 2022).

Mimiyana. "Zhongguo qingnian nüquan yundong jianshi—xia (2014–2019)" (Short History of China's Movement of Young Feminists, 2nd part, 2014–2019). chinesefeminism.org (April 5, 2021). https://tinyurl.com/yc7tck5h (accessed April 20, 2022).

Monthly Review. "On December 24, 2004, Maoists in China Get Three Year Prison Sentences for Leafleting." MR online, January 21, 2005. https://tinyurl.com/5bc36zu6 (accessed April 20, 2022).

Moody, Peter R. "The New Anti-Confucian Campaign in China: The First Round." *Asian Survey*, vol. 14, no. 4 (April 1974), pp. 307–324.

Mulvad, Andreas Møller. "China's Ideological Spectrum: A Two-dimensional Model of Elite Intellectuals' Visions." *Theory and Society*, vol. 47 (2018), pp. 635–661.

Murphy, Rachel, and Tao Ran. "No Wage and No Land: New Forms of Unemployment in Rural China," in *Unemployment in China: Economy, Human Resources and Labour Markets*, edited by Grace O.M. Lee and Malcolm Warner, pp. 128–148. London/New York: Routledge, 2007.

Naughton, Barry. *The Chinese Economy: Adaptation and Growth*, 2nd edn. Cambridge/London: MIT Press, 2018.

O'Brien, Kevin J., and Li Lianjiang. "Campaign Nostalgia in the Chinese Countryside." *Asian Survey*, vol. 39, no. 3 (May–June 1999), pp. 375–393.

O'Brien, Kevin J., and Li Lianjiang. *Rightful Resistance in Rural China*. Cambridge: Cambridge University Press, 2006.

Okudera, Atsushi, and Nozomu Hayashi. "Mao References in Anti-Japan Protests a Concern for Chinese Authorities." *Asahi Shimbun*, September 18, 2012. https://tinyurl.com/ms2b7aru (accessed July 31, 2022).

Opletal, Helmut. "Der 'Pekinger Frühling'—Erinnerungen an die chinesische Demokratiebewegung 1978 bis 1981." University of Vienna website, 2020. https://tinyurl.com/yckwn66z (accessed April 20, 2022).

Paltemaa, Lauri. "The Democracy Wall Movement, Marxist Revisionism, and the Variations on Socialist Democracy." *Journal of Contemporary China*, vol. 16, no. 53 (2007), pp. 601–625.

Perry, Elizabeth J. "Shanghai's Strike Wave of 1957." *The China Quarterly* 137 (March 1994), pp. 1–27.

Perry, Elizabeth J. "'To Rebel is Justified': Cultural Revolution Influences on Contemporary Chinese Protest," in *The Chinese Cultural Revolution Reconsidered: Beyond Purge and Holocaust*, edited by Law Kam-yee, pp. 262–281. Basingstoke/New York: Palgrave Macmillan, 2003.

Perry, Elizabeth J. "Masters of the Country? Shanghai Workers in the Early People's Republic," in *Dilemmas of Victory: The Early Years of the People's*

Republic of China, edited by Jeremy Brown and Paul G. Pickowicz, pp. 59–79. Cambridge/London: Harvard University Press, 2007.

Pun Ngai. *Migrant Labor in China: Post-socialist Transformations*. Cambridge: Polity Press, 2016.

Pun Ngai and Chris Chan King-Chi. "The Subsumption of Class Discourse in China." *boundary* 2, vol. 35, no. 2 (2008), pp. 75–91.

Pun Ngai and Li Wanwei. *Dagongmei: Arbeiterinnen aus Chinas Weltmarktfabriken erzählen*—Übersetzt und herausgegeben von Ralf Ruckus. Berlin/Hamburg: Assoziation A, 2008.

Pun Ngai and Chris Smith. "Putting Transnational Labour Process in Its Place: The Dormitory Labour Regime in Post-socialist China." *Work, Employment and Society*, vol. 21, no. 1 (2007), pp. 27–45.

Pun Ngai, Lu Huilin, Guo Yuhua, and Shen Yuan, eds. *iSlaves: Ausbeutung und Widerstand in Chinas Weltmarktfabriken*—Übersetzt und herausgegeben von Ralf Ruckus. Vienna: Mandelbaum. 2013.

Qian Benli. "Jasic Struggle: Debate among Chinese Maoists." *Against the Current*, no. 200 (May–June 2019). https://tinyurl.com/89d84e8t (accessed April 20, 2022).

Qin, Amy. "Qiu Jin (1875–1907)—A Feminist Poet and Revolutionary Who Became a Martyr Known as China's 'Joan of Arc.'" *The New York Times*, March 8, 2018. https://www.nytimes.com/interactive/2018/obituaries/overlooked-qiu-jin.html (accessed April 20, 2022).

Qin Ling. "Introduction: The Survival and Collective Struggles of Workers in China's Coastal Private Enterprises since the 1990s," in *China on Strike: Narratives of Workers' Resistance*, edited by Hao Ren et al., pp. 1–26. Chicago: Haymarket Books, 2016.

Rho Sungmin. "The Workers' Dilemma: Collective Action and Factory Workers in China." PhD diss., Department of Political Science of Stanford University, 2015. https://tinyurl.com/3dtx5t8f (accessed April 20, 2022).

Riskin, Carl. *China's Political Economy: The Quest for Development since 1949*. Oxford: Oxford University Press, 1987.

Rosen, Stanley. "Guangzhou's Democracy Movement in Cultural Revolution Perspective." *The China Quarterly* 101 (March 1985), pp. 1–31.

Ruckus, Ralf. "Out of Control—Hong Kong's Rebellious Movement and the Left." nqch.org, September 10, 2019. https://tinyurl.com/2p8tm2x8 (accessed September 11, 2019).

Ruckus, Ralf. "Critical Perspectives on the 'Jasic Movement'—Suitable Tactics of Intervention?" nqch.org, January 18, 2020. https://tinyurl.com/yeycuts3 (accessed April 20, 2022).

Ruckus, Ralf. *The Communist Road to Capitalism: How Social Unrest and Containment Have Pushed China's (R)evolution since 1949*. Oakland: PM Press, 2021.

Ruckus, Ralf. "Leitplanken für den Kapitalismus." *WOZ*, September 9, 2021. https://tinyurl.com/v3r7bupx (accessed April 20, 2022).

Saich, Tony. "Workers in the Workers' State: Urban Workers in the PRC," in *Groups and Politics in the People's Republic of China*, edited by David S.G. Goodman, pp. 152–175. Cardiff: University College Cardiff Press, 1984.

Saich, Tony, ed. *The Chinese People's Movement: Perspectives on Spring 1989*. Armonk: M.E. Sharpe, 1990.

Sargeson, Sally. "Violence as Development: Land Expropriation and China's Urbanization." *Journal of Peasant Studies*, vol. 40, no. 6 (2013), pp. 1063–1085.

Schling, Hannah. "Gender, Temporality, and the Reproduction of Labour Power: Women Migrant Workers in South China." *Sozial.Geschichte Online* 14 (2014), pp. 42–61. https://tinyurl.com/5n6bd4wh (accessed April 20, 2022).

Schurmann, Franz. *Ideology and Organization in Communist China*. Berkeley: University of California Press, 1968.

Scott, James, C. *Weapons of the Weak: Everyday Forms of Peasant Resistance*. New Haven/London: Yale University Press, 1985.

Selden, Mark. "The Social Origins and Limits of the Democratic Movement," in *Chinese Democracy and the Crisis of 1989: Chinese and American Reflections*, edited by Roger V. Des Forges, Luo Ning, and Wu Yen-Bo, pp. 107–130. Albany: State University of New York Press, 1993.

Sheehan, Jackie. *Chinese Workers: A New History*. London: Routledge, 1998.

Shengwulian. "Whither China?" [1968], in *Peking and the New Left : At Home and Abroad*, edited by Klaus Mehnert, pp. 82–100. Berkeley: University of California Press, 1969.

Shenker, Jack. "This Wave of Global Protest Is Being Led by the Children of the Financial Crash." *Guardian*, October 29, 2019. https://tinyurl.com/yy76gfw8 (accessed July 31, 2022).

Shi Anshu, François Lachapelle, and Matthew Galway. "The Recasting of Chinese Socialism: The Chinese New Left since 2000." *China Information*, vol. 32, no. 1 (2018), pp. 139–159.

Silver, Beverly J. *Forces of Labor: Workers' Movements and Globalization since 1870*. Cambridge: Cambridge University Press, 2003.

Silver, Beverly J., and Zhang Lu. "China as an Emerging Epicenter of World Labor Unrest," in *China and the Transformation of Global Capitalism*, edited by Hung Ho-fung, pp. 174–187. Baltimore: Johns Hopkins University Press, 2009. https://tinyurl.com/47359s9u (accessed April 20, 2022).

Solinger, Dorothy J. "Labour Market Reform and the Plight of the Laid-off Proletariat." *The China Quarterly* 170 (June 2002), pp. 304–326.

Spakowski, Nicola. "Socialist Feminism in Postsocialist China." *positions*, vol. 26, no. 4 (2018), pp. 561–592.

Stacey, Judith. *Patriarchy and Socialist Revolution in China*. Berkeley/Los Angeles: University of California Press, 1983.

Statista. "Degree of Urbanization in China from 1980 to 2021." statista.com, 2022. https://tinyurl.com/2p8c9rr7 (accessed April 20, 2022).

Tan Jiangying. "Truckers on Strike and the Structural Contradictions of China's Logistics Industry." China Change, June 15, 2018. https://tinyurl.com/mtpy37cz (accessed April 20, 2022).

Teiwes, Frederick C., and Warren Sun. "China's New Economic Policy under Hua Guofeng: Party Consensus and Party Myths." *The China Journal* 66 (2011), pp. 1–23.

That Faint Light. "A People's History of the Cultural Revolution." That Faint Light Blog, July 14, 2012. https://tinyurl.com/37dx4cts (accessed April 20, 2022)

Tian Liujia, Ian. "Socialism from the Grassroots: New Directions of Leftist Organizing in Post-socialist China." *Upping the Anti*, issue 22 (January 30, 2022). https://tinyurl.com/2p9uvha8 (accessed April 20, 2022).

Unger, Jonathan, ed. *The Pro-democracy Protests in China: Reports from the Provinces*. Armonk: M.E. Sharpe, 1991.

Walder, Andrew G. *Chang Ch'un-Ch'iao and Shanghai's January Revolution*. Ann Arbor: Center for Chinese Studies. The University of Michigan, 1978.

Walder, Andrew G. "Workers, Managers and the State: The Reform Era and the Political Crisis of 1989." *The China Quarterly* 127 (September 1991), pp. 467–492.

Walder, Andrew G., and Gong Xiaoxia. "Workers in the Tian'anmen Protests: The Politics of the Beijing Workers' Autonomous Federation." *Australian Journal of Chinese Affairs*, 29 (January 1993), pp. 1–29.

Walker, Kathy L. "'Gangster Capitalism' and Peasant Protest in China: The Last Twenty Years." *Journal of Peasant Studies*, vol. 33, no. 1 (January 2006), pp. 1–33.

Walker, Kathy L. "From Covert to Overt: Everyday Peasant Politics in China and the Implications for Transnational Agrarian Movements." *Journal of Agrarian Change*, vol. 8, nos 2 and 3 (April and July 2008), pp. 462–488.

Wang Feng. *Boundaries and Categories: Rising Inequality in Post-socialist Urban China*. Stanford: Stanford University Press, 2008.

Wang Hui. "The Rumour Machine: Wang Hui on the Dismissal of Bo Xilai." *London Review of Books*, vol. 34, no. 9 (2012), pp. 13–14.

Wang Jiangsong. "The Significance of Crane Operators across China Going on Strike." China Change, May 7, 2018. https://tinyurl.com/s5fntx5a (accessed April 20, 2022).

Wang Shaoguang. "Deng Xiaoping's Reforms and the Chinese Workers' Participation in the Protest Movement of 1989," in *Research in Political Economy*, vol. 13, edited by Paul Zarembka, pp. 163–197. London: JAI Press, 1992.

Wang Shaoguang. "From a Pillar of Continuity to a Force for Change: Chinese Workers in the Movement," in *Chinese Democracy and the Crisis of 1989: Chinese and American Reflections*, edited by Roger V. Des Forges, Luo Ning, and Wu Yen-Bo, pp. 177–190. Albany: State University of New York Press, 1993.

Wang Yingyi, Stephanie. "Unfinished Revolution: An Overview of Three Decades of LGBT Activism in China." *Made in China Journal*, vol. 6, no. 1 (2021), pp. 90–95. https://tinyurl.com/56ej7u3d (accessed April 20, 2022).

Wang Zheng. "'State Feminism'? Gender and Socialist State Formation in Maoist China." *Feminist Studies*, vol. 31, no. 3 (2005), pp. 519–551.

Wang Zheng. "Detention of the Feminist Five in China." *Feminist Studies*, vol. 41, no. 2 (2015), pp. 476–482.

Wasserstrom, Jeffrey N. "Student Protests and the Chinese Tradition, 1919–1989," in *The Chinese People's Movement: Perspectives on Spring 1989*, edited by Tony Saich, pp. 3–24. Armonk: M.E. Sharpe, 1990.

Weber, Isabella. *How China Escaped Shock Therapy: The Market Reform Debate*. London/New York: Routledge, 2021.

Wedeman, Andrew. "Stealing from the Farmers: Institutional Corruption and the 1992 IOU Crisis." *The China Quarterly* 152 (December 1997), pp. 805–831.

Weil, Robert. "Conditions of the Working Classes in China." *Monthly Review*, vol. 58, issue 2 (June 2006). https://tinyurl.com/4xdtuv6b (accessed April 20, 2022).

Wen Dale. *China Copes with Globalization: A Mixed Review*. San Francisco: International Forum on Globalization, 2006. https://www.yumpu.com/en/document/read/26201346/china-report-with-cover-international-forum-on-globalization (accessed April 20, 2022).

Wesoky, Sharon R. "Bringing the Jia Back into Guojia: Engendering Chinese Intellectual Politics." *Signs: Journal of Women in Culture and Society*, vol. 40, no. 3 (2015), pp. 647–666.

Widor, Claude, ed. *Documents on the Chinese Democratic Movement, 1978–1980: Unofficial Magazines and Wall Posters*, vol. 2. Paris : Éditions de l'École des Hautes Études en Sciences Sociales, 1984.

Williams, Philip S. "Some Provincial Precursors of Popular Dissent Movements in Beijing." *China Information*, vol. 6, no. 1 (June 1991), pp. 1–9.

Wilson, Jeanne L. "'The Polish Lesson': China and Poland 1980–1990." *Studies in Comparative Communism*, vol. XXIII, nos 3–4 (Autumn/Winter 1990), pp. 259–279.

Wong Sue-Lin. "Chinese Students Assaulted at Pro-Marxist Society Protest." Reuters, November 2, 2018. https://tinyurl.com/2k2vew9z (accessed April 20, 2022).

Wu Yiching. *The Cultural Revolution at the Margins: Chinese Socialism in Crisis*. Cambridge/London: Harvard University Press, 2014.

Wu Yiching. "The Great Retreat and its Discontents: Re-examining the Shengwulian Episode in the Cultural Revolution." *The China Journal* 72 (July 2014), pp. 1–28.

Wu, Jason Y. "Categorical Confusion: Ideological Labels in China." SSRN, September 9, 2020. https://tinyurl.com/yskye96d (accessed April 20, 2022).

Wu Xiao, Angela, and Dong Yige. "What is Made-in-China Feminism(s)? Gender Discontent and Class Friction in Post-socialist China." *Critical Asian Studies*, vol. 51, no. 4 (2019), pp. 1–22.

Xiao Suowei. "Women's Work: How 'Ernai' Mistresses Bolster Fragile Masculinity (Part 1)." *Sixth Tone*, May 15, 2019. https://tinyurl.com/5c5xh8rd (accessed April 20, 2022).

Xiao Suowei. "For Love or Money: What Drives China's Migrant Mistresses? (Part 2)." *Sixth Tone*, May 21, 2019. https://tinyurl.com/6y96ph62 (accessed April 20, 2022).

Xiong Jing and Dušica Ristivojević. "#MeToo in China: How Do the Voiceless Rise Up in an Authoritarian State?" *Politics & Gender*, vol. 17, no. 3 (2021), pp. 490–499.

Xu Zhun and Chen Ying. "Spatial Shift in China's Labor Struggles: Evidence and Implication." *Journal of Labor and Society*, vol. 22, no. 1 (March 2019), pp. 129–138.

Yan Hairong. *New Masters, New Servants: Migration, Development, and Women Workers in China*. Durham/London: Duke University Press, 2008.

Yang Guobin. "The Liminal Effects of Social Movements: Red Guards and the Transformation of Identity." *Sociological Forum*, vol. 15, no. 3 (September 2000), pp. 379–406.

Yang Guobin. "China's Zhiqing Generation: Nostalgia, Identity, and Cultural Resistance in the 1990s." *Modern China*, vol. 29, no. 3 (July 2003), pp. 267–296.

Yang Guobin. *The Red Guard Generation and Political Activism in China*. New York: Columbia University Press, 2016.

Yang Yuan. "Inside China's Crackdown on Young Marxists: Why is the Communist Power Arresting and Detaining Leftist Students?" *Financial Times*, February 14, 2019. https://tinyurl.com/bdhwxrxd (accessed April 20, 2022).

Yi Xi. "New Foundations for Struggle and Solidarity: The Culmination of Development and Privatization on a Guangzhou Island." libcom.org, October 7, 2014. https://tinyurl.com/e5frz8jx (accessed April 20, 2022).

Young, Marilyn B. "Chicken Little in China: Women after the Cultural Revolution," in *Promissory Notes: Women in the Transition to Socialism*, edited by Sonia Kruks, Rayna Rapp, and Marilyn B. Young, pp. 233–247. New York: Monthly Review Press, 1989.

Yu Luoke. "On Family Background." *Contemporary Chinese Thought*, vol. 32, no. 4 (Summer 2001), pp. 17–36.

Zarrow, Peter. "He Zhen and Anarcho-feminism in China." *Journal of Asian Studies*, vol. 47, no. 4 (November 1988), pp. 796–813.

Zeng Jinyan. "Chinese Feminism under (Self-)Censorship: Practice and Knowledge Production." *Made in China Journal*, vol. 6, no. 2 (2021), pp. 166–169. https://tinyurl.com/2p8y75kc (accessed April 20, 2022).

Zhang Qin. "Negotiating Change: The Emergence and Development of the Women's Movement in Contemporary China." PhD diss., Rutgers, State University of New Jersey, New Brunswick, 2008.

Zhang Taisu. "What it Means to Be 'Liberal' or 'Conservative' in China: Putting the Country's Most Significant Political Divide in Context." China File, April 24, 2015. https://tinyurl.com/yv34sfn5 (accessed April 20, 2022).
Zhang Weihong. "A Typology of the Mao Craze," in *Shades of Mao: The Posthumous Cult of the Great Leader*, edited by Geremie R. Barmé, pp. 158–161. New York/London: M.E. Sharpe, 1996.
Zhang Yiqi. "Sheng wa shi jiashi yeshi guoshi" (Having a Child Is Not Only a Family Affair but Also a State Affair). *Renmin Ribao* (People's Daily), August 6, 2018. http://politics.people.com.cn/n1/2018/0806/c1001-30210179.html (accessed April 13, 2022).
Zhang Yueran. "The Jasic Struggle and the Future of the Chinese Labour Movement." *Made in China Journal*, vol. 3, no. 3 (July–September 2018), pp. 12–17. https://tinyurl.com/mvwbvpzz (accessed April 20, 2022).
Zhang Yueran. "Leninists in a Chinese Factory: Reflections on the Jasic Labour Organising Strategy." *Made in China Journal*, vol. 5, no. 2 (May–August 2020), pp. 82–88. https://tinyurl.com/2s49czxy (accessed April 20, 2022).
Zhang Yueran. "Workers on Tian'anmen Square," in *Proletarian China: A Century of Chinese Labour*, edited by Ivan Franceschini and Christian Sorace, pp. 151–159, London/New York: Verso, 2022.
Zhao Suisheng. "Xi Jinping's Maoist Revival." *Journal of Democracy*, vol. 27, no. 3 (July 2016), pp. 83–97.
Zheng Tiantian. *Red Lights: The Lives of Sex Workers in Postsocialist China*. Minneapolis/London: University of Minnesota Press, 2009.
Zheng Yongnian. *Globalization and State Transformation in China*. Cambridge: Cambridge University Press, 2004.
Zhuang Wenjia and Chen Feng. "'Mediate First': The Revival of Mediation in Labour Dispute Resolution in China." *The China Quarterly* 222 (2015), pp. 380–402.

Index

#Metoo (#mitu), 134, 136, 139, 165, 198
50 Cent Army, 167, 201

abolitionists, 60–1; *see also democracy movements*
absenteeism, 26, 38, 73
activism (activists), xiii, 5, 13, 15, 114, 120, 147, 162, 177, 191, 199, 201
  activists in democracy movements, 52, 54–7, 59, 61–2, 69–70, 75–6; labor/worker activism, 16, 17, 19, 39, 60, 69, 88–9, 96, 99–100, 108, 113, 116–8, 120, 137–9, 147, 151, 156, 179, 188, 191–2; left-wing (and Maoist) activism, xi, xii, xiii, 63, 92, 93, 96, 99, 101, 103, 104, 114–5, 117, 121, 123, 137–8, 142, 146–7, 151, 156–7, 160, 163, 191–2; feminist activism, xi, xii, xiii, 18, 19, 104, 129, 132, 133–7, 139, 147, 152–3, 156, 169, 198; in the 2019 Hong Kong movement, 2; LGBTIQ* activism, 11, 191; Red Guard/rebel activists, 34, 40, 42–3, 48–9, 57, 199; rural activism, *see peasants*; student activism, 104, 117–8; *see also demonstrations; feminism; strikes; struggles (from below); women*'s struggles*
agriculture, 22, 65, 84–5, 102, 107, 175, 199
  and taxes, 79, 80, 83, 102; feminization of, 125; *see also land reform; reforms (after 1978)*
All-China Federation of Trade Unions (ACFTU), 23, 26–30, 37, 46, 53, 62, 69–70, 74–6, 88–9, 96, 100, 110, 112–3, 118, 167, 171, 191; *see also cadres, union cadres*
All-China Women's Federation (ACWF), 27, 130–1, 135, 136, 138, 139, 142, 167, 196, 197; *see also feminism, state feminism*
anarchism (anarchists), xiii, 3, 7, 9–10, 11, 13, 44, 129, 169
Andreas, Joel, 171, 172, 173, 175
anti-colonial struggles, 6, 7, 13, 130
anti-communist, 14
anti-corruption campaign, *see campaigns*
anti-imperialist, 11–2, 162
anti-Japanese protest, *see Japan*
anti-leftism (by the CCP), 19, 94, 154–8, 164, 169, 199
Anti-Restoration Society, 41, 164
Anti-Rightist Campaign, *see campaigns*
apprentices, 21, 26, 36, 37, 44, 46, 174
April 3 Faction, 41, 166
April 5 Forum, 57, 166
April 5 Movement 1976, *see democracy movements*
arbitration, 108, 109, 112, 138, 190
Arbitration Law, *see laws*
army, *see People's Liberation Army*
authoritarian, xi, xiv, 2, 10–1, 14–5, 18, 21, 24, 28, 30, 33, 47–8, 51, 53–5, 64, 77, 97, 101, 119, 130, 134, 136, 138–40, 142–4, 150–4, 158–9, 161–2, 198, 201, 202
authoritarianism, 3, 18, 66, 155
  flexible authoritarianism, 143, 144
autonomy, *see self-determination*

bargaining power
  of workers, 108, 160; of women*, 126, 128–9, 160

Beijing, 34, 37, 41, 49, 51–3, 55, 57–8, 60–1, 64, 66–74, 91, 94–5, 115, 117, 131, 164, 174, 176, 178–9, 190
Beijing Spring (journal), 57, 164
benefits (wage supplements), 8, 25–6, 31, 35–6, 46, 59, 90, 106, 119, 200; *see also social insurances; wages; welfare*
Benton, Gregor, 176, 177, 178, 179
big alliance (*dalianhe*), 38, 44, 164
big character posters (*dazibao*), 26, 51, 53, 56, 180
Big Dipper Society, 41, 164
big freedoms, *see four big freedoms*
birth control, 81, 127, 128, 138, 195
  One-Child-Policy, 81, 105, 124, 126, 127, 129, 131, 138, 164, 181, 195; Two-Child Policy, 127; Three-Child Policy, 127; *see also gender gap*
birth rate, 127, 195; *see also birth strike; fertility rate*
birth strike, 127, 137–8, 146; *see also birth rate; fertility rate*
black categories, 22, 34, 40; *see also class system*
blood-line theory, 34, 167, 174
Bo Xilai, 99, 119, 120, 139, 153, 157, 193
boundary-spanning resistance (of migrant workers), *see resistance*
bourgeoisie (bourgeois), 34, 43, 75, 92, 94, 111
  bourgeois class, 44; bourgeois democracy, 59, 61; bourgeois feminism, 11; bourgeois (reactionary) line, 34, 44; bourgeois revolution, 42; red (newborn) bourgeoisie, 21, 42, 44, 50, 75, 142, 143, 149; *see also capitalist roaders; ruling class*
Brodsgaard, Kjeld Erik, 173, 175, 176, 177
bureaucracy (bureaucratic), 14, 21, 180
  bureaucratic apathy, 30; bureaucratic leadership/class, 34, 42–3, 44, 53, 59, 61, 177; bureaucratism (*guanliaozhuyi*), 37, 45, 63, 76, 164; bureaucratization, 33; *see also cadres; management*

cadres, 14, 26, 27–30, 33–41, 43–4, 47, 50, 52–3, 55–60, 65, 68–9, 71, 75–6, 80–2, 86, 89, 91, 102, 113, 130, 142–3, 156, 164, 170, 197, 200
  union cadres, 27, 29–30, 53, 69, 88; cadre corruption, xiv, 16, 18, 49, 65, 78, 82, 85, 92, 93, 102, 144; cadre arbitrariness, 3, 20, 30, 39, 50, 58, 78, 80, 100, 142–3; *see also bureaucracy; management*
campaign
  against the "two illegals," 62; anti-corruption campaign, 121; Anti-Rightist Campaign, 20, 29, 37, 55, 155, 164, 177, 200; Campaign to Criticize Lin Biao and Confucius, 50, 166; Campaign to Suppress Counterrevolutionaries, 23, 167; Cleansing the Class Ranks campaign, 40, 166; Democratic Reform Movement, 23, 165; Five Antis campaign, 23, 24, 167; Four Cleanups Movement, *see campaign, Socialist Education Movement*; One Strike, Three Antis campaign, 40, 167, 174; Socialist Education Movement (SEM), 33, 166; Three Antis campaign, 23, 24, 166
capitalism, xi, xii, 2, 6, 9, 19, 77–9, 85, 88, 95–6, 117, 122–3, 128, 141, 143–5, 152, 159, 161–2, 170
  global capitalism, xi, 92, 95, 189; patriarchal capitalism, 9, 133, 139, 197; terror capitalism, 168
capitalist class, 6, 8, 14, 143

capitalist roaders, 33, 34, 38–40, 44, 97, 156, 167
capitalist period (in the PRC), xiv, 2–3, 7, 12, 15–6, 19, 21, 64, 75, 77–8, 87, 103, 105, 114, 121, 126, 128, 141–4, 146, 149–50, 152–4, 163, 175, 200; *see also reform period; socialist period; transition(al) period*
CCP leadership, *see Chinese Communist Party (CCP) leadership*
Central Cultural Revolution Group (CCRG), 33, 36–41, 43, 44, 167
Chan King-Chi, Chris, 190
Chan, Anita, 176, 179, 180
Charity Law, *see laws*
Che Guevara (theater play), 95–6, 186, 201
Chen Chih-Jou, Jay, 183, 189
Chen Erjin, 177
Chen Feng, 171–3, 185–6, 190–2, 200
Chen Ruoxi, 177
Chile, 162
China Labour Bulletin, 117, 184, 189, 190, 192
China Workers Net (website), 167, 192
Chinese Communist Party (CCP) leadership, 2, 20–2, 28, 32, 34, 39–40, 45, 47–51, 53, 55, 61–68, 70, 72–76, 80, 84, 87, 89, 92, 94–6, 98–100, 106, 114, 119–20, 122, 124, 130–1, 133, 137–9, 145, 153, 155–7, 158, 161, 173, 194
Chinese Communist Youth League (CCYL), 27, 167
Chinese Human Rights Alliance, 57, 167
Chongqing Model, 119, 158, 193; *see also Bo Xilai*
Civil Code, *see laws*
class
  class struggle, 2, 11, 42, 74, 97, 99, 111, 119, 121, 123, 130, 142, 143, 155, 163, 165, 192, 194, 200; class struggle rhetoric, 65, 82, 92, 156; class struggle without class organization, 111; socialist class system, 20, 22, 32, 142; *see also black categories; bourgeoisie; capitalist class; landlord class; ruling class; working class*
Cleansing the Class Ranks campaign, *see campaigns*
collective bargaining, 75, 108, 112, 116–7
collectivist, *see left-collectivist*
collectivization, 20, 79
colonialism, xiv, 2, 6, 7, 8, 13, 130, 168, 191, 197, *see also anti-colonial struggles*
Comintern (Communist International), 13, 14, 170
commandism (*minglingzhuyi*), 45, 165
common prosperity, 122, 157, 164, 195, 201
communism (communists), xi, 7–9, 14, 21
Communist Party of the Soviet Union, 13, 40, 67
concessions, 19–20, 27, 37–9, 45–7, 50, 62–4, 73, 76–7, 81, 83, 85, 90, 99, 102–5, 110, 112, 124, 135, 139, 145–6, 148, 199; *see also cooptation; countermeasures; repression*
Confucianism (Confucian), 13, 129, 138, 157, 175, 187, 201; *see also Harmonious Society*
conservative, 9–11, 130
  conservatives (late 1960s/early 1970s), *see factions, Red Guards*; conservatives (since the late 1970s), *see factions*
contained resistance (of migrant workers), *see resistance*
contract workers, *see workers*
cooperatives, 22, 25, 35, 84
cooptation, 19–20, 39–40, 44–5, 55, 64, 71, 73, 77, 102, 112, 115, 123, 139, 146, 148, 155, 177, 181, 199;

see also concessions; countermeasures; repression
corruption, *see cadre corruption*
countermeasures (from above), xiii, 15, 27, 29, 84, 111, 140, 141, 145–6, 149, 162, 170; *see also concessions; cooptation; repression; struggles (from below)*
counter-revolutionary, 23, 34, 38, 43, 50, 53, 56, 62, 67, 167, 174; *see also revolutionary*
countryside, 25–6, 29, 32, 35–6, 39, 49, 57, 65, 79, 83, 102, 106, 107, 125, 182, 195
New Socialist Countryside, 83, 85, 119, 165, 182; *see also agriculture; land reform; peasants*
Covid-19 pandemic, xii–xiii, 162
crisis, 31, 56, 90, 92, 138, 162
of social reproduction, 137, 195; of the economy, 38, 84, 92, 160,62
Cui Zhiyuan, 98, 187, 193; *see also New Left*
Cultural Revolution, 3, 16–7, 21, 31–46, 48–53, 55, 57–8, 60, 62–3, 73–6, 82, 93, 96–9, 106, 117, 119, 122, 139, 142, 145, 147–9, 151, 155–6, 159–61, 167, 173–5, 177, 180–1; *see also Central Cultural Revolution Group (CCRG); Red Guards*
Custody and Repatriation system, 107, 166

danwei, see work unit
Day, Alexander F., 181
dazibao, see big character posters
de-Dengization, 95
de-Maoization, 32
de-Stalinization, 32
decollectivization, *see Household Contract Responsibility System*
democracy (democratic), 28, 66, 140, 152, 153
organizational democracy, 9–10, 199; social democracy, 122, 200; socialist democracy, 16, 59, 77, 174, 176, 177; ultra-democracy (extreme democratization), 41, 43, 61; Western (liberal) democracy, 9, 12, 56, 60, 77, 97, 98, 159, 177; workers' democracy, 41, 59, 173, 180; *see also democracy movements*
democracy movements, 46, 54, 93, 151
April 5 Movement 1976, 16, 17, 48, 49–57, 63, 71, 75–7, 142, 166, 176; Democracy Wall Movement (DWM), 16, 17, 48, 51, 54–64, 75–78, 142, 145, 147, 165, 174, 176–8, 200; Tian'anmen Square movement, 16, 18, 49, 52, 64–75, 76, 77, 80, 86, 91, 94, 98, 99, 139, 143, 145, 152, 156, 166, 179; *see also activism*
Democratic Reform Movement, *see campaigns*
demonstrations, 5, 17, 37, 48, 50, 52, 58, 64, 66–8, 70–1, 74, 78, 81, 83, 85, 88, 96, 102–3, 118, 146–8, 178; *see also activism; discontent; strikes; struggles (from below)*
Deng Liqun, 95
Deng Xiaoping, 2, 32, 33, 35, 37, 40, 44, 46, 48, 50, 52, 54–7, 59–63, 66–7, 71, 73, 76–7, 92, 94–5, 97, 142, 148, 156, 176, 179, 180, 185
dictatorship, 8, 61, 64
dictatorship of the proletariat, 2, 7, 8, 21, 61, 160
Dirlik, Arif, 176, 194, 201
discontent, 5, 15–7, 19, 21, 23, 25–6, 28, 30–2, 35, 46–9, 51, 61, 63–4, 66, 75–6, 79, 81, 89, 91, 99, 104, 141, 147, 155, 160, 170, 174, 184, 196; *see also activism; demonstrations; strikes; struggles (from below)*
discrimination, xiv, xv, 1, 2, 5, 7, 10, 12, 14, 17, 18, 20–1, 24, 30, 33–5,

46–7, 56, 58, 90, 104–5, 142, 143, 148, 158, 160
of black categories, 34; of women*, 1, 7, 17, 23, 26, 105, 107, 125, 127–39, 146, 158–9, 168; of migrant workers, ruralites, 42, 106, 113, 116, 125, 145–6; *see also exploitation; hukou; oppression; patriarchy; racism; repression; sexism*
Dong Limin, 132, 197
Dong Yige, 173, 195, 196, 198
dormitory labor regime, 107–8, 188
dual-track pricing system, 65, 165

eastern bloc, 92
Eastern Europe, xiii, 12, 73, 177, 197
economic crisis, *see crisis*
economism (economist), 16–7, 21, 27, 31, 36–40, 43–5, 106, 142, 145, 155, 165
egalitarian, 10–1, 71, 74, 144, 150–4, 158–9, 170, 200
egalitarianism, 74
Elfstrom, Manfred, 189, 190, 191, 192, 198, 202
Enlightenment Society, 57, 166
environmental crisis (issues, groups), xi, xv, 115, 137, 158, 160, 199
European Union (EU), 159
exploitation (exploitative), xiv, xv, 1, 2–3, 6, 10–2, 24, 28–30, 34, 41–3, 46–7, 59, 79, 82, 95, 100–1, 104–5, 107, 113, 125, 133, 136, 138–9, 141, 145, 150–4, 157–61, 200
Exploration (journal), 57, 166

factions
centrist faction, 50, 55, 60; conservative faction (late 1960s/early 1970s), 34, 37, 39, 41, 43–5, 50–3, 57, 60, 164; conservative faction (since the late 1970s), 66, 151–2, 156, 187, 201; factionalism, 72; rebel faction (movement), 16–17, 21, 31–46, 48–50, 52–3, 57, 59, 63, 75–7, 79, 93, 98, 117, 119, 142, 145, 147, 149, 155, 167, 175, 177, 181, 193; reform(er) faction, 48–9, 51, 55, 59–2, 63, 67, 70, 73, 76–7, 89, 91–2, 151–2; whateverist faction, 55, 60; *see also ultra-left*
Factory Director Responsibility System, 65, 164
feminism (feminists), xi, xiii, 7, 13, 17–19, 103, 104–5, 118, 123–4, 129–35, 138–9, 147, 156, 169, 193–5, 197–8
anarcho-feminism, 196; critical socialist feminists, 19, 132–3, 152–3, 197; Feminist Five, 198; feminist NGOs, 19, 105, 115, 129, 131–7, 139, 147, 152–3, 191, 197; Feminist Voices, 133, 165; social feminism (from below), 124–7, 137, 196; state feminism, 105, 130–1, 133, 136, 138–9, 196–7, *see also All-Chinese Women's Federation (ACWF);* Western feminism, 105, 132–3, 135–6, 139, 197; young feminist activism, 19, 133–4, 136, 152–3; *also see activism; discrimination, gender, patriarchy, sexism*
fertility rate, 124, 127–8; *see also birth control; birth rate; birth strike*
Five Antis campaign, *see campaigns*
Five-Year Plan, 22, 24, 83, 171
four big freedoms, 53, 61, 166
Four Cleanups Movement, *see campaigns*
Four Modernizations, 50, 52, 55, 59, 166, 175
Foxconn, 118, 192
Fraser, Nancy, 133, 197
freedoms, *see four big freedoms*
French Revolution, 5, 169
Friedman, Eli, 191

Gan Yang, 98, 187; *see also New Left*

Gang of Four, 3, 48, 54, 55–6, 59, 62, 155–6, 166, *see also ultra-left*
gender, 113, 130–3, 139, 146, 158, 168, 170, 195–7, 199, 201
gender asterisk (explanation), 168; gendered division of labor, 14, 105, 125, 128, 130; gender equality, 7, 131, 196, 198; gender gap, 126; gender regime/polices, 23, 123–4, 130, 132, 137; *see also discrimination, of women*; patriarchy; sexism*
Germany, 3, 6, 11, 149, 150, 169, 199
German left, 11–12
Gipouloux, François, 171–2
Global North, 8, 11, 12
Global South, 7, 12
Gongzilian (Beijing Workers' Autonomous Federation), 64, 69–72, 75, 164, 179; *see also Workers' Autonomous Federations (WAF)*
Gorbachev, Mikhail, 67
Great Leap Forward (GLF), 31–3, 35–7, 42, 60, 74, 80, 156, 164, 171, 182, 199
Guangdong, xii, 50, 107, 108, 110, 115, 183, 191
Guangzhou, 50, 51, 57, 61, 68, 69, 107, 116, 118, 177, 192

Hangzhou, 50, 68, 69, 180
Harmonious Society, 91, 112, 119, 133, 143, 144, 165, 184, 185, 194
Hebei, 88
Heilmann, Sebastian, 175–6
Heilongjiang, 88
historical nihilism, 133, 165
Hong Kong, xiv, 115, 117, 123, 191
2019 Hong Kong movement, 2, 162, 169; *see also activism*
hostile foreign forces, 135, 165
housing, 22, 25, 35, 50, 58, 84, 107, 119, 172, 195
Household Contract Responsibility System, 80, 165
Hu Jintao, 83, 112, 119, 133, 144, 153, 184, 194
Hu Yaobang, 66, 67, 70
Hua Guofeng, 48, 50, 55, 60, 176
hukou (household registration), 32, 37, 79, 84, 106–7, 109, 111, 113, 116, 119, 125, 165, 173, 175
Hunan, 42, 82, 165, 166, 174, 180
Hundred Flowers Movement (HFM), 20, 28, 155, 164, 200
Hungary 1956 uprising, 20, 28, 32
Hurst, William, 183, 184

imperialism, 158, 159
U.S. imperialism, xi, 95; PRC imperialism, 187, 202
industrialization, 8, 14, 24, 48, 55, 56, 79, 81, 84, 103, 127, 137, 142, 143, 154
inequality, xiv, 2, 9, 17, 30, 58, 83, 92–3, 98, 100, 113, 121, 157, 174, 180
inside the system (*tizhinei*), 144, 147, 166
iron rice-bowl, 78, 81, 85, 87, 90, 94, 100, 166, 178, 191

Japan, 13, 187, 194
anti-Japanese protest, 187, 194; Japanese army, 13–4, 22
Jasic incident, xii, 118, 120, 168, 191–3
Jiang Qing, 49, 55; *see also Gang of Four*
Jiang Zemin, 68, 87, 89, 92, 97, 111, 144, 153, 156

Keynesianism, 157, 201
Kuomintang (KMT, Nationalist Party), 13–4, 22, 79, 155, 164, 170

labor
Labor Contract Law, *see laws*; labor contracts, 26, 65, 86, 107; Labor Law, *see laws*; labor-NGOs,

17–8, 104, 110, 112, 115–22, 138, 145, 147, 152–3, 191, 192; labor reform (punishment), 29, 173; labor shortage, 108, 113, 160; *see also activism; protests; strikes; struggles (from below); workers*
land theft (seizure), 16, 18, 78, 83–5, 102, 144, 183, 199
land reform, 14, 22, 79
landlord class, 14, 22, 79, 82
laws
Arbitration Law, 89; Charity Law, 134; Civil Code, 136, 198; labor laws, 89, 90, 107, 108, 112; Marriage Law, 22, 124; National Security Law, 134; Overseas NGO Law, 134; Trade Union Law, 89; *see also martial law*
Lee, Ching-Kwan, 184, 188, 189, 191
Left Bank (website), 167, 192
left, the (definition), 1, 3–5, 9, 168–9
left-collectivist, 10–11, 150–4
left-exploitative, 150–2
left/right spectrum (graph), 5, 6, 9–10, 19, 141, 149, 155, 169
legacy, *see socialist legacy*
Leninism, *see Marxism-Leninism*
LGBTIQ*, 11, 12, 115, 191, 193; *see also activism; Pepper Tribe; Queer Workers*
Li Junpeng, 186, 187, 200
Li Peng, 67, 68, 73, 77
Li Yi Zhe, 50–1, 53, 59, 75, 176, 177
Liaoning, 88
liberalism (liberals), 2, 9, 11, 29, 94, 95, 97–8, 103, 117, 122, 153, 159, 169, 170, 177, 186–7, 200
Lide strike, 116, 192
Little Pink, 167, 201
Liu Guokai, 173, 174
Liu Shaoqi, 32–5, 37, 40, 44, 46, 156
Lü Pin, 133–4, 198

management (manager), 3, 23–8, 30, 39, 44, 47, 53, 59, 61–2, 65, 74–5, 86, 89, 96, 107–8, 110, 124, 126, 128, 134; *see also bureaucracy; cadres*
Mao Zedong, 2, 21, 28, 32–5, 39–40, 44–6, 51, 55, 58, 71, 74, 85, 93, 103, 114, 132, 142, 146, 151, 152, 155, 156, 172, 185, 200
Mao cult, 50; Mao nostalgia/revival/craze/fever, 18, 74, 82, 93–4, 99–101, 103, 117, 144, 182, 185, 194; Mao Zedong-ism, 45; Mao Zedong Thought, 61, 96, 187
Maoflag (website), 165, 192
Maoism, (Maoists), xiii, xiv, 2, 3, 11, 16, 18, 74, 78, 82, 85, 89–103, 114, 117–23, 132, 137–8, 144–5, 152–3, 155–6, 158–9, 161, 175, 185–6, 191, 193, 196
exhaustion of, 48, 50; Maoist dissidents, 16, 17, 151, 155; Maoist Left, xii, 115, 118–9, 123, 159–60, 165; Maoist patriarchy, 124, 126, 138, 171; Maoist Right, 115, 118–9, 123, 159, 165, 194; revival of, 93–7, 115, 139, 144, 194; *see also activism*
marketization, 70, 97–8, 100, 102–3, 125, 142–6; *see also reforms*
Marriage Law, *see laws*
martial law (1989), 68–71, 74, 76
Marx, Karl, 139
Marxism (Marxists), 105, 117
and feminism, 132, 136; tamed/domesticated (CCP), 1, 92, 99, 120–2, 139, 157–8, 194, 201; in the Democracy Wall Movement, 58–61, 63
Marxism-Leninism, xiii, 2, 7–11, 14, 54, 61, 120, 154–6, 159, 187, 200
Marxist Theoretical Research and Development Project, 121, 165
Masses' Reference News, 57, 166
masters of the work unit (society), 21, 25, 29, 31, 47, 54, 86, 88, 90, 171
May 4 Movement, 13, 129, 167
Meisner, Maurice, 176, 180

middle class, 76, 128
migrant workers, *see workers*
migration (rural/urban) 32, 79, 84, 104, 106, 113, 119, 125, 126, 128, 173, 188, 199
migration regime, *see Custody and Repatriation system; hukou*
military, 12, 39, 41, 68, 72–4, 162; *see also peasant army; People's Liberation Army (PLA); soldiers*
minorities, 14, 157, 166, 168, 170; *see also Uyghurs*
modernity, 65, 98, 187, 201
modernization, 8, 13, 84, 129, 156, 175; *see also Four Modernizations*
moral economy, 31, 74, 90, 149
movements (from below), *see struggles*

Nanjing, 51, 52, 57, 69
National Security Law, *see laws*
nationalism, nationalist, 8, 92, 98, 99, 101, 121–3, 138, 139, 159, 161, 194
Nationalist Party, *see KMT*
nationalization, 14, 17, 20, 22, 24–5, 29, 46, 145
neoliberalism, neoliberal, 79, 95, 98–9, 101, 103, 143–4
nepotism, 67, 76
New Left, 3, 16, 18, 85, 91, 96–101, 103, 118–9, 132–3, 144, 153, 158–60, 167, 187, 193; *see also left*
new trends of thought, 40–3
New Workers (website), 167, 192
NGOs (non-governmental organizations), 115, 148
  feminist/women*'s NGOs, *see feminism*; labor NGOs, *see labor*; NGO-ization, 115; Overseas NGO Law, *see laws*
nihilism, *see historical nihilism*
nostalgia, *see Maoism, revival of*

October Revolution Group, 41, 166
One-Child Policy, *see birth control*
One-Man Regiment, 23, 25, 28, 31, 32, 171
One Strike, Three Antis campaign, *see campaigns*
oppression, 2, 6, 9, 12, 50, 59, 82, 95, 124, 168; *see also discrimination; repression*
outside the system (*tizhiwai*), 106, 147, 166
Overseas NGO Law, *see laws*

pandemic, *see Covid-19 pandemic*
Paris Commune, 41, 59, 169
patriarchy, 1, 6, 17–8, 24, 123–4, 126, 128–9, 131, 136, 138, 143, 145, 161, 168, 195, 197
  patriarchal capitalism, 9, 139; patriarchal Confucian practices, 129; patriarchal family, 124–5; *see also sexism*
peasant army, 14, 21; *see also military; People's Liberation Army (PLA); soldiers*
peasants, xiv, 2, 3, 13–4, 17, 25, 32, 42, 50, 52, 54, 56, 58, 63, 65–6, 69, 73, 76, 78, 83–6, 91–5, 102, 113–4, 119, 121, 124, 134, 142, 144, 146, 170–1, 182, 200
  landless peasants, 83, 107, 126; peasant protests/struggles, xi, xiv, 3, 16, 18, 58, 60, 76, 78–85, 91, 98–103, 143, 146–7, 157, 160–1, 171–2, 181–3, 189, 199; peasant workers, *see workers; see also ruralites*
pensions, 87–8, 90, 109
People's Liberation Army (PLA), 38–9, 67–8, 71–2
PLA officers, 39, 43–4, 68; *see also peasant army; military; soldiers*
people's literature (*minkan*), 54, 165; *see also underground journals*
Pepper Tribe, 165, 193; *see also LGBTIQ**
permanent (urban, state) workers, *see workers*

Perry, Elizabeth, 171–3, 181, 182, 184, 188, 199
petition movement (*shangfang*), 26, 58, 165
planned economy, 2, 14, 17, 20–2, 25, 46, 86, 101, 142–3, 156
Poland, 61–2, 73–4, 178
  1956 uprising, 20, 28, 32; *see also Solidarność*
police, 52, 67, 69, 81, 84, 88–9, 102, 107, 111–2, 118, 135, 148, 192, 199; *see also repression; state security forces*
poverty, poor, 65, 73, 79, 87, 91, 95, 121, 126, 144, 157, 200
power from below, 83, 122
power seizures (*duoquan*), 38, 40–1, 164
precarious workers, *see workers*
pressure (from below), *see struggles*
privatization, 87, 90, 92, 98, 102, 125, 131, 143–4, 192
privileges, 10, 33–4, 37, 43, 72, 90
  privileged cadres, 16, 17, 29, 40–4, 50–1, 59, 70, 72, 159, 177
proletarian, 4, 20, 30, 124, 166, 173, 174, 177, 178, 187; *see also workers*
proletarianization, 107
protest, *see activism; demonstrations; discontent; strikes; struggles (from below)*
Pun Ngai, 188–90, 192, 197

Qin Ling, 189
Queer Workers, 165, 193; *see also LGBTIQ**

racism, 2, 5, 73, 107, 158, 161, 168; *see also discrimination; sexism*
rebels, *see factions, Red Guards*
red bourgeoisie, 21, 42, 44, 142, 143, 149
Red China (website), 97, 119, 165
Red Guards, 33–4, 36, 38, 53, 165, 199
  conservative (old) Red Guards, 34, 40, 44; former Red Guards, 50–51, 53, 57, 60, 77, 93, 177, 180, 185; rebel (new) Red Guards, 34, 41, 44; *see also activism; factions*
Red Song Society, 167, 192
red terror, 34, 165
reformism, reformist, 7, 8, 43, 70, 73, 75, 98, 117, 122, 154
reformist faction, *see factions*
reforms, 6, 13, 15, 16–8, 26, 29, 31, 49–50, 55–7, 59–66, 69, 71, 74–80, 84, 87, 90, 94–5, 97, 99, 100, 102–3, 106, 119, 121–2, 124, 128, 139, 141–3, 145–6, 148–9, 176–9, 181, 185, 195
  democratic reforms, 16, 17, 48, 58, 67; GLF reforms, 32; market reforms, 2, 16, 18, 65, 77–8, 85–6, 91–2, 94–5, 101–2, 106, 119, 125, 131, 133, 148, 156, 159, 176; political reforms, 16, 18, 48–9, 56, 58–9, 64, 67, 76, 97, 143, 152; post-1978 reforms in the countryside, 65, 78–80, 83, 84; post-1978 reforms in the cities, 86, 183; post-1978 reform effects, 70, 74, 77, 79, 91, 143; *see also countermeasures (from above); Factory Director Responsibility System; Four Modernizations; Household Contract Responsibility System; land reform; restructuring*
reform period, 122, 128, 197; *see also capitalist period; socialist period; transition(al) period*
rehabilitation, 37, 50–1, 54–6, 58, 76
repression, xi–xiii, 10–12, 19–20, 30, 37, 39, 45, 50, 60–1, 63–4, 72, 76–7, 83–6, 102, 104–6, 110–11, 113, 115, 118, 120–1, 123, 132–4, 136, 138–9, 141, 143–5, 148, 150–6, 160, 163, 168, 181, 182, 186, 189, 198, 199; *see also concessions; cooptation; countermeasures; police*
reproduction, 10, 138

reproductive labor, 23, 26, 124–5, 127–8, 138, 145–6; social reproduction (of labor power), 107, 137, 195, 200
resistance (of migrant workers)
boundary-spanning resistance, 109–10, 190; contained resistance, 109–10, 190; transgressive resistance, 110, 113, 191
restructuring, 16, 18, 24, 74, 78–9, 81, 86–90, 94, 96, 100–3, 109, 125, 143–4, 146, 183; *see also countermeasures (from above); reforms*
revolution, revolutionary, xv, 1, 6–8, 13, 17, 20–2, 25, 27, 29, 34, 38, 40, 43, 74–5, 79, 95, 119, 121–3, 130, 148, 154–6, 158–60, 167, 168, 177, 186
1911 revolution 13, bourgeois revolution, 42; continuous revolution, 42, 43, 148; *see also counter-revolutionary; Cultural Revolution; French Revolution; reformism*
Revolutionary Committees, 38–40, 43–44, 164
right (right-wing, rightist), 5–6, 8–11, 14, 22, 29, 64, 77, 97, 101, 115, 119, 121, 150, 152–6, 161, 169–70, 185, 200; *see also left/right spectrum; Maoist Right; right-exploitative*
right-exploitative, 10–11, 152–53
right to rebel, 52
right to strike, 62
rightful resistance, 18, 80–83, 103, 181, 182
rights, 9, 16–7, 22, 28, 52, 57, 58, 59, 62, 64, 67, 70, 72, 75, 76, 83, 86, 88, 91, 96, 106, 116, 124, 129–32, 143, 151, 165, 166, 173, 182, 191; *see also weiquan*
ruling class
former (old) ruling class, 22, 34, 40, 42; socialist (new) ruling class, 8, 40, 44, 59–60, 63, 74–5, 77, 142–4, 148, 150; capitalist ruling class, 2, 91–92, 144, 148, 150; *see also bourgeoisie; capitalist class*
Russia, 7, 162, 163
ruralites, 42, 80, 104, *see also peasants*
rustication, rusticated, 21, 26, 34–40, 42, 45–7, 50–1, 56–8, 60, 63, 93, 149

sabotage, 107, 147
self-determination, 18, 56, 99, 170
Seventy Articles, 32, 39
Sixteen Points, 34
sexism, 2, 5, 17, 107, 124, 126, 129, 131, 135, 137, 138, 145, 197
sexualized violence, 23, 128, 131–2, 138–9, 146; sexual harassment, 105, 129, 131, 134–6; *see also discrimination; patriarchy*
SEZ (special economic zone), 106
Shaanxi, 96, 186
Shandong Bohai Battle Regiment, 41, 166
Shanghai, 21, 23–6, 35–42, 51, 57, 68–9, 171–4
Shanghai People's Commune, 38, 41, 166
Sheehan, Jackie, 171–4, 176–7, 179–80, 183, 209, 215
Shengwulian, 42–5, 51, 59, 63, 75, 165, 166, 174
Shenzhen, xii, 105, 118, 189, 193
Silver, Beverly, 188, 189
social democracy (social democrats), 3, 7–8, 10–11, 98, 117, 122, 152, 154, 200
social insurances, 109, 112, 116; *see also benefits; wages; welfare*
socialism (socialists), xi, xiv, 1–3, 6–9, 11–14, 16–8, 20, 23–5, 28–9, 31–4, 36, 40–3, 45–7, 58–9, 61, 63, 73–5, 77, 79, 82–3, 85–6, 88–90, 92, 94–101, 103, 119–22, 124, 133, 138, 142, 148–52, 154–7, 159–63, 168, 170, 175, 177, 187, 194–5, 200

critical socialist feminists, *see feminism*; democratic socialism, *see democracy*; socialist class system, *see class*; socialist development, 86, 138, 155; socialist industrialization, 79, 142, 143; socialist market economy, 87; socialist modernization, 156; socialist (planned) economy, *see planned economy*; socialist ruling class, *see ruling class*; socialist (settler) colonialism, xiv; socialist working class, *see working class*; actually existing socialism, 8, 59, 90, 158–9, 175
Socialist Education Movement (SEM), *see campaigns*
socialist (leftist, Maoist) legacy, xiii, 17, 78, 82, 98, 100–2, 121, 158, 168, 186
socialist period (in the PRC), xii, xiv, 2–3, 12, 15–8, 20, 63–4, 82, 85, 91–4, 99–100, 102–6, 128, 130, 132, 136, 139, 141–3, 145–6, 149–50, 154–6, 158, 178, 194, 200*; see also capitalist period; reform period; transitional period*
soldiers, 68, 71
demobilized, 37; *see also military; peasant army; People's Liberation Army*
Solidarność, 61–2, 73–4
Solinger, Dorothy, 183, 184
Song Shaogang, 132
Soviet Union, 13, 23, 25, 28, 31, 32, 40, 56, 67, 163, 170, 171; *see also Communist Party of the Soviet Union*
Spakowski, Nicola, 197
Sri Lanka, 162
Staff and Workers Congresses (SWC), 28, 62, 167
Stalin, Joseph, 32
Stalinism, 11, 22; *see also de-Stalinization*
state security forces, xii, 118, 120, 192
state workers, *see workers*
strikes, 86, 107, 109, 111, 112, 116, 117, 118, 155, 164, 189–90, 192
1956–57 wave, 25–7, 46, 142, 151, 155, 171–3; 1980–81 wave, 61–2; 2010 wave, 108; general strike, 72; hunger strike, 67; right to strike, 62; *see also activism; birth strike; demonstrations; discontent; struggles (from below)*
struggles (from below), xiii, 3, 7, 8, 15, 27, 28, 43, 46, 49, 60, 77, 83, 92, 104, 106, 108, 111, 114, 115, 119, 122, 123, 135, 139, 141, 142, 148, 149, 154, 155, 159, 161, 170, 199; *see also activism; countermeasures (from above); demonstrations; discontent; strikes; women*'s struggles*
students, 3, 11, 13, 64, 93, 95, 97, 147, 176, 179, 185–6
in feminist groups, 134; in labor support/Maoist groups (2000s, 2010s), 104, 114–5, 117–8, 120–1, 138, 193; in the 1986–87 student movement, 66; in the April 5 Movement, 52; in the Cultural Revolution, 33, 36, 40, 42, 43, 45; in the Tian'anmen Square Movement 1989, 64, 66–70, 72–3, 76–7, 151–2, 180–1; *see also activism*

Taiwan, xiv
temporary workers, *see workers*
Third Front Construction, 33, 166
Three Antis campaign, *see campaigns*
Three-Child Policy, *see birth control*
Tian'anmen Square Movement 1989, *see democracy movements*
Tibet, xiv, 123, 169, 170
Today (journal), 57, 165
Tongmenghui (Revolutionary Alliance), 13, 166
town and village enterprises (TVE), 80, 181

Trade Union Law, *see laws*
transgressive resistance (of migrant workers), *see resistance*
transition(al) period (in the PRC), xii, xiv, 2, 3, 7, 12, 15–6, 18, 21, 24, 63, 75, 77, 78, 86, 103, 105, 114, 126–7, 129, 130, 136, 138, 142–6, 149–55, 175; *see also capitalist period; reform period; socialist period*
Trotskyism (Trotskyists), xiii, 3, 11, 117, 122, 152, 192
Two-Child Policy, *see birth control*

uprising 1956, *see Poland, Hungary*
U.S. imperialism, *see imperialism*
Ukraine, 162, 169, 202
ultra-democracy, 41, 43, 44
ultra-left, 3, 32, 39, 40, 45, 48, 54, 148, 151–2, 156, 165, 174; *see also Gang of Four*
underground resistance, 135, 139, 143, 145, 147, 149
underground journals, 57–60, 164, 175–6; *see also people's literature (minkan)*
unemployment, unemployed, 24, 25, 26, 33, 38, 65, 69, 73, 87, 126, 144, 183–4, 196; *see also xiagang*
union, *see All-China Federation of Trade Unions (ACFTU); Solidarność*
unified purchasing and marketing, 79, 166
United Nations Fourth World Conference on Women (1995), 131
United States, U.S., xi, 6, 32, 50, 60, 95, 98, 99, 159, 162, 194, 197; *see also imperialism*
unrest, *see activism; demonstrations; discontent; strikes; struggles (from below)*
urban workers, *see workers*
Utopia (website), 97, 100, 119, 167, 186, 192
Uyghurs, 168

wages, 26, 52, 54, 125, 171
  minimum wage, 91, 108, 113; wage arrears, 88, 108, 113, 189; wage cuts, 24, 26, 94; wage freeze, 31, 50, 52, 61; wage increase, 38, 91, 108, 112; wage labor, 124, 128, 131; work according to the wage, 27, 164; *see also benefits; social insurances*
Walder, Andrew, 174–5, 178–80
Walker, Kathy, 181–2
Wang Hongwen, 55; *see also Gang of Four*
Wang Hui, 98, 187, 193; *see also New Left*
Wang Shaoguang, 98, 179–80, 185, 187; *see also New Left*
Wang Zheng, 196–8
weapons of the weak, 107, 172, 189
Weber, Max, 111
Wei Jingsheng, 61, 177
weiquan (safeguarding rights), 116, 166; *see also rights*
welfare, 2, 8, 10, 14, 17–8, 25–6, 28, 52, 59, 74, 78, 83, 87, 89–92, 94, 98, 100, 102, 114–6, 119, 122–3, 125, 139, 143–4, 150, 157–8, 172–3, 197, 200–1; *see also benefits; social insurances*
West (Western), 14, 56, 59, 95, 98, 200
  Western capitalism, 159; Western democracy, 8, 12, 92, 97, 98, 140, 159; Western feminism, *see feminism*; Western influences, 122–3, 139, 157; Western modernity, 98
Western Europe, xiii
whateverist faction, *see factions*
Wickedonna blog, 164, 192
women*
  women*'s struggles (resistance), 103, 123, 128–9, 134, 137–9, 146–7, 160; women*'s strike, 127; *see also birth strike; discrimina-*

*tion; feminism; sexism; workers, women**; working class, women* as part of the*
work units (*danwei*), 23, 25–30, 32, 34, 36–42, 44, 46–7, 50, 53, 59, 63, 65, 69–70, 74–5, 77–8, 86–90, 125, 164, 176, 178; *see also management*
workers
contract workers, 30, 35–7, 39, 42, 44, 46; migrant workers, 17–9, 73, 86, 91, 97, 100, 103, 104–17, 119, 122, 136–7, 139, 145–7, 152, 159, 188–92, 195, *see also hukou; outside the system (tizhiwai); resistance (of migrant workers)*; peasant workers, 111, 165, *see also hukou; migrant workers*; permanent (urban, state) workers, 25–6, 35–8, 43, 50, 74, 102, 143–4, 175, 178, 184, *see also inside the system (tizhinei); iron rice-bowl*; precarious workers, 16, 17, 35, 106–7, 142, 146, 200; temporary workers, 21, 26, 30, 35–9, 42, 44, 46, 50, 86, 106, 111, 137, 175, 178; women* workers, 26, 110, 116; *see also activism; proletarian; strikes; struggles (from below); working-class*
worker-peasant system (*yi gong yi nong*), 35, 167
Workers' Autonomous Federations (WAF), 69–75, 179; *see also Gongzilian*
Workers' General Headquarter, 38, 164
working class, 6, 7, 8, 28, 29, 63, 64, 74, 77, 88, 92, 96, 97, 103, 119, 122–3, 134, 173, 180, 188
new working class (of rural migrants), 103–11, 112–4, 122, 128; old socialist working class (of urban state workers), 18, 47, 74, 89–90, 97, 117, 122, 144; women* as part of the working class, 124, 128, 134; *see also class, class struggle; ruling class*
working conditions, 24, 36, 87, 98, 109, 114, 116, 118, 119, 146; *see also wages*
Wu Yiching, 171, 173–5
Wuhan, xii, 41, 50, 51, 57, 68, 69

Xi Jinping, 84, 99, 112, 119–21, 128, 139, 144, 153, 158–9, 162, 186, 187, 194, 201
xiagang (redundant state workers), 87–9, 167, 184
Xinjiang, xiv, 88, 123, 157, 168, 169, 170, 201

Yang Guobin, 180, 185, 199
Yao Wenyuan, 55; *see also Gang of Four*
Yu Luoke, 41, 174
youth, 17, 34, 76, 93, 125, 167
rusticated youth, 21, 34–5, 37–8, 42, 46, 50, 56–8, 60, 63, 93; youth unemployment, 33, 38

Zhang Chunqiao, 55; *see also Gang of Four*
Zhang Yueran, 168, 178–81, 193
Zhao Ziyang, 67–8, 70, 73, 76–7
Zhengzhou, 51, 96
Zhengzhou Four, 96
Zhou Enlai, 48, 50–3, 76, 175

Thanks to our Patreon subscribers:

Ciaran Kane

Who have shown generosity and comradeship in support of our publishing.

Check out the other perks you get by subscribing to our Patreon – visit patreon.com/plutopress.

Subscriptions start from £3 a month.